ESSENTIALS OF CONTRACT LAW IN TEXAS

AF735213

1ST EDITION

PERFORMANCE
PROGRAMS
COMPANY

STEPHEN METTLING
RYAN METTLING
DAN HAMILTON

Material in this book is not intended to represent legal advice and should not be so construed. Readers should consult legal counsel for advice regarding points of law.

6810 190th Street East, Bradenton, FL 34211
info@performanceprogramscompany.com
www.performanceprogramscompany.com

ISBN: 978-1965482582

Essentials of Contract Law in Texas

Table of Contents

PREFACE

Welcome to Essentials of Contract Law in Texas published by Performance Programs Company. This course is one of the six required 30-hour prelicense education courses that every candidate for a Texas real estate salesperson license must complete before sitting for the state licensing examination administered by the Texas Real Estate Commission (TREC). Together, the six courses total 180 hours of qualifying education and are designed to give new licensees a thorough foundation in the law, ethics, and professional practice of Texas real estate.

About This Course

Contracts are the instruments through which every real estate transaction is created, modified, and concluded. A licensee who cannot read a contract carefully, complete a form correctly, explain provisions clearly to clients, and recognize when something is wrong before it becomes a problem will not serve clients well regardless of how skilled that licensee is in every other dimension of practice. This course treats contract law not as an abstract legal subject but as the practical core of professional real estate work in Texas.

The course covers 11 chapters organized to build understanding progressively: from the foundational legal principles that govern all contracts, through the ownership rights that contracts convey and limit, through the specific forms Texas licensees use in residential transactions, through the financing structures that support those transactions, through the conveyance and closing process that completes them, and finally through the common mistakes that derail transactions when contracts are prepared carelessly.

Topics Covered

The course opens with the regulatory framework that governs Texas real estate practice. You will study the history and authority of TRELA and TREC, the role of the Texas Real Estate Broker-Lawyer Committee in drafting promulgated forms, the boundary between permissible brokerage activity and the unauthorized practice of law, and the provisions of the Texas Deceptive Trade Practices Act that most directly affect licensees.

The next chapters build the legal foundation for understanding real property. You will study how Texas law defines land, real estate, and property; the bundle of rights that accompany ownership; surface, subsurface, air, and water rights; fixtures, trade fixtures, and emblements; the physical and economic characteristics of real property; the major forms of ownership recognized in Texas including community property; and the governmental powers, freehold estates, encumbrances, and environmental disclosure obligations that limit and shape ownership.

From that foundation the course moves to contract law itself. You will study the six essential elements of a valid contract, the legal statuses a court may assign to a contract, the difference between executed and executory contracts, the Texas Property Code requirements that apply to contracts for deed and other executory arrangements, performance and breach, and the remedies available when a party fails to perform.

The course then examines the contracts most commonly used in Texas residential transactions in detail. You will study the full range of listing agreements, buyer representation agreements, leasehold estates, the TREC temporary lease forms, options, contracts for deed, and lease purchase agreements. Two chapters address the One to Four Family Residential Contract (Form 20-19) in depth: one covering the offer and acceptance process, seller's disclosure obligations, lead-based paint disclosure, property conveyance, and breach of contract remedies; and a second covering the contingency structure, the major addenda including Forms 39-11, 40-11, 41-3, 26-8, and 12-3, and how each addendum interacts with the main contract.

The financing portion of the course covers the legal theories of mortgage ownership, the three basic financing instruments used in Texas, the deed of trust and its foreclosure mechanics, lien priority, short sales, the secondary mortgage market, conventional and government-backed loan programs, private mortgage insurance, and the major federal lending laws including RESPA and TRID, Regulation Z, ECOA, the Community Reinvestment Act, the Fair Credit Reporting Act, and HMDA

The conveyance and closing chapters cover the voluntary and involuntary methods of alienating title, the types of deeds and their levels of protection, adverse possession, the probate process, the public recording system, chain of title, marketable title, title insurance, and the full transaction process from accepted offer through post-closing IRS reporting, including proration calculations using both the 12-month/360-day and 365-day methods.

The course closes with a chapter dedicated entirely to the common mistakes licensees make when completing the One to Four Family Residential Contract. This chapter examines errors in party identification, legal descriptions, checkbox elections, the Special Provisions paragraph, the default provisions, signatures and effective dates, addenda identification, and the real property versus personal property disputes that arise when neither agent clarifies in writing what conveys with the sale.

How to Use This Text

Each chapter opens with a set of learning objectives and closes with a Snapshot Review summarizing the key rules, definitions, and principles introduced in that chapter. These summaries are designed for focused review and exam preparation. The case study discussion questions at the end of each chapter present realistic scenarios drawn from the topics covered and are followed by a debrief explaining how the chapter's concepts apply to each situation. Working through the case studies is one of the most effective ways to move from knowing what the rules are to understanding how to apply them in practice.

About the Authors

For over forty years, Stephen Mettling has operated one of the nation's most successful custom training organizations specializing in real estate program development. Mr. Mettling has also served as vice president and author for a major real estate training and publishing organization. Under various capacities, he has managed the acquisition, development, and sale of national real estate textbooks and publications, as well as directed the country's largest affiliated group of real estate schools.

Ryan Mettling, partner and publisher of Performance Programs, is an experienced online curriculum designer, author, and course developer.

Dan Hamilton is recognized nationally as a real estate author, educator and broker. During a Texas career spanning over 25 years, he has owned and operated many brokerages and received numerous professional awards and honors. Dan has operated his own school of real estate and currently teaches courses throughout the state. He has served on the board of the national Real Estate Educators Association (REEA) and as President of the Texas Real Estate Teachers Association (TRETA).

CHAPTER 1:

TEXAS CONTRACT LAW

Chapter Overview

Learning Objectives

Upon completing Chapter 1, the student will be able to:

1. Highlight the history of the Texas Real Estate License Act from its origins in 1939 through its current form, and explain the composition and authority of the Texas Real Estate Commission.
2. Define key property terms and contract-related terms used in Texas real estate transactions, and apply those definitions correctly when working with promulgated contract forms.
3. Distinguish between permissible license holder activity and the unauthorized practice of law, and identify the consequences of crossing that line.
4. Describe the history, membership structure, and functions of the Texas Real Estate Broker-Lawyer Committee, and explain how contract forms move from the committee to promulgation by TREC.
5. Define fraud and misrepresentation, explain the difference between the two, and describe best practices for avoiding both in daily real estate practice.
6. Explain the purpose and key provisions of the Texas Deceptive Trade Practices Act, including notice requirements, the statute of limitations, available defenses, and the damages a court may award.
7. Identify the current TREC promulgated contracts and their appropriate uses, and summarize the function of each paragraph in the One to Four Family Residential Contract (Form 20-19).
8. Describe the purpose and correct use of the major promulgated addenda, amendments, and temporary lease forms, referencing current TREC form numbers and effective dates.

Contents

- The Texas Real Estate License Act
- Key Property Terms
- Key Contract-Related Terms
- Unauthorized Practice of Law
- The Texas Real Estate Broker-Lawyer Committee
- Fraud, Misrepresentation, and the Deceptive Trade Practices Act
- Promulgated Contract Forms: Authority and Use
- Understanding the One to Four Family Residential Contract
- Specialized Contracts
- Contract Addenda
- Temporary Leases and Other Promulgated Forms

The Texas Real Estate License Act

The Texas Real Estate License Act, commonly known as TRELA, serves as the foundation for regulating real estate practice in Texas. Understanding its history, authority, and reach is essential for every license holder working with contracts.

Historical Background

In 1939, the Texas legislature enacted the Real Estate Dealer's License Act, requiring real estate agents to obtain licenses before conducting business. The secretary of state administered this act until 1949, when the Texas Real Estate Commission (TREC) assumed administrative responsibility. The commission's initial duties included issuing and renewing licenses, revoking licenses for cause, and instituting proceedings against persons who practiced without a license.

In 1955, the legislature renamed the law the Texas Real Estate License Act. Today TRELA's stated purpose is to safeguard the public interest and protect consumers of real estate services. In accordance with state and federal law, TREC oversees real estate brokerage, appraisal, inspection, and timeshare interest providers. Through education, licensing, and regulation, the agency works to ensure the availability of qualified and ethical service providers.

Commission Membership and Authority

The commission was originally composed of six members. In 1979 the membership was expanded to nine: six must have been active as licensed real estate brokers for at least five years before their appointment, and three must have no financial interest in the real estate business. This balance ensures that both experienced industry professionals and members representing the public interest participate in governance.

TREC holds full rule-making authority, and any rules it adopts carry the full force and effect of law. This authority extends to the forms that license holders are required to use when negotiating real estate transactions.

TRELA Rules Relating to Contract Forms

TRELA addresses the use of contract forms directly. Under the relevant provisions, the commission may adopt rules requiring license holders to use contract forms prepared by the Texas Real Estate Broker-Lawyer Committee and adopted by the commission. At the same time, TRELA prohibits the commission from preventing a license holder from using a contract form for the sale, exchange, option, or lease of real property if that form was prepared by the property owner or prepared by an attorney and required by the property owner.

Listing contract forms adopted by the commission must include a provision informing the parties that real estate commissions are negotiable, and, where appropriate, a provision explaining the availability of Texas coastal natural hazards information important to coastal residents.

Before any license holder attempts to complete contract forms that are binding on the sale, lease, or rental of real property, that person should take time to become comprehensively familiar with what the rules permit and what they do not allow.

Key Property Terms

The following terms relate to property rights and ownership concepts that arise frequently in real estate contracts. License holders should be able to define and apply each term correctly.

Air rights The right to control, occupy, or use the vertical space above a property, subject to necessary and reasonable use by neighbors and others such as aircraft.

Bilateral contract A reciprocal arrangement between two parties where each promises to perform an act in exchange for the other party's act.

Bundle of rights A set of legal rights held by the real estate title holder, including the right of possession, the right of control, the right of exclusion, the right of enjoyment, and the right of disposition.

Easement A right to cross or otherwise use someone else's land for a specified purpose.

Eminent domain The power of a state, municipality, or authorized private entity to take private property for public use following payment of just compensation to the owner.

Encroachment A situation where a property owner violates the property rights of a neighbor by building on the neighbor's land or allowing something to hang over onto the neighbor's property.

Encumbrance A claim against, limitation on, or liability against real estate, including liens, deed restrictions, easements, assessments, and taxes.

Equitable title The portion of control held by a buyer who is a party to a contract for deed or installment contract; the ability to gain full control and title to property while someone else holds legal title.

Estate at sufferance An arrangement in which a property renter is permitted to remain in a property after a lease term has expired, but before the landlord demands that the tenant vacate.

Estate at will A tenancy arrangement where a tenant occupies property with the owner's consent but without an agreement specifying a definite rental period or regular payment of rent.

Estate for years An interest in real property held under a rental agreement by which the owner grants another party the right to occupy or use the land for a defined period of time.

Estate from period to period An interest in leased property that continues from one period to the next, such as week to week, month to month, or year to year.

Executed contract A contract that has been fully performed by both parties.

Executory contract A contract under which one or more parties has not yet performed.

Express contract A contract whose terms are clearly spelled out, usually in writing.

Freehold estate An estate in which ownership is for an undefined length of time.

Homestead A legal life estate occupied as the family home.

Involuntary alienation The loss of property due to an adverse action such as a foreclosure or tax sale.

Leasehold estate A form of property tenure where one party buys the right to occupy land or a building for a given length of time.

Legal description The geographical description of a real estate property used to identify the property for legal transactions.

Legal life estate A form of life estate created by state law.

Littoral rights Rights relating to the ownership of property that abuts an ocean, sea, or lake.

Marketable title Ownership and possession of real property that is readily transferable because it is free from valid claims by outside parties.

Personal property Any asset other than real estate.

Primary mortgage market The market where borrowers and mortgage originators negotiate terms and complete mortgage transactions, including mortgage brokers, bankers, credit unions, and banks.

Real property Any property attached directly to land, as well as the land itself.

Riparian rights A system for allocating water among those who possess land along its path.

Secondary mortgage market A market for buying and selling mortgages.

Subsurface rights A landowner's rights to water and other substances below the surface of land.

Surface rights Ownership rights in a parcel of real estate limited to the surface, not including air rights or subsurface rights.

Survey An assessment of property lines to determine the exact amount of land that a property owner holds.

Title A legal document evidencing a person's right to or ownership of a property.

Unilateral contract A contract created by an offer that can only be accepted by performance.

Valid contract A contract that meets all requirements of law, is binding upon its parties, and is enforceable in a court of law.

Void contract A formal agreement that is illegitimate and unenforceable from the moment it is created.

Voidable contract A formal agreement between two parties that may be rendered unenforceable for a number of legal reasons.

Voluntary alienation A transfer of real property through one's intentional actions.

Water rights Interests that may attach to real estate ownership, pertaining to the rights to use adjacent bodies of water.

Key Contract-Related Terms

The following terms relate directly to real estate contracts and the transaction process. Mastery of these definitions is foundational to working effectively with promulgated forms.

Acceleration clause A contract provision that allows a lender to require a borrower to repay all or part of an outstanding loan if certain requirements are not met.

Addendum A document attached to and made part of the original contract. It may be explanatory, informational, or may indicate requirements of the parties not fully addressed in the contract itself.

Amendment A document that makes a change to a ratified sales contract after the contract has been executed by all parties.

Amortized loan An installment loan in which monthly payments are applied first toward reducing the interest balance, with any remaining amount applied to the principal balance.

Appraisal The process of valuing real property using one of three approaches: the cost approach, the income capitalization approach, or the sales comparison approach.

Balloon payment A final loan installment that is disproportionately larger than the regular installment payments.

Closing The completion of a transaction involving the sale or exchange of real estate.

Computer loan origination (CLO) An electronic network for handling loan applications through remote computer terminals linked to various lenders' computers.

Contingency A provision in a real estate contract specifying that the contract would cease to exist upon the occurrence of a certain event.

Counteroffer An offer made in response to a previous offer by the other party during negotiations for a final contract.

Deed of trust A type of secured real estate transaction used in Texas instead of a mortgage, involving the borrower, lender, and a trustee.

Earnest money A deposit made to a seller showing the buyer's good faith in a transaction.

Exclusive agency listing An agency agreement in which the seller reserves the right to sell the property independently without paying a commission to the agent.

Exclusive right-to-sell listing An agency agreement under which a real estate agent holds the sole right to sell a specified property.

Land contract A contract between a seller and buyer of real property in which the seller provides financing to the buyer at an agreed-upon price, with the buyer repaying the loan in installments.

Lease A legal document outlining the terms under which one party agrees to rent property from another party.

Mortgage A debt instrument secured by the collateral of specified real estate property, obligating the borrower to repay according to a predetermined schedule.

Net listing A listing in which the broker's commission is the excess of the sale price over an agreed-upon net price to the seller. Net listings are legal in Texas but uncommon.

Offer to purchase A preliminary agreement, secured by earnest money, between a buyer and seller as an offer to purchase real estate.

Open listing A property listing that uses multiple real estate agents; the agent who sells the property collects the commission.

Option An agreement in which one party buys the right to have the first chance of purchasing a piece of property at a specific price at some point in the future.

Promissory note A written, signed, unconditional promise to pay a certain amount of money on demand or at a specified time.

Proration The act of determining the portion of a cost or benefit to be allocated between two parties.

Rescission The unmaking or termination of a contract between parties.

Short sale Any sale of real estate that generates proceeds less than the amount owed on the property.

Underwriter A person, typically employed by a lender, who reviews required paperwork and gives final approval for a loan.

Unauthorized Practice of Law

One of the most important compliance areas for Texas real estate license holders involves knowing where the line falls between brokerage activity and the practice of law. Both TRELA and the rules of TREC exist, at their core, to protect the public, and that protection includes guarding against unqualified legal advice.

What Constitutes Unauthorized Practice

Regulation of real estate brokers and sales agents includes the prohibition of the unauthorized practice of law. This prohibition covers two related activities: constructing legal documents and giving legal advice or opinions. A license holder may help a party understand what a document says but must not offer legal advice or opinions about the effect of that document. The distinction matters enormously in practice.

TREC has made various forms available to license holders. Those forms must be used according to a strict set of rules. Certain exceptions allow the use of forms prepared by property owners, government agencies, and attorneys. Forms published by the Texas REALTORS for its members also fall within permissible use.

A Texas license holder must be careful to avoid writing language into an agreement that grants legal rights or remedies to any party. Business details and factual statements may be added, but a promulgated addendum must be used when one addresses the particular circumstance. A license holder may never draw lines through contract language, cross out portions, or add words, phrases, or sentences beyond what the form permits. Doing so would constitute acting as an attorney and is prohibited.

The National Association of REALTORS Code of Ethics, Article 13, reinforces this obligation: REALTORS shall not engage in activities that constitute the unauthorized practice of law and shall recommend that legal counsel be obtained when the interest of any party requires it. Avoiding the unauthorized practice of law is not only a legal obligation but an ethical one. It is wrong to provide guidance in a field where one is not qualified.

Suspension or Revocation of License

TRELA establishes that it is a direct violation of the license act to write contracts or verbiage in a contract or addendum that gives legal rights or remedies to the principals of the agreement. Giving legal advice in the role of a real estate broker or sales agent is equally prohibited. TREC has the authority to suspend or revoke the license of a violator.

Under TRELA, the commission shall suspend or revoke the license of a holder who is not a licensed attorney and who, for consideration or in connection with their employment or agency relationship, drafts an instrument that transfers or otherwise affects an interest in real property, or advises a person regarding the validity or legal sufficiency of an instrument or the validity of title to real property.

Despite this rule, a license holder who completes a contract form for the sale, exchange, option, or lease of real property incidental to acting as a broker is not engaged in the unauthorized practice of law if the form was adopted by the commission for the type of transaction for which it is used, prepared by a Texas-licensed attorney and approved by that attorney for the type of transaction, or prepared by the property owner or by an attorney and required by the property owner.

Texas Administrative Code Rules

The Texas Administrative Code (TAC) contains rules and regulations set by various state commissions and agencies. TREC rules governing real estate license holders are found in TAC Chapter 537. These rules reinforce TRELA by specifying that when negotiating contracts binding the sale, exchange, option, lease, or rental of any interest in real property, a license holder shall use only those contract forms promulgated by TREC for that kind of transaction, with limited exceptions.

Those exceptions include transactions in which the license holder is functioning solely as a principal rather than as an agent, transactions in which a United States government agency requires a different form, transactions for which a contract form has been prepared by the property owner or by an attorney and required by the property owner, and transactions for which no standard contract form has been promulgated and the license holder uses a form prepared by a Texas-licensed attorney or by the Broker-Lawyer Committee with TREC's consent.

Limitations on What License Holders May Do

A license holder may not practice law, offer, give, or attempt to give advice directly or indirectly regarding the legal effect of any contracts or instruments affecting title to real estate. A license holder may not give opinions concerning the status or validity of title, and must never discourage any party from seeking legal counsel. In fact, best practice is to strongly encourage clients to consult an attorney whenever they have doubts about legal issues.

When filling in an authorized form, the license holder may only fill in the blanks provided. The license holder may not add to or remove language from the form except to add factual statements and business details requested by the principals, and to strike only what the principals want removed and what is necessary to conform the instrument to their intent. A license holder may not add to a promulgated contract form any factual statements or business details for which a separate promulgated addendum, lease, or other form exists for mandatory use.

When a party to a contract wishes to add, delete, or change language, best practice is to allow the party or that party's attorney to make the actual change. Any deletions or additions must be agreed to and initialed by all parties to satisfy the requirement of mutual agreement. The Special Provisions paragraph in the standard contract form provides a place for license holders to add factual statements and business details that have no other designated paragraph.

The Texas Real Estate Broker-Lawyer Committee

Historical Background

Texas is distinctive among all states in having a well-developed system of standardized residential sales contracts. In many states, attorneys are deeply involved in residential transactions. In Texas, it is rare for an attorney to participate in a residential sale other than to prepare the deed or loan documents. Commercial transactions are different: it is customary for both buyers and sellers, as well as tenants and landlords, to have legal counsel throughout a commercial sale or lease.

In the late 1960s and early 1970s, a significant controversy arose between Texas lawyers and Texas REALTORS. The State Bar of Texas argued that when real estate brokers and sales agents used contract forms to construct transactions for which they were being paid, they were practicing law without a license. The Bar maintained that purchasing real estate is a complex legal transaction and that contracts should be prepared by attorneys.

Real estate brokers countered that lawyers were often unfamiliar with market conditions and that writing real estate contracts was itself a form of brokerage for which lawyers were not licensed. The Texas REALTORS strongly opposed efforts to transfer contract preparation from licensees to attorneys, arguing it would increase costs and delay closings.

Rather than litigate the matter, the two sides agreed to cooperate. The State Bar and the Texas REALTORS formed a joint committee to resolve the conflict. The result was a compromise that still operates today: a committee of both lawyers and brokers would draft standardized forms that REALTORS could use without risking unauthorized practice of law. Because both organizations were private entities, initially only TXR members could use these forms.

Committee Membership

The Broker-Lawyer Committee today operates according to TRELA and under the jurisdiction of TREC. The Texas Real Estate Broker-Lawyer Committee consists of 13 members appointed as follows:

- Six members appointed by the Texas Real Estate Commission
- Six members of the State Bar of Texas appointed by the president of the State Bar
- One public member appointed by the governor

Appointments are made without regard to race, creed, sex, religion, or national origin. The six members appointed by TREC must be brokers with certain experience qualifications. The six members appointed by the president of the State Bar typically have specialties in contracts and real estate. The public member represents the general public's interest in the drafting of the forms. Each member serves a six-year term, with two lawyer and two broker terms expiring every two years and the public member's term expiring every six years.

Committee Duties and the Promulgation Process

The Broker-Lawyer Committee is an advisory body. It drafts and recommends contract forms to TREC for use by license holders. After the committee prepares or revises a form, the TREC board of directors reviews the committee's recommendations and then decides whether to approve and promulgate the form. To promulgate in this context means to put into force under the law.

In addition to drafting original forms, the committee revises promulgated forms as necessary to reflect changes in the law or in real estate and financing practices. All promulgated forms must contain safeguards protecting the principals in the transaction, and they must not favor either the buyer or the seller. TREC promulgated contract forms are available for use by the general public as public records and may be accessed at the TREC website.

Occasionally the Broker-Lawyer Committee and TREC ask selected brokers to use proposed contracts or addenda on a trial basis before promulgating them for all licensees. When TREC promulgates a new form or a revision to an existing form, it typically allows two to three months for all licensees to study and become familiar with the change. During that period, either the old form or the new form may be used. After the allowed period, the new form is mandatory and the old one is retired permanently.

Fraud, Misrepresentation, and the Deceptive Trade Practices Act

Fraud

Fraud is an act of deception done deliberately by someone to gain an unfair advantage over another person. The concept of intention is always central to fraud. A mistake is not fraud because a mistake is not intentional. Fraud is more difficult to prove in court than misrepresentation because the plaintiff's attorney must prove that the plaintiff was damaged, that the damages were caused by the licensee's acts, and that the licensee performed those acts intentionally. Proving intent is the most difficult part.

Because of this higher burden of proof, most licensees are sued for misrepresentation rather than fraud. The fact that a lawsuit has been filed does not mean that fraud or misrepresentation actually occurred. Anyone may file a lawsuit for any reason, and the license holder may ultimately be cleared of any wrongdoing. In our legal system, a person is presumed innocent until proven guilty.

Misrepresentation

Misrepresentation arises when a license holder makes a misleading or false statement that a customer or client accepts as fact and then suffers damages as a result of relying on that information. License holders should not copy information directly from prior MLS listings, including room measurements, because the earlier licensee may have made errors. Copying that information duplicates the mistake.

License holders should not rely on unverified internet data about a property. If quoting a fact about a property, the license holder should also identify the source: for example, 'According to the county appraisal district, the square footage of this home is 1,700 square feet.' License holders should share only verifiable facts accompanied by their source. This practice reduces the likelihood of a lawsuit and demonstrates professionalism.

The Deceptive Trade Practices Act

The Deceptive Trade Practices Consumer Protection Act is a law that applies broadly to business in Texas, not just real estate, to ensure that fraud and misrepresentation do not occur as companies provide products and services. When a real estate license holder is involved in litigation, the suit is often brought under this law. The Texas version of the Act is commonly called the DTPA.

The Texas DTPA was created to protect consumers. Its goal is to make consumers whole after a consumer transaction has damaged them. The central question is whether any false, misleading, or deceptive act or statement was the producing cause of damages to the consumer. The Act also serves to punish business people who engage in deceptive conduct and to protect the public from breaches of warranty.

A large part of avoiding fraud and misrepresentation is the disclosure process that real estate agents facilitate. Years ago the concept in real estate was 'let the buyer beware.' The goal today is 'make the buyer aware.' Agents work to ensure that sellers and buyers have the information necessary to make informed decisions. DTPA and TREC both exist, at their core, to protect the public from license holders who might cause harm.

License holders can create liability by answering questions without the knowledge to answer them accurately. Best practice is to state only facts and, when the facts are not known, to seek out information from an expert. If a question falls outside the license holder's knowledge, the client or customer may need to consult an expert directly.

Recommending Repair and Service Providers

Clients and customers often ask license holders to recommend professionals ranging from lenders to home inspectors to repair contractors. If a license holder recommends only one provider and the consumer later alleges that fraud or misrepresentation occurred in connection with that recommendation, the attorney may pursue the license holder and the broker as well. For this reason, brokers should maintain an office list of acceptable professionals working in the fields surrounding real estate transactions, including attorneys, title companies, lending institutions, home inspectors, appraisers, surveyors, plumbers, electricians, and general contractors.

When a consumer asks for a personal recommendation, the license holder's best approach is to hand the consumer the office list and indicate that the office does not recommend one provider over another. If the consumer asks specifically which provider's work the agent has observed firsthand, the agent may name that person but should follow immediately with a clear statement that this does not constitute a recommendation of that provider over others. This approach reduces liability for both the agent and the broker.

Notice, Inspection, and Time Limits Under the DTPA

Under the DTPA, the plaintiff must give the potential defendant 60 days' notice of the intention to file, along with an outline of the complaint and the claimed damages, including both economic damages and mental anguish. The list must also include anticipated expenses and attorney's fees. The defendant must be given the opportunity to inspect the property and to settle the matter before the case proceeds to court.

A defendant may make an offer to settle without admitting guilt. If the plaintiff declines the offer and proceeds to trial, the defendant may file the offer with the court as evidence of a reasonable effort to resolve the dispute. If the judge determines that the offer was reasonable and close to the actual damages and legal fees, the judge may end the case and award the amount in the offer.

The DTPA has a statute of limitations. A consumer must file suit within two years from the date of the event or from the date of discovery of the event. In one instructive case, buyers who had lived in a home for five years discovered evidence of a prior fire when they removed wall paneling. They had two years from the date of discovery to file their lawsuit. The court dismissed the case against the real estate agent because a reasonable person would not have known about the concealed fire, but it ruled against the sellers, who had disclosed 'No' on the seller's disclosure notice next to 'Previous Fires' and had covered the evidence with paneling.

Successful Defenses and Damages

When sellers complete all required disclosures and give buyers the opportunity to inspect the property, courts generally find that the sellers did what could reasonably be expected. A seller cannot disclose what the seller does not know. If a problem exists that the seller was genuinely unaware of, it cannot be held against that seller. Similarly, agents are not held responsible for material defects in a property that they have no knowledge of. This does not, however, eliminate the agent's obligation to go through the seller's disclosure thoroughly and impress upon the seller the importance of full and honest disclosure.

The DTPA allows a winning consumer to recover economic damages, attorney's fees, and court costs. A judge or jury may also award additional damages for mental anguish if the act was committed knowingly or intentionally. In cases of knowing or intentional conduct, the plaintiff may receive up to three times the economic damages for mental anguish. Some brokers include provisions in their independent contractor agreements allowing recovery of these costs from future commissions earned by the sales agent who caused the problem. The best defense against any of these outcomes is to do the right thing from the beginning: state facts, cite sources, and use experts when necessary.

Promulgated Contract Forms: Authority and Use

When negotiating contracts binding the sale, exchange, option, lease, or rental of any interest in real property, a Texas real estate license holder must use only those contract forms promulgated by TREC for that kind of transaction, subject to the exceptions described earlier in this chapter. All TREC forms state at the top that they are promulgated by the Texas Real Estate Commission. The form name appears in bold capital letters, and a notice often appears beneath the name clarifying the form's intended use.

TREC contract forms are intended for use by trained license holders. Mistakes in the use of a form may result in financial loss or an unenforceable contract. TREC does not promulgate listing agreements, buyer representation agreements, property management contracts, forms for commercial property, or residential leases other than the temporary residential leases used in connection with a sale. For those forms, license holders should contact an attorney or a real estate trade association.

As public records, all TREC contract forms are available to any person and may be accessed at the TREC website. If a member of the public obtains a form for use in a real estate transaction, that person should contact a license holder or an attorney for assistance. TREC cannot provide legal advice on private contractual matters.

Current Promulgated Contracts

TREC promulgates the following contract forms for use by license holders:

- One to Four Family Residential Contract (Resale) -- Form 20-19
- Unimproved Property Contract -- Form 9-18
- New Home Contract (Incomplete Construction) -- Form 23-20
- New Home Contract (Completed Construction) -- Form 24-20
- Farm and Ranch Contract -- Form 25-17
- Residential Condominium Contract (Resale) -- Form 30-18

In addition to contracts, TREC promulgates a substantial library of addenda, notices, and other forms. A complete and current list is available at the TREC website at trec.texas.gov.

Understanding the One to Four Family Residential Contract

The One to Four Family Residential Contract (Form 20-19) is the form license holders use most frequently. It applies to the resale of single-family homes, duplexes, triplexes, and fourplexes. The current version became effective July 1st, 2026. The following summarizes the purpose of each paragraph.

Parties Identifies the buyers and sellers who are parties to the contract.

Property Identifies the property to be sold by its legal description and lists items included in or excluded from the sale.

Sales Price States the offer amount, including the down payment, loan amount, and total sales price.

Financing Identifies the type of financing the buyer intends to obtain. Details are specified in the appropriate financing addendum.

Earnest Money and Termination Option Allows the buyer to demonstrate good faith. If the buyer performs and the transaction closes, the earnest money is applied to closing costs. This paragraph identifies the option fee and how the option will operate. This paragraph also identifies the escrow agent.

Title Policy and Survey Addresses which party pays for the title policy, the title company to be used, the title commitment conditions, survey options, objection procedures, and required notices.

Property Condition Addresses the buyer's right to inspections, the seller's responsibility to provide the Seller's Disclosure Notice, lead-based paint disclosure obligations, buyer's acceptance of the property, and provisions for repairs, treatments, and residential service contracts.

Broker Disclosure Notes that certain disclosures must be made in accordance with the Broker's ownership of a property.

Closing Sets the closing date and describes the parties' responsibilities at closing.

Possession Sets the date on which occupancy transfers to the buyer.

Special Provisions Allows the parties to include factual statements or business details for which no other paragraph of the contract provides a designated place.

Settlement and Other Expenses Specifies the expenses each party is responsible for paying.

Prorations Divides certain expenses between the buyer and seller as of the closing date.

Casualty Loss Describes the rights and obligations of the parties if the property is damaged or destroyed before closing.

Default Addresses the remedies available to the non-defaulting party in the event of a breach of contract.

Mediation Provides an option for resolving disputes through mediation, a non-binding process in which a neutral mediator helps the parties reach agreement. Costs are split equally.

Attorney's Fees Specifies how the expenses of a court proceeding will be paid.

Escrow Explains the conditions under which the escrow agent holds funds and how those funds are handled if the transaction does not close.

Representations States that all covenants, representations, and warranties survive closing. If any representation is untrue at closing, the seller is in default.

Federal Tax Requirements Addresses tax withholding obligations when real estate transactions close.

Notices States that all notices between parties must be in writing and are effective when mailed, hand-delivered, emailed, or faxed.

Agreement of Parties Lists the most frequently used addenda and includes a space for any additional addendum the parties wish to attach.

Termination Option Allows the buyer to terminate the contract for any reason during an agreed period in exchange for an agreed option fee. The option fee may be credited at closing if agreed.

Consult an Attorney Reminds all parties that real estate license holders cannot give legal advice and urges parties to consult an attorney before signing if anything is unclear.

The final page of the contract provides space for the effective date, signatures, broker information, option fee receipt, and earnest money receipt.

Specialized Contracts

Unimproved Property Contract (Form 9-18)

This form is intended for vacant land that has been subdivided into lots and blocks rather than large tracts of raw land. The property identification paragraph calls for lot and block numbers but accommodates an exhibit for lengthy metes and bounds descriptions. A key provision informs the buyer of the responsibility to determine whether utilities are available to meet the buyer's needs. The seller discloses any knowledge of flooding, pending litigation, environmental hazards, dumpsites, landfills, underground storage tanks, wetlands, or endangered species. The seller is not required to inspect or investigate, only to disclose what is known.

New Home Contracts (Forms 23-20 and 24-20)

Two separate forms address new construction: one for incomplete construction and one for completed construction. Neither form may be used for condominiums or for closings prior to completion of construction.

The Incomplete Construction form (23-20) is for houses to be built from the ground up. It includes provisions for construction specifications, change orders, and allowances for buyer-selected materials, along with start and completion dates.

The Completed Construction form (24-20) applies to newly built homes where construction is finished at the time of the contract. Both forms include a Federal Trade Commission required disclosure about the R-value of insulation and provisions for builder warranties. Any builder warranty must be set out in a separate document, and any manufacturer's warranties pass from the builder to the buyer.

Most Texas home builders use contract forms prepared by their own attorneys. Builder contracts may favor the builder, unlike TREC forms, which are neutral between the parties. License holders should never attempt to interpret a builder's contract or give legal opinions about it. Buyers should be strongly advised to seek legal counsel before signing any builder contract.

Farm and Ranch Contract (Form 25-17)

This form serves any property from a small farm or country getaway to a large working ranch. It covers farm homes, barns, and other outbuildings. The legal description section accommodates metes and bounds descriptions and addresses water rights and easements. Improvements are divided between farm and ranch improvements such as windmills, barns, and fencing, and residential improvements such as flooring and lighting. Accessories include hunting blinds, game feeders, livestock feeders, and irrigation equipment.

Crops are specifically addressed: the seller retains the right to harvest all growing crops until title passes. The reservations provision allows the seller to retain mineral, water, royalty, timber, or other interests. The sales price paragraph allows for adjustment if a survey reveals more or less acreage than originally believed. The seller must list any government subsidy programs currently in force and provide documentation. Rollback taxes are also addressed: these may be levied when property that has been receiving an agricultural tax rate loses that benefit and additional taxes become due. Farm and ranch real estate is a specialty, and license holders entering this area should seek additional education before attempting to broker such properties.

Residential Condominium Contract (Form 30-18)

The Texas Property Code defines a condominium as a form of real property ownership that combines separate ownership of individual apartments or units with common ownership of all other elements. This form may not be used where the seller owns fee simple title to the land beneath the unit.

The property paragraph not only identifies the unit and building but also references the Condominium Declaration, Bylaws, Rules of the Association, and the Resale Certificate. Prorations include maintenance fees, special condominium assessments, and cash reserves from assessments. The casualty loss provisions are more detailed than in other forms because some damage may be the responsibility of the condominium association rather than the individual seller. TREC does not promulgate a form for new condominium construction.

Contract Addenda

Addenda expand or modify contracts to address circumstances not fully covered in the main form. TREC promulgates addenda for mandatory use in specific situations. The following describes the major promulgated addenda and their current form numbers.

Addendum for Sale of Other Property by Buyer (Form 10-6)

This addendum creates a contingency contract based on the sale of the buyer's current property. It protects buyers who must sell an existing home before completing the purchase of a new one. If the sale of the buyer's other property falls through by the specified date, the buyer is released from the contract and the earnest money is returned. The seller retains the right to continue showing the property and to accept another offer. If the seller does accept a second offer, the seller must give the original buyer a set number of days to either remove the contingency or withdraw and have the earnest money returned.

Addendum for Back-Up Contract (Form 11-9)

This form is used when a property is already under contract and a second buyer wants to be positioned to purchase if the first contract falls through. The back-up buyer must deposit required earnest money and pay an option fee if a termination option is desired. If the first contract terminates within the specified time limits, the back-up contract becomes the primary contract. If the first contract does not terminate, the back-up buyer's earnest money is refunded and the back-up contract ends. Back-up contracts are common when inventory is low and buyer demand is strong. TREC has also promulgated a companion notice for use with this addendum, the Seller's Notice to Buyer of Removal of Contingency Under Addendum for Back-Up Contract (Form 62-0, effective May 28, 2026). The seller uses this notice to inform the back-up buyer that the first contract has terminated and that the back-up contract has moved into the primary position, the event that begins the performance periods under the now-primary contract.

Addendum for Release of Liability on Assumed Loan (Form 12-3)

This form is used only when a buyer is assuming the seller's existing loan. It is appropriate when the seller wants to be released from liability after the buyer assumes the loan. The buyer must apply for approval based on income and creditworthiness. If the existing loan is a VA loan, restoration of the seller's VA entitlement may be obtained only if the buyer is a veteran who substitutes his or her VA entitlement for the seller's.

Seller Financing Addendum (Form 26-8)

Seller financing is available when the seller owns the property free and clear and does not require the full sales price in cash at closing. The seller acts as the lender, with the property serving as collateral. If the buyer fails to pay, the seller may foreclose. The addendum addresses the buyer's creditworthiness, credit approval, the promissory note, the deed of trust, and tax and insurance escrow arrangements. The seller should be advised to have an attorney prepare the loan documents and deed of trust.

Third Party Financing Addendum (Form 40-11)

This addendum, effective January 3, 2025, addresses conventional financing, Texas Veterans loans, FHA-insured loans, VA-guaranteed loans, and USDA-guaranteed financing. It is concerned solely with financing approval: the buyer must apply promptly, use diligence in securing financing, and notify the seller within a specified number of days if financing cannot be obtained. Failure to provide timely notice binds the buyer to the contract. If the buyer properly notifies the seller of an inability to obtain financing, the contract terminates and the earnest money is refunded.

Loan Assumption Addendum (Form 41-3)

When a buyer assumes an existing loan, title transfers to the buyer, but the seller may remain liable if the buyer later defaults. Loan assumptions are uncommon today because most loan documents from the past several decades do not permit assumptions, and current loan programs make new financing more attractive. The addendum addresses the buyer's creditworthiness and credit approval, loan details, and lender transfer fees. This addendum is used for assumptions of existing loans; the Third Party Financing Addendum is used for new loans.

Environmental Assessment, Threatened or Endangered Species, and Wetlands Addendum (Form 28-2)

When a buyer has concerns about environmental issues, this addendum is used. It covers three categories: environmental assessment, threatened or endangered species, and wetlands. Environmental issues that may require assessment include mold, asbestos, radon gas, water contamination, electromagnetic fields, carbon monoxide, toxic waste sites, and leaking underground storage tanks. The buyer is given a specified period to arrange formal inspections by qualified inspectors. If an adverse report is received, the buyer may terminate the contract.

Notice of Buyer's Termination of Contract (Form 38-8)

This promulgated notice, effective April 1, 2025, is not part of the contract itself. It serves as the vehicle by which a buyer notifies the seller of termination under one of the contract's contingency provisions. It applies to termination under the Termination Option, to situations where financing approval cannot be obtained under the Third Party Financing Addendum, to cases where the property does not meet loan underwriting requirements, and to termination under the seller's disclosure notice provision. Timeliness of delivery is critical in any of these situations.

Coastal Area Addenda

Two addenda are required for properties along the Texas Gulf coast, where storm damage may erode beaches and alter property boundaries in ways an owner could not anticipate.

The Addendum for Coastal Area Property (Form 33-2) must be attached to contracts involving land abutting tidally influenced waters. It warns that property boundaries may shift because of tidal forces. Coastal areas submerged by tides belong to the state of Texas, and no structures are permitted in such areas without a state permit.

The Addendum for Property Located Seaward of the Gulf Intracoastal Waterway (Form 34-4) informs buyers of land on or near the coast that all Texas beaches are open to the public as a public easement and that no structures may be placed on any beach. Due to hurricane-driven erosion, property owners in these areas may be required by the state to remove structures that end up on the beach.

Addendum for Property Subject to Mandatory Membership in a Property Owners Association (Form 36-11)

When the main contract indicates that the property is located in a mandatory homeowners association, this addendum is required. A buyer may request that the seller provide subdivision information within a specified number of days, including subdivision restrictions, rules, and association bylaws. If the seller fails to deliver the requested information on time, the contract becomes voidable and the buyer may choose to terminate. If the seller becomes aware of material changes in the subdivision information, the seller must notify the buyer immediately. The addendum also addresses association transfer fees and procedures for repairs that are the association's responsibility.

Addendum for Reservation of Oil, Gas and Other Minerals (Form 44-3)

Standard TREC sales contracts convey title to the property without addressing subsurface mineral rights. This addendum is used only when the seller intends to reserve all or part of the mineral estate, including oil, gas, and other minerals, along with any royalty under existing leases. It also addresses surface rights connected to those mineral interests, such as production and drilling rights, easements, and lease payments. Because oil and gas law is a specialized area, license holders should strongly advise all parties to consult an attorney about the legal implications.

Addendum for Property in a Propane Gas System Service Area (Form 47-0)

This addendum must be included in the contract if the property is located in an area served by a propane gas system authorized to provide service under Texas Utilities Code Chapter 141. It informs the buyer of potential costs associated with propane gas service, including special charges, facility fees, and line charges, giving the buyer the opportunity to investigate these costs before proceeding.

Short Sale Addendum (Form 45-2)

This addendum creates a contingency based on the lender's approval of the short sale. It is used when the seller's net proceeds at closing will be insufficient to pay off the existing mortgage balance and the seller requires the lienholder's consent to sell. The addendum provides that the contract is contingent on the lienholder's agreement to accept the seller's net proceeds as full satisfaction of the loan and to deliver an executed release of lien in recordable form.

Amendment to Contract (Form 39-11)

An amendment is specifically drafted to reflect changes negotiated after the original contract has been signed. Unlike addenda, which are attached to the original contract at execution, an amendment modifies an already-ratified agreement. Each amendment is signed by the parties and takes effect as of its signing date. Current TREC rules identify ten permissible reasons to amend a contract:

- Changing the sales price, down payment, or amount financed
- Specifying additional repairs
- Extending the closing date
- Changing the seller's contribution to the buyer's closing costs
- Reallocating the amounts the parties agree to pay for lender-required repairs
- Extending the Termination Option period with the amount of any additional option fee
- Waiving the right to the remainder of an existing option period
- Extending the date by which the buyer must give notice regarding the securing of financing
- Adding or deleting factual statements or business details concerning the existing contract
- Making any other modification agreed to by the parties that is not addressed by the preceding nine paragraphs, provided the modification does not require the licensee to draft language creating legal rights or remedies

License holders should not make changes to a contract for any reason other than those listed on the amendment form.

Additional Promulgated Addenda

TREC promulgates several additional addenda that license holders will encounter in appropriate transactions. The Addendum Concerning Right to Terminate Due to Lender's Appraisal (Form 49-1) addresses the buyer's rights when an appraisal comes in below the contract price. The Addendum Containing Notice of Obligation to Pay Improvement District Assessment (Form 53-0) discloses improvement district obligations to buyers. The Addendum for Authorizing Hydrostatic Testing (Form 48-1) is used when the buyer wants to authorize testing of the sewer system. The Addendum for Section 1031 Exchange (Form 60-0), effective January 3, 2025, facilitates tax-deferred exchanges under the Internal Revenue Code. The Addendum Regarding Residential Leases (Form 51-1) and the Addendum Regarding Fixture Leases (Form 52-1) address existing tenant leases and leased fixtures, respectively.

Temporary Leases and Other Promulgated Forms

Seller's Temporary Residential Lease (Form 15-7)

When a seller needs to remain in possession of the property after closing, this temporary lease is used. The form is an addendum to a TREC contract form and may never be used as a stand-alone lease agreement. The Seller's Temporary Residential Lease applies to both home and condominium sales. The possession paragraph of the sales contract provides that possession occurs at closing and funding, or according to a temporary residential lease promulgated by TREC. This temporary lease must be used any time the seller remains in possession after title transfers, even for a single day. The buyer becomes the landlord and the seller becomes the tenant.

The temporary lease covers daily rent charges, lease term, security deposit, repairs, holdover penalties, insurance, default, and other standard lease provisions. The temporary lease may not extend beyond 90 days. If the parties need a longer occupancy period, a regular lease form must be used instead. As with all forms, license holders should remind clients to consult an attorney about any provisions they do not fully understand.

Buyer's Temporary Residential Lease (Form 16-7)

Occasionally a buyer takes possession of a property before closing. This occurs only in limited circumstances, typically when the seller has already vacated. Before allowing a buyer to take early possession, the seller and the seller's agent should be reasonably confident that closing will occur. In this arrangement, the seller becomes the landlord and the buyer is the tenant. The 90-day limit applies here as well.

The buyer-tenant may use the property only for residential purposes and may not assign the lease or sublet any portion of the property. The buyer-tenant may not make holes in or drive nails into woodwork, floors, walls, or ceilings; alter, paint, or decorate the property; or install improvements or fixtures without the prior written consent of the seller-landlord. Any improvements or fixtures installed during the lease period become part of the property.

Other Promulgated and Optional Forms

TREC also provides several other forms that license holders use in appropriate circumstances. The Seller's Disclosure Notice (Form 55-1) is a disclosure of the seller's knowledge of the property's condition as of the date signed. It is not a warranty by the seller or the seller's agent. The Non-Realty Items Addendum (Form 57-0), effective September 3, 2025, facilitates the transfer of personal property between the parties. The Notice to Prospective Buyer (Form 58-0), effective September 3, 2025, advises buyers to obtain an attorney's opinion or title insurance. The Notice of Seller's Termination of Contract (Form 50-0) provides the vehicle for sellers to notify buyers of contract termination under applicable circumstances. The Seller's Disclosure about Groundwater and Surface Water Rights (Form 61-0, effective July 1, 2026) provides prospective buyers with information about the groundwater and surface water rights associated with the property.

The Condominium Resale Certificate (Form 32-5) and the Subdivision Information, Including Resale Certificate for Property Subject to Mandatory Membership in a Property Owners' Association (Form 37-5) provide important financial and operational information about associations to prospective buyers. Both must be requested in writing from the relevant association, which is required by law to comply. The association may charge a fee.

The Disclosure of Relationship with Residential Service Company (Form RSC-4) requires disclosure of any relationship the license holder has with a residential service company. Texas law requires all real estate license holders to provide buyers, tenants, sellers, and landlords with information about brokerage services as part of the first substantive communication in a transaction.

Chapter 1: Snapshot Review

The following review summarizes the key rules and concepts from Chapter 1.

TRELA and TREC

- The Texas Real Estate License Act (TRELA) was enacted in 1939 as the Real Estate Dealer's License Act, renamed in 1955, and exists to safeguard the public and protect consumers of real estate services
- The Texas Real Estate Commission (TREC) assumed administration of the license act in 1949 and holds full rule-making authority; its rules carry the full force and effect of law
- TREC is composed of nine members: six active brokers with at least five years of licensed experience, and three members with no financial interest in the real estate business
- TREC oversees real estate brokerage, appraisal, inspection, home warranty, and timeshare interest providers
- TRELA requires listing contract forms to include a notice that real estate commissions are negotiable

Unauthorized Practice of Law

- Unauthorized practice of law covers two activities: constructing legal documents and giving legal advice or opinions about the effect of a document
- A license holder may help a party understand what a document says but must not offer legal opinions about its legal effect
- License holders may only fill in the blanks provided on promulgated forms; they may not add language granting legal rights or remedies, cross out existing language without authorization, or alter the form beyond what the rules permit
- The Special Provisions paragraph is the only place to add factual statements and business details not addressed elsewhere in the contract
- TREC may suspend or revoke the license of a holder who drafts legal instruments, gives legal opinions, or advises on title validity in connection with employment or for consideration
- A license holder completing a TREC promulgated form incidental to acting as a broker is not engaged in the unauthorized practice of law
- TAC Chapter 537 reinforces TRELA: license holders must use only TREC promulgated forms when negotiating contracts binding the sale, exchange, option, lease, or rental of any interest in real property, with limited exceptions
- Exceptions to the promulgated form requirement include: license holder acting as a principal, government agency form required, form prepared by the property owner or owner's attorney, or no promulgated form exists and an attorney or the Broker-Lawyer Committee prepared the form

The Texas Real Estate Broker-Lawyer Committee

- The committee was formed in the late 1960s and early 1970s as a compromise between the State Bar of Texas and the Texas REALTORS to resolve the unauthorized practice of law controversy
- The committee consists of 13 members: six brokers appointed by TREC, six State Bar attorneys appointed by the president of the State Bar, and one public member appointed by the governor

- Each member serves a six-year term; the committee is an advisory body only -- it drafts and recommends forms but TREC's board of directors approves and promulgates them
- To promulgate means to put a rule or form into force under the law
- All promulgated forms must protect both principals and must not favor either buyer or seller
- When a new or revised form is promulgated, TREC typically allows a two-to-three month transition period during which either the old or new form may be used; after that period the new form is mandatory
- All TREC promulgated forms are public records available at trec.texas.gov

Fraud, Misrepresentation, and the DTPA

- Fraud is a deliberate act of deception; intent must be proven in court, making it harder to establish than misrepresentation
- Misrepresentation is a misleading or false statement accepted as fact that causes damages; intent need not be proven
- Best practice: state only verifiable facts, always cite the source (e.g., 'According to the county appraisal district...'), and never copy unverified data from prior MLS listings
- When recommending service providers, give clients the office list of professionals and avoid singling out one provider; do not accept referral fees from any service provider
- The Texas Deceptive Trade Practices Consumer Protection Act (DTPA) protects consumers from false, misleading, or deceptive business practices in any Texas business context
- DTPA procedure: the plaintiff must give the defendant 60 days' written notice before filing suit; the defendant may make a settlement offer without admitting guilt; if the offer is reasonable and the plaintiff rejects it and loses, the court may award only the settlement amount
- DTPA statute of limitations: two years from the date of the event or from the date of discovery
- DTPA damages: economic damages, attorney's fees, and court costs; up to three times the economic damages for mental anguish in cases of knowing or intentional conduct
- Successful defense: sellers who complete all required disclosures and give buyers the opportunity to inspect generally satisfy their legal obligation; sellers and agents are not responsible for defects they did not know about

Promulgated Contract Forms

- Six current TREC promulgated contracts: One to Four Family Residential Contract (Form 20-19), Unimproved Property Contract (Form 9-18), New Home Contract Incomplete Construction (Form 23-20), New Home Contract Completed Construction (Form 24-20), Farm and Ranch Contract (Form 25-17), and Residential Condominium Contract (Form 30-18)
- TREC does not promulgate listing agreements, buyer representation agreements, property management agreements, commercial forms, or stand-alone residential leases
- Form 20-19 (effective July 1st, 2026) is the most commonly used form; it applies to the resale of one-to-four family residential properties
- The Termination Option in Paragraph 23 of Form 20-19 allows the buyer to terminate for any reason during the option period in exchange for an option fee paid to the seller
- The Special Provisions paragraph (Paragraph 11) allows only factual statements and business details; legal rights and remedies may not be added by a license holder

Contract Addenda and Amendments

- An addendum is attached to and made part of the original contract at execution; it addresses circumstances not fully covered in the main contract form
- An amendment (Form 39-11, effective July 1, 2026) modifies a ratified contract after execution; it is used for only ten specified purposes including price changes, repair requests, closing date extensions, and related adjustments
- Every addendum checked in Paragraph 22 of Form 20-19 must be physically attached; every attached addendum must be identified in Paragraph 22
- Key addenda: Third Party Financing Addendum (Form 40-11, eff. January 3, 2025) for new loans; Loan Assumption Addendum (Form 41-3) for assumed loans; Seller Financing Addendum (Form 26-8) for seller-carried notes; Short Sale Addendum (Form 45-2) for lienholder-approval contingencies
- Coastal addenda (Forms 33-2 and 34-4) are required for properties abutting tidally influenced waters or located seaward of the Gulf Intracoastal Waterway
- The Addendum for Mandatory HOA Membership (Form 36-11) is required when the property is in a mandatory property owners association

Temporary Leases and Other Forms

- Seller's Temporary Residential Lease (Form 15-7, eff. January 5, 2026): used when the seller remains in possession after closing; buyer becomes landlord, seller becomes tenant; maximum term 90 days; may not be used as a stand-alone lease
- Buyer's Temporary Residential Lease (Form 16-7, eff. January 5, 2026): used when the buyer takes possession before closing; seller becomes landlord, buyer becomes tenant; maximum term 90 days
- Seller's Disclosure Notice (Form 55-1, eff. May 28, 2026): disclosure of seller's knowledge of property condition; not a warranty
- Seller's Disclosure about Groundwater and Surface Water Rights (Form 61-0, eff. July 1, 2026): provides prospective buyers with information about the groundwater and surface water rights associated with the property
- Non-Realty Items Addendum (Form 57-0, eff. September 3, 2025): facilitates transfer of personal property between parties
- Notice of Buyer's Termination of Contract (Form 38-8, eff. April 1, 2025): the vehicle for notifying the seller of contract termination under applicable contingency provisions; timeliness of delivery is critical
- Seller's Notice to Buyer of Removal of Contingency Under Addendum for Back-Up Contract (Form 62-0, eff. May 28, 2026): notifies the back-up buyer that the first contract has terminated and the back-up contract has become the primary contract
- All current TREC promulgated forms are public records available at trec.texas.gov and are updated periodically; license holders should always verify they are using the current version of any form

CHAPTER 1 QUIZ:
TEXAS CONTRACT LAW

1. In what year did the Texas legislature first enact the law that is now known as the Texas Real Estate License Act?
   a. 1955
   b. 1979
   c. 1939
   d. 1949

2. Which agency assumed administrative responsibility for the Texas real estate license act in 1949?
   a. The Texas Real Estate Commission
   b. The Texas Department of Licensing and Regulation
   c. The Office of the Secretary of State
   d. The Texas State Bar

3. How many members currently serve on the Texas Real Estate Commission?
   a. Six
   b. Twelve
   c. Thirteen
   d. Nine

4. Among TREC's members, how many must have no financial interest in the real estate business?
   a. Two
   b. Three
   c. Six
   d. Four

5. Which of the following activities is prohibited under the unauthorized practice of law rules that govern Texas real estate license holders?
   a. Giving a client a legal opinion about the effect of a contract provision
   b. Explaining to a buyer the definition of a given term in a contract
   c. Adding factual statements about a property to the Special Provisions paragraph
   d. Using a TREC promulgated form when representing a seller

6. The Texas Real Estate Broker-Lawyer Committee drafts contract forms and then submits them to which body for final approval and promulgation?
   a. The Texas State Bar
   b. The Texas Legislature
   c. The Office of the Governor
   d. The Texas Real Estate Commission

7. How many members does the Texas Real Estate Broker-Lawyer Committee have in total?
   a. Nine
   b. Thirteen
   c. Eleven
   d. Fifteen

8. Which of the following best describes fraud in a real estate context?
   a. A false statement made by a licensee who did not know the information was incorrect
   b. A mistake in the legal description of a property
   c. A deliberate act of deception committed to gain an unfair advantage over another person
   d. A breach of contract that results in financial harm to the buyer

9. Misrepresentation differs from fraud primarily because misrepresentation does not require the plaintiff to prove which of the following?
   a. That the statement was false
   b. That the plaintiff suffered damages
   c. That the licensee made the statement to the client
   d. That the licensee acted with intent to deceive

10. Under the Texas Deceptive Trade Practices Act, how many days' written notice must a plaintiff give a defendant before filing suit?
    a. 60 days
    b. 30 days
    c. 45 days
    d. 90 days

11. What is the statute of limitations for filing a claim under the Texas Deceptive Trade Practices Act?
    a. Four years from the date of the event
    b. Three years from the date of closing
    c. Two years from the date of the event or from the date of discovery
    d. One year from the date of injury

12. In cases where a DTPA defendant acts knowingly or intentionally, a court may award the plaintiff up to how many times the economic damages as an additional award for mental anguish?
    a. Two times
    b. Three times
    c. Four times
    d. Five times

13. Which TREC promulgated form is most commonly used for the resale of a single-family home in Texas?
    a. One to Four Family Residential Contract (Form 20-19)
    b. Unimproved Property Contract (Form 9-18)
    c. Farm and Ranch Contract (Form 25-17)
    d. Residential Condominium Contract (Form 30-18)

14. The Termination Option in Form 20-19 allows the buyer to do which of the following?
   a. Extend the closing date without paying any additional fee
   b. Waive the seller's disclosure requirement
   c. Transfer the contract to a new buyer without seller approval
   d. Terminate the contract for any reason during an agreed period in exchange for an option fee

15. Which of the following does TREC NOT promulgate?
   a. The Farm and Ranch Contract
   b. The Buyer Representation Agreement
   c. The One to Four Family Residential Contract
   d. The Unimproved Property Contract

16. How long does TREC typically allow licensees to study and become familiar with a newly promulgated form before it becomes mandatory?
   a. Two to three weeks
   b. Six months
   c. Two to three months
   d. One full year

17. An addendum differs from an amendment in that an addendum is executed at which point in the transaction?
   a. After the contract has been ratified by all parties
   b. Only after the closing date has passed
   c. When the lender requests a change to the financing terms
   d. At the same time as the original contract

18. The TREC Amendment to Contract (Form 39-11) may be used for how many permissible categories of changes to a ratified contract?
   a. Nine
   b. Five
   c. Seven
   d. Twelve

19. What is the maximum number of days that either the Seller's Temporary Residential Lease or the Buyer's Temporary Residential Lease may extend beyond the closing date or before closing?
   a. 30 days
   b. 90 days
   c. 60 days
   d. 120 days

20. When a client asks a license holder for a legal opinion about a contract provision, what is the best practice response?

   a. Explain the legal effect based on the licensee's years of experience
   b. Write the interpretation into the Special Provisions paragraph of the contract
   c. Encourage the client to consult a licensed attorney for any legal questions
   d. Contact TREC directly for an official ruling on behalf of the client

Chapter 1: Case Study
Texas Contract Law

The Situation

Sandra Meyers has held a Texas real estate sales agent license for three years and works under broker Dale Hutchins at PPC Realty. Sandra recently listed a property owned by Carl and Donna Renfro, a couple who are going through a contentious divorce. Carl signed the listing agreement, but Sandra was unable to reach Donna and listed the property without her signature.

After two weeks on the market, Sandra received an offer from buyer Marcus Webb that was very close to the asking price. Before presenting the offer to Carl, Sandra received a phone call from another buyer she had been working with for several months who said he planned to submit a competing offer within a day or two. Wanting to give her long-time buyer a fair shot, Sandra waited 48 hours before presenting Marcus Webb's offer to Carl.

Carl accepted Marcus Webb's offer and signed the contract. During the option period, Marcus asked Sandra to explain what would happen legally if he terminated the contract on day eight of a ten-day option period versus what would happen if he waited until day eleven. Sandra provided a detailed verbal explanation of both scenarios, including her opinion on which approach would give Marcus the strongest legal position.

Marcus ultimately decided to proceed with the purchase. As the closing approached, a title search revealed that Donna Renfro had never signed any document related to the sale. The title company declined to insure the transaction without Donna's signature, and the closing was postponed indefinitely. Marcus Webb, who had already given notice at his apartment, suffered financial harm as a result of the delay.

Discussion Questions

Question 1

Sandra listed the property without Donna Renfro's signature on the listing agreement. Why was this an error, and what specific steps should Sandra have taken at the outset to prevent the title problem that surfaced at closing?

____

____

____

____

____

Question 2

Sandra delayed presenting Marcus Webb's offer for 48 hours while waiting for her other buyer to submit a competing offer. Identify the specific TREC rule Sandra violated, explain the legal and ethical consequences of that violation, and describe the harm that could result from this type of delay.

Question 3

When Marcus asked Sandra to explain the legal effect of terminating on day eight versus day eleven of the option period, Sandra gave him a detailed verbal opinion. Explain why Sandra's response crossed the line into unauthorized practice of law, what she should have done instead, and what disciplinary consequences she could face under TRELA.

CHAPTER 2:

BASICS OF TEXAS REAL ESTATE LAW

Chapter Overview

Learning Objectives

Upon completing Chapter 2, the student will be able to:

1. Explain how federal, state, local, and judicial regulation governs real property interests in Texas, and identify the six major areas subject to regulation.
2. Define the legal concepts of land, real estate, and property, and describe the bundle of rights associated with real property ownership.
3. Distinguish surface rights, subsurface rights, air rights, and water rights, and explain how each may be separately held or transferred.
4. Differentiate real property from personal property and classify fixtures, trade fixtures, and emblements correctly.
5. Describe the physical and economic characteristics of real property and explain how each influences value.
6. Identify and compare the major forms of real property ownership in Texas, including ownership in severalty, tenancy in common, joint tenancy, community property, and ownership in trust.
7. Describe how business organizations including partnerships, corporations, limited liability companies, and syndicates may hold real property.
8. Explain the distinguishing features of condominium, cooperative, and time-share ownership and identify the principal laws that affect real estate practice.

Contents

- Regulation of Real Property Interests
- Legal Concepts of Land, Real Estate, and Property
- Real Property Rights
- Surface, Subsurface, Air, and Water Rights
- Classification of Property
- Fixtures, Trade Fixtures, and Emblements
- Physical and Economic Characteristics of Real Property
- Forms of Ownership
- Co-Ownership in Texas
- Ownership by Business Organizations
- Condominium, Cooperative, and Time-Share Ownership
- Laws Affecting Real Estate

Regulation of Real Property Interests

Although the United States Constitution guarantees private ownership of real estate, laws and regulations at every level of government qualify and limit individual real property ownership and the bundle of rights associated with it. Real property law addresses both the tangible and intangible aspects of a property. Tangible aspects include land, buildings, structures, trees, and minerals. Intangible aspects include the rights above and below the land, zoning considerations, and all the rights that accompany ownership.

Regulations vary across state, county, and local jurisdictions, so a rule in one city will not necessarily apply to a neighboring city. In general, regulation takes the form of federal and state laws and regulations, county and local ordinances and codes, and court decisions from the judicial system. Regulation therefore draws from statutes, civil law, and case law.

Areas of Regulation

Government entities regulate the following aspects of real property interests:

- Bundle of rights -- possession, usage, transfer, encumbering, and exclusion
- Legal descriptions
- Financing
- Insurance
- Inheritance
- Taxation

Bundle of Rights

Ownership of real estate includes a set of rights that are transferred from seller to buyer during a sale. Ownership of these rights belongs to the person whose name appears on the title to the property. The bundle of rights is examined in detail later in this chapter.

Legal Descriptions

A property deed must include a written legal description of the property. The most common legal description formats used in the United States are lot and block, metes and bounds, and the U.S. Public Land Survey System.

Financing

Financing regulations address lending requirements and establish standards for lending, underwriting, and loan management practices.

Insurance

Insurance regulations govern insurance requirements, available policies, and the process for filing claims associated with real property.

Inheritance

Inheritance regulation addresses the logistics of transferring ownership of real property through an estate and the associated tax obligations.

Taxation

Taxation regulations govern all aspects of taxing real property. Real property taxation occurs at the local level, so tax amounts differ across cities, counties, and districts even within the same state.

Federal, State, Local, and Judicial Regulation

Federal Regulation

In regulating real property rights, the federal government is primarily concerned with broad standards of real property usage, natural disaster response, land description, and discrimination. Federal agencies such as the Federal Housing Administration promote and regulate homeownership. The Environmental Protection Agency establishes usage restrictions and guidelines for hazardous materials and environmental concerns. Federal flood insurance legislation requires certain homeowners to carry flood insurance. The Federal Fair Housing Act of 1968 prohibits discrimination in housing based on race, religion, color, or national origin. The Americans with Disabilities Act prescribes design and accessibility standards. The federal government does not levy real estate taxes.

State Regulation

State governments are the primary regulatory entities of the real estate business. They establish real estate license laws and qualifications, and they create real estate commissions to administer license laws and oversee licensee activities. State governments also exert regional influence over the use and environmental control of real estate within their borders, including laws relating to flood zones, waste disposal, drainage control, shore preservation, and pollution standards.

States define how real property may be owned, transferred, encumbered, and inherited. In some states, a mortgaged property becomes the legal property of the lender until the loan is paid off. States have the power to levy real estate taxes, but they generally pass this authority to local government.

Local Regulation

County and local government regulation focuses on land use control, control of improvements, and taxation. Land use regulations and ordinances govern how all property within a jurisdiction may be developed, improved, demolished, and managed. County and local governments have the power to zone land, exercise eminent domain for public purposes, issue building permits, and establish rules for all development projects. County and local governments, along with school districts and other local jurisdictions, have the power to levy real estate taxes.

Regulatory laws created at the federal, state, and local levels are considered statutory law because they originate from legislation. Statutory laws may never contradict constitutional law. Once statutes are in place, agencies at all government levels use them as a basis for creating regulations.

Judicial Regulation

The judicial system influences real estate ownership and use through decisions based on case law and common law, as distinguished from statutory law. Case law consists of decisions based on judicial precedent. Common law is the collective body of law derived from custom and generally accepted practice in society. Together, these sources of law shape the legal framework within which real property is owned and used in Texas.

Legal Concepts of Land, Real Estate, and Property

To understand real estate rights and interests, it is necessary to recognize the distinctions between land and real estate, real estate and property, and real property and personal property.

Land

The legal concept of land encompasses all of the following:

- The surface area of the earth
- Everything beneath the surface extending downward to the center of the earth
- All natural things permanently attached to the earth
- The air above the surface extending outward to infinity

Land therefore includes minerals beneath the earth's surface, water on or below the surface, the air above, and all plants attached to or growing in the ground. A parcel, or tract, of land is a portion of land delineated by boundaries.

Real Estate

The legal concept of real estate encompasses land plus all man-made structures that are permanently attached to the land. Real estate therefore includes fences, streets, buildings, wells, sewers, sidewalks, and piers, in addition to land itself. Such man-made structures are called improvements.

The phrase permanently attached refers primarily to intent. Very few man-made structures can be permanently attached to land in a literal sense, but if a person constructs a house intending to create a permanent dwelling, the house is considered real estate. By contrast, if a camper stakes a tent to the ground intending to move it in a week, the tent is not real estate.

Property

Property is both the item owned and the set of legal rights the owner holds in that item. These rights are commonly called the bundle of rights. In owning property, a person has the right to possess and use it as the law allows, the right to transfer ownership, the right to encumber it as collateral for debt, and the right to exclude others from its use.

Simple example: when a buyer purchases a home, that buyer acquires not only the structure but also all the legal rights associated with it. The bundle of rights passes from seller to buyer through the deed.

Private ownership rights in the United States are not absolute. The government may impose taxes and restrictions on private ownership and may even take private property for public use through eminent domain. Other private parties may also hold enforceable interests in a person's property. A lender, for example, may foreclose if the owner fails to pay a mortgage. A neighbor may hold an easement across the property by long-standing use.

Real Property Rights

Real property rights consist of the bundle of rights associated with owning a parcel of real estate. The five primary rights are described below.

Right of Possession

The right of possession is the foremost right in the bundle. The owner holds legal title and may occupy or control the property.

Right of Use

The right to use a property refers to the right to use it in certain ways, including mining, cultivating, landscaping, demolishing, and building. The right is subject to local zoning restrictions and the requirement that the use be lawful. An owner's right of use may not infringe on adjacent property owners' rights to use and enjoy their own property.

Right of Transfer

The right to transfer includes the right to sell, bequeath, lease, donate, or assign ownership interests. An owner may transfer individual rights without transferring total ownership. For example, a person may sell mineral rights while retaining the right of possession, or may convey all rights except mineral rights. A seller can only transfer the rights the seller actually holds.

Right to Encumber

The right to encumber means the right to mortgage the property as collateral for debt. Certain restrictions may apply, such as a spouse's homestead rights, which can limit the degree to which a homestead may be mortgaged.

Right of Exclusion

The right of exclusion gives the owner the legal right to keep others off the property and to prosecute trespassers.

Divisibility of Rights

The bundle of rights applies separately to the individual components of real estate: the air, the surface, and the subsurface. An owner can transfer subsurface rights without transferring air rights, and can lease air space without encumbering surface or subsurface rights. If a municipality wants to construct a subway beneath an owner's land, it must acquire the subsurface rights to do so.

A standard lease is a common example of the partial transfer of the bundle of rights. The landlord relinquishes the right to possess a portion of the surface in exchange for rent. The tenant enjoys the rights to possess and use the leased space for the term of the lease. When the lease expires, those rights revert to the landlord. During the term, the tenant holds no rights to the subsurface or airspace beyond what the structure occupies, and the tenant does not acquire any other rights in the bundle of rights.

Surface, Subsurface, Air, and Water Rights

Land can be laterally severed into distinct categories of rights. Each category may be held, sold, or leased separately.

Surface Rights

Surface rights apply to the real estate contained within the surface boundaries of a parcel. This includes the ground, all natural things affixed to the ground, all improvements, and water rights associated with the surface. Surface rights do not automatically include subsurface or air rights.

Subsurface Rights

Subsurface rights apply to land beneath the surface extending from the surface boundaries downward to the center of the earth. Notable subsurface rights are the rights to extract mineral deposits, gas, and subsurface water. In Texas, oil, gas, and other mineral rights are recognized as separate estates. This means a landowner may sell mineral rights to an oil company while retaining all other interests, creating multiple ownerships in a single parcel. The City of Houston, for example, has issued licenses granting subsurface rights to downtown businesses, allowing them to construct underground pedestrian tunnels connecting buildings.

Air Rights

Air rights apply to the space above the surface boundaries of a parcel, defined by imaginary vertical lines extended to infinity. Since the development of commercial aviation, air rights have been limited to allow aircraft to fly over private property, provided the flights do not unreasonably interfere with the owner's use and enjoyment of the property.

In Texas, large amounts of available land mean that air rights are more commonly licensed through a fee arrangement than sold outright. In cities such as Houston, the city issues licenses when hospitals or high-rise buildings build walkways or sky bridges over public streets. Texas law has also created air easements over land near commercial airports, including height restrictions on surrounding buildings to prevent interference with flight paths.

Water Rights

Water rights concern the rights to own and use water found in lakes, streams, rivers, and the ocean. In Texas, the classification of the water determines who holds the rights. Surface water includes ponds, rivers, streams, and bays. The state of Texas publicly owns and governs all surface water. Groundwater filters down through the earth's surface and belongs to the landowner. Riparian rights govern water use along a waterway, and littoral rights apply to property abutting an ocean, sea, or lake.

Classification of Property

The legal system recognizes two classifications of property: real property and personal property.

Real property Ownership of real estate together with the bundle of rights associated with owning that real estate.

Personal property Ownership of anything that is not real estate, together with the rights associated with owning that item. Personal property items are also called chattels or personalty.

Manufactured Homes

Manufactured homes are typically classified as personal property because they are movable. In Texas, however, a manufactured home may be converted to real property through a Statement of Ownership and

Location filed with the Texas Department of Housing and Community Affairs. A manufactured home may also be treated as real property when it is permanently connected to utilities and affixed to the land.

Tangible and Intangible Property

Both real and personal property may be further categorized as tangible or intangible. Tangible property is physical, visible, and material. All real estate is tangible by its physical nature. Intangible property is abstract and has no physical existence in itself beyond serving as evidence of an ownership interest.

Personal property may be either tangible or intangible. Boats, jewelry, coins, appliances, and artwork are tangible personal property. Stocks, copyrights, bonds, trademarks, patents, and franchises are intangible personal property.

Real Versus Personal Property: The Attachment Test

The primary test for distinguishing real from personal property is whether the item is permanently attached to the land or to structures attached to the land. This classification is not fixed and may be changed through conversion.

> **Severance** The conversion of real property to personal property by detaching it from the real estate, such as cutting down a tree or removing an antenna from a roof.
>
> **Affixing** The conversion of personal property to real property by attaching it to the real estate, such as assembling bricks into a built-in barbecue or constructing a dock.

Additional Criteria for Classification

When the attachment test alone is insufficient, a court may apply one or more of the following additional criteria:

- Intention -- if a person attached an item to real property intending to remove it later, the item may still be deemed personal property
- Adaptation -- if an item is uniquely adapted to the property, it may be deemed real property regardless of how easily it could be removed; examples include house keys, custom-fitted window screens, and purpose-built cabinetry
- Functionality -- if an item is vital to the operation of the building, it may be treated as a fixture even if easily removable; window-unit air conditioners and detachable solar panels are examples
- Relationship of parties -- a tenant-installed item used for business purposes may be a trade fixture, which is personal property
- Contract provisions -- the listing of an item in a sale or lease contract as personal property or a fixture overrides all other tests; unless exceptions are stated, all fixtures are included in the sale

When listing a home, it is good practice for the agent to walk the property with the seller and discuss what items are fixtures. If the seller intends to keep a fixture, it is often best to remove and replace it before the property goes on the market. What buyers do not see, they cannot negotiate over.

Fixtures, Trade Fixtures, and Emblements

Fixtures

A personal property item that has been converted to real property by attachment to real estate is called a fixture. Common examples include chandeliers, toilets, water pumps, septic tanks, and window shutters. Texas standard sales contract forms typically specify what items are deemed fixtures. The owner of real property owns all fixtures belonging to that property. When the property is sold, the buyer acquires all fixtures unless specific items are excluded in the contract.

Trade Fixtures

Trade fixtures, also called chattel fixtures, are items of a tenant's personal property that the tenant has temporarily affixed to a landlord's real property for business purposes. Trade fixtures may be detached and removed before or upon surrender of the leased premises. If a tenant fails to remove a trade fixture, it may become the property of the landlord through accession and be treated as real property thereafter.

Examples of trade fixtures include a grocer's refrigeration units, a merchant's clothing racks, a restaurant owner's bar equipment, a dairy's milking machines, and a printer's printing press.

Emblements

Growing plants and agricultural crops may be classified as either real property or personal property. Plants and crops that grow naturally without requiring human labor are real property. Plants and crops that require human intervention and labor to plant and cultivate are called emblements Emblements are treated as personal property despite being attached to the land.

If emblements belong to a tenant farmer, the tenant retains the right to harvest the crop even after the lease has expired. The landlord may not claim a tenant's growing crops.

Physical and Economic Characteristics of Real Property

Real property has two general types of characteristics: physical and economic. Understanding these characteristics helps agents, buyers, sellers, and investors understand the real estate market and the factors that influence property value.

Physical Characteristics

The three physical characteristics of real property are immobility, indestructibility, and heterogeneity.

Immobility Land cannot be moved from one site to another. The geographical location of a parcel is fixed. One can transport portions of land such as mined coal or excavated soil, but once those elements are detached from the land they are no longer land.

Indestructibility Land is essentially permanent. One would have to remove a segment of the planet all the way to its core to destroy it. Even then, the vertical column extending to infinity would remain. This quality also makes land a reliable long-term investment.

Heterogeneity No two parcels of land are identical. Even adjacent parcels with similar characteristics are inherently different because each occupies a unique location. Differences in soil composition, shape, elevation, and surrounding uses make every parcel one of a kind.

Economic Characteristics

The four economic characteristics of real property are scarcity, improvements, permanence of investment, and area preference.

Scarcity The total supply of land is fixed. Buildings can be built taller, but the supply of land in any given location cannot increase. In areas where population is large relative to the available land, prices rise accordingly.

Improvements Any change to a parcel of land, whether a modification or a new construction, can affect the value and use of that land. Improvements may affect the parcel itself and the surrounding neighborhood, either favorably or unfavorably. A new employer opening in a struggling area, for example, often raises surrounding property values.

Permanence of investment Resources and capital invested in improvements represent a large, fixed commitment. Infrastructure investments such as sewage systems, drainage, water lines, and electrical systems tend to remain in place over the economic life of the improvement, providing relatively stable long-term returns.

Area preference Area preference refers to people's preferences for certain locations and their characteristics. Different preferences produce different values for otherwise similar properties. This is the principle behind the phrase location, location, location. Area preference is the most important economic characteristic of real property because it explains why similar homes sell for very different prices in different neighborhoods.

Forms of Ownership

Real property may be owned in a number of different ways depending on how many parties share the ownership and how they share it. It is essential for a license holder to understand how a property is held, because the form of ownership determines who must sign every document in a transaction, from the listing agreement through the deed.

Ownership in Severalty

When a single party owns a fee or life estate, the ownership is called an estate in severalty, also known as sole ownership or tenancy in severalty. This form of ownership is severed, or separate, from any form of co-ownership. When the sole owner is a married person, the property is that spouse's separate property, and the owning spouse holds title independently of the other spouse. Upon the death of a sole owner, the estate passes to heirs through probate.

Ownership in Trust

In an estate in trust, a fee owner (the grantor or trustor) transfers legal title to a fiduciary (the trustee), who holds and manages the estate for the benefit of another party (the beneficiary). A trust may be created by a deed, a will, or a trust agreement. The trustee holds fiduciary duties to the trustor and beneficiary, including the obligation to maintain the condition and value of the property. The specific responsibilities and authorities of the trustee are set out in the trust agreement.

Living trust A living trust allows the trustor, during his or her lifetime, to convey title to a trustee for the benefit of a third party. The trustee manages the property, protects its value, and may be directed to sell the property at a designated time. The beneficiary receives all income and sales proceeds, net of the trustee's fees.

Land trust A land trust allows the trustor to convey the fee estate to the trustee while naming himself or herself as the beneficiary. The land trust applies only to real property. The trust agreement grants the beneficiary-trustor the rights to possess and use the property and to direct the trustee's actions.

Co-Ownership in Texas

Co-ownership means that a parcel is owned by two or more persons or organizations. Co-owners are called co-tenants. Texas recognizes three forms of co-ownership: tenancy in common, joint tenancy, and community property.

Tenancy in Common

Tenancy in common, also called an estate in common, is the most common form of co-ownership when the owners are not married. It is also the default form of co-ownership when a deed does not specify otherwise. The key defining features are:

- Two or more owners may hold any number of shares
- Co-tenants share an indivisible right to possess and use the entire property
- Each co-tenant's interest is individually owned and may be sold, encumbered, or transferred without the consent of the others
- Ownership shares are electable; parties may agree on unequal shares such as 40 percent, 35 percent, and 25 percent
- There is no survivorship right; a deceased co-tenant's interest passes by probate to heirs
- Co-tenants need not acquire their interests at the same time

In Texas, a spouse married to a tenant in common is typically required to sign a deed conveying the property to release the spouse's potential interest. For a married couple, a deed of conveyance creates a community property interest rather than a tenancy in common.

A partition suit may be used to terminate a tenancy in common when co-owners cannot agree. The court may order the property physically divided or, if that is not feasible, sold and the proceeds distributed among the co-owners. Foreclosure and bankruptcy may also terminate these estates.

Joint Tenancy

In a joint tenancy, two or more persons collectively own a property as though they were a single person. Rights and interests are indivisible and equal. In Texas, a joint tenancy must be created by a written agreement that expressly states the intent to create a joint tenancy.

The defining characteristics are:

- Unity of ownership -- joint tenants together hold a single title to the property
- Equal ownership -- each joint tenant holds an identical share; four joint tenants each own 25 percent
- Transfer of interest -- a joint tenant may transfer his or her interest to an outside party, but only as a tenancy in common interest; the remaining joint tenants continue as joint tenants among themselves
- Survivorship -- upon the death of a joint tenant, that tenant's interests and rights pass automatically to the surviving joint tenants, free from the claims of creditors or heirs

Creation of Joint Tenancy

To create a joint tenancy, the four unities must generally be satisfied:

- Unity of time -- all parties must acquire their interests at the same time
- Unity of title -- all parties must acquire the property in the same deed
- Unity of interest -- all parties must receive equal undivided interests
- Unity of possession -- all parties must receive the same rights of possession

Although the Texas legislature authorized written joint tenancy agreements in 1987 without specifically mentioning the four unities, courts have generally upheld them. A joint tenancy can only be created by agreement between parties, not by operation of law.

When the last surviving joint tenant dies, the survivalty owner's interest becomes an estate in severalty. That estate will pass through probate upon the surviving owner's death.

Community Property

Texas is a community property state. Community property law defines the property rights of married persons before, during, and after marriage, and after the death of either spouse. Texas community property laws apply to all married couples, regardless of where they were married.

Community property law divides property into two categories: separate property and community property.

> **Separate property** Property owned by one spouse before the marriage, property acquired by gift or inheritance during the marriage, property purchased with separate-property funds, and income from separate property. A spouse may gain an equitable interest in separate property if its value increases during the marriage or if community property funds were used to pay down a debt on it.
>
> **Community property** All other property earned or acquired by either spouse during the marriage. Both spouses own community property equally.

In practice, Texas title companies and attorneys require the signatures of both spouses on a conveyance of separate property to eliminate any question about whether it is actually community property. Community property cannot be transferred or encumbered without the signatures of both spouses. Homestead rights may be conveyed only by a joint deed of both spouses, even when the homestead is the separate property of one spouse.

Upon the death of one spouse, half of the deceased's community property passes to the surviving spouse and the other half passes to the decedent's heirs.

Community Property Right of Survivorship

In 1987, the Texas legislature created a community property right of survivorship. Unlike a joint tenancy, in which a surviving party is responsible for only half the debt, in a community property arrangement both spouses are responsible for all debt. If one spouse dies, the surviving spouse remains responsible for the full amount.

An agreement to create a community property right of survivorship must be in writing, signed by both spouses, describe the community property covered by the agreement, and include language expressing the intent that the property will pass to the survivor. However, these agreements are not widely accepted by Texas title insurance companies or mortgage lenders, so their use is discouraged in practice.

Tenancy in Partnership

Tenancy in partnership is a form of ownership held by business partners as provided by the Uniform Partnership Act. All partners have equal rights to use partnership property for partnership purposes, but individual interests are not assignable without the consent of the other partners.

Ownership by Business Organizations

Businesses may purchase, hold, and sell real property in much the same way as private individuals. The form of business organization determines how the property is held and who has authority over transactions.

Sole Proprietorship

In a sole proprietorship, one person owns the entire business and reports all profits and losses on a personal income tax return. This structure is easy to organize and operate, and many Texas real estate brokers choose it. The owner may use a personal name or a registered fictitious business name. Because certain tax advantages available to corporations are not available to sole proprietors, it is increasingly common for sole proprietors to incorporate to access benefits such as pension and profit-sharing plans.

General Partnership

When two or more people associate to carry on a business for profit, they form a partnership. Because partnership interests can be bought and sold by members entering or leaving the partnership, real estate ownership by a partnership is treated as a tenancy in common. A general partner is an active partner with unlimited personal liability for the partnership's debts. Under the Uniform Partnership Act, general partners have equal rights to use partnership property for partnership purposes and may not transfer their interests without the consent of the other partners. Creditors of the partnership have first claim on partnership assets.

Limited Partnership

In a limited partnership, limited partners have liability only to the extent of their investment. At least one general partner must exist with unlimited liability. The partnership agreement must be in writing, and the partnership must file a formal certificate of limited partnership. Limited partners may not allow their names to be used in ways that suggest they are general partners. The Tax Reform Act of 1986 eliminated many tax advantages previously associated with limited partnerships in real estate investment, but many real estate limited partnerships continue to operate.

Joint Venture

A joint venture is a partnership formed for a single undertaking rather than an ongoing business. The most common joint venture structure in real estate is the limited partnership. Limited partners typically provide most of the equity capital while general partners manage the assets. A joint venture member does not automatically have the authority to bind the other members. Unlike a general partnership, the death of a joint venture member does not automatically dissolve the joint venture. A managing partner typically controls the venture's operations.

Corporation

A corporation is a separate legal entity established under state law through the filing of articles of incorporation with the Secretary of State. Because a corporation is a distinct legal person, real estate owned by a corporation is owned in severalty. Shareholders have limited liability and elect a board of directors to set corporate policy. Directors hire officers who operate the corporation. Because a corporation has unlimited theoretical life, it does not terminate on the death of a shareholder. If the corporation wishes to sell all or a majority of its assets, the majority of stockholders must approve. Closely held corporations, where a small number of shareholders actively control the business, can reduce corporate tax exposure through salary and benefit arrangements to officer-shareholders.

Limited Liability Company

A limited liability company (LLC) is a hybrid business entity combining characteristics of both a corporation and a partnership. It provides the limited liability protection of a corporation without the full regulatory burden, making it a flexible structure for real estate ownership. Owners are called members, and each member's liability is limited to the capital contribution. An LLC may be managed by its members in proportion to their membership interests, or an operating agreement may designate a manager or board of managers. All LLCs must file evidence of existence with the secretary of state and must disclose the company name, appoint a statutory agent, and state a valid business purpose.

Syndicate

A syndicate is a group of two or more people who combine their financial resources to achieve specific investment objectives, typically acquiring real estate that no individual could purchase alone. Syndication is a descriptive rather than a legal term; the syndicate is governed by whatever legal business form the participants adopt, most commonly a limited partnership, general partnership, corporation, or real estate investment trust. Because most syndicates intend to generate profit for many investors through the efforts of a few sponsors, they must comply with Securities and Exchange Commission rules and regulations.

Condominium, Cooperative, and Time-Share Ownership

Condominium Ownership

A condominium is a hybrid form of ownership combining a fee simple interest in the airspace within an individual unit with an undivided tenancy-in-common interest in the property's common elements, such as lobbies, hallways, elevators, and swimming pools. Under Texas law, condominium unit boundaries are the interior surfaces of the perimeter walls, floors, and ceilings.

The Texas Uniform Condominium Act (Chapter 81 of the Texas Property Code) states that a unit owner holds fee simple title to the unit and a share of the common elements as a tenant in common. Common elements include the land, structural components, building systems such as plumbing and electrical, recreational facilities, and non-exclusive building and ground areas. Unit owners may not partition the common elements.

A condominium unit may be owned jointly, in severalty, in trust, or in any manner allowed by state law. Units can be individually sold, mortgaged, or foreclosed without affecting other units. Condominium units are individually assessed and taxed based on the value of the unit plus the owner's pro rata share of the common elements. Resale may require prior approval of the condominium association.

A condominium differs from a townhouse in that a condo unit consists of bounded airspace within a larger building, while a townhouse owner holds fee simple title to both the structure and the land beneath it. Condominiums are governed by the Texas Uniform Condominium Act; townhouses are not. Condominium associations manage the maintenance of exteriors and common areas; homeowners associations perform a similar function for townhouse communities. TREC does not promulgate a contract form for new condominium construction.

Cooperative Ownership

In a cooperative (co-op), a person owns shares in a nonprofit corporation or cooperative association that in turn holds title to an apartment building as its principal asset. Along with the stock, the shareholder acquires a proprietary lease granting the right to occupy one of the units. The number of shares purchased reflects the unit's proportional value relative to the total property value and establishes the owner's share of operating expenses.

The cooperative association is the only party with a real property interest. Unit owners hold personal property interests (stock and a lease) rather than real property interests. There is no separate ownership of individual units as with condominiums. The proprietary lease has no fixed rent; instead, each owner-tenant pays a monthly pro rata share of the association's operating expenses. When the unit is sold, the lease and stock certificates are both assigned to the buyer.

Because the association owns the property as a whole, the financial failure of individual shareholders can jeopardize the entire cooperative. If the corporation cannot meet its obligations, creditors may foreclose on the entire property, terminating all shareholders' proprietary leases. This risk distinguishes cooperatives from condominiums, where a single owner's financial failure affects only that owner's unit.

Time-Share Ownership

Time-share ownership is a fee or leasehold interest in a property where owners or tenants agree to use the property on a periodic, non-overlapping basis. Time-shares most commonly apply to vacation and resort properties.

In a leasehold time-share, the tenant agrees to rent the property on a scheduled basis according to the terms of a lease, typically denominated in weeks or months over the lease term. In a freehold time-share (also called an interval ownership estate), tenants in common own undivided interests in the property, with expense proration and rules governing interval usage established by a separate agreement.

Before a developer can sell a time-share interest in Texas, the time-share plan must be registered with the Texas Real Estate Commission. Any person selling a time-share who is not associated with the developer or the current owner must hold a TREC license.

Laws Affecting Real Estate

A broad range of laws governs real estate practice in Texas. The following overview identifies the major categories and selected federal laws that every license holder should know.

Property Law

Historically, all property was owned by monarchs, and land use controls date at least as far back as the Roman Empire. In modern property law, a title is a bundle of rights in a piece of property that may be held in whole by one party or divided among several parties. Evidence of title in the United States is established through title reports prepared by title insurance companies, documenting the history of ownership through public records. The most common way to acquire an interest in property is through a consensual transaction with the existing owner.

Agency Law

The law of agency governs contractual, fiduciary relationships in which an agent is authorized to act on behalf of a principal to create legal relations with a third party. In Texas, all agency relationships are established at the broker level. An agent owes the principal several duties:

- Undertake the tasks specified by the terms of the agency
- Discharge duties with care and due diligence
- Avoid conflicts of interest between the principal's interests and the agent's own interests
- Refrain from accepting obligations inconsistent with duties owed to the principal
- Refrain from self-dealing

In return, the principal must make full disclosure of all information relevant to the transactions the agent is authorized to conduct and must pay the agreed compensation.

License Law

Each state maintains real estate license laws designed to regulate the industry and protect the public. In Texas, TRELA and TREC rules govern license holders. Unlicensed real estate activity is illegal; however, buyers and sellers acting as principals in their own transactions are not required to hold licenses. To obtain a real estate license in Texas, an applicant must generally meet the following requirements:

- Be at least 18 years of age
- Be a citizen of the United States or a lawfully admitted alien
- Be a legal resident of Texas
- Successfully complete all required qualifying education
- Pass the Texas real estate licensing examination
- Submit a completed application with required fees
- Submit to a background and fingerprinting review
- Obtain a sponsoring broker

Federal Laws Affecting Real Estate

License holders should be familiar with the following federal laws, regulations, and programs that affect real property transactions:

- Federal Fair Housing Act (Title VIII of the Civil Rights Act of 1968) -- prohibits discrimination in housing based on race, color, religion, national origin, sex, disability, and familial status
- Americans with Disabilities Act -- prescribes design and accessibility standards for commercial properties
- Real Estate Settlement Procedures Act (RESPA) -- governs settlement services and requires disclosure of closing costs

- Truth in Lending Act (TILA) -- requires lenders to disclose the true cost of credit
- Equal Credit Opportunity Act -- prohibits discrimination in credit transactions
- Fair Credit Reporting Act -- regulates the use of consumer credit information
- National Flood Insurance Program -- requires flood insurance for properties in designated flood zones
- Residential Lead-Based Paint Hazard Reduction Act -- requires disclosure of known lead-based paint for housing built before 1978
- Dodd-Frank Wall Street Reform and Consumer Protection Act -- established the Consumer Financial Protection Bureau and reformed mortgage lending practices
- Secure and Fair Enforcement for Mortgage Licensing Act (SAFE Act) -- establishes minimum standards for mortgage loan originator licensing
- Community Reinvestment Act -- encourages lending institutions to meet the credit needs of all segments of their communities
- Home Mortgage Disclosure Act -- requires financial institutions to maintain and disclose data about home purchases and improvement loans
- USA PATRIOT Act -- imposes anti-money-laundering compliance obligations on real estate-related businesses
- CAN-SPAM Act, Do Not Call Act, and Junk Fax Prevention Act -- regulate commercial communications by real estate licensees

Chapter 2 Snapshot Review

The following review summarizes the key rules and concepts from Chapter 2.

Regulation of Real Property

- The Constitution guarantees private ownership of real estate, but government at every level may qualify, limit, tax, and even take private property; private ownership is not absolute
- Federal regulation: broad usage standards, Fair Housing Act, ADA, flood insurance, environmental rules; no real estate taxes
- State regulation: license laws, TREC authority, regional usage and environmental standards; primary regulator of the real estate business in Texas
- Local regulation: zoning, permits, development rules, real estate taxes; the most specific level
- Judicial regulation: case law and common law; interpretive rather than legislative

Property Rights and Classification

- Bundle of rights: possession, use, transfer, encumbrance, exclusion
- Land includes the surface, everything beneath it to the earth's core, natural attachments, and air above to infinity
- Real estate adds man-made improvements permanently attached to land; real property adds the bundle of rights
- Surface rights do not automatically include subsurface or air rights; each may be separately held in Texas
- Primary test to distinguish real from personal property: permanent attachment to land
- Fixture: personal property attached to real estate and converted to real property; passes with a sale unless specifically excluded
- Trade fixture: business item temporarily attached by a tenant; remains personal property; must be removed before lease surrender
- Emblements: cultivated crops requiring human effort; personal property of the tenant who grew them
- Severance converts real property to personal property by detaching it; affixing converts personal property to real property by attaching it

Physical and Economic Characteristics

- Physical characteristics: immobility (land cannot be moved), indestructibility (land is essentially permanent), heterogeneity (no two parcels are identical)
- Economic characteristics: scarcity (fixed total supply), improvements (man-made attachments), permanence of investment (large stable commitments), area preference (location preference)
- Area preference is the most important economic characteristic; it is the principle behind location, location, location

Forms of Ownership

- Severalty (sole ownership): one owner; estate passes by probate at death
- Living trust: trustor conveys title to trustee for benefit of a third party; may allow probate avoidance
- Land trust: trustor conveys title to trustee and names self as beneficiary; applies only to real property; used for privacy
- Tenancy in common: default co-ownership form in Texas; no survivorship right; interests are individually transferable
- Joint tenancy: survivorship right; must be expressly created by written agreement in Texas; requires the four unities of time, title, interest, and possession
- Community property: all property earned or acquired by either spouse during marriage; both spouses own it equally; both must sign any conveyance or homestead transfer
- Community property with right of survivorship: must be in writing, signed by both spouses, describing the property; not widely accepted by Texas title insurers or lenders
- Separate property: owned before marriage or received as gift or inheritance during marriage; not subject to equal spousal ownership
- Partnership, LLC, corporation, and REIT: business entity ownership forms with distinct liability and tax characteristics

Special Ownership Forms

- Condominium: fee simple title to a unit's airspace combined with tenancy-in-common interest in common elements; governed by Texas Uniform Condominium Act (Property Code Chapter 81)
- Cooperative: shareholder owns stock in a corporation that holds title to the building; receives proprietary lease to occupy a unit
- Time-share: periodic use rights in a property by multiple parties; must be registered with TREC before sale in Texas
- Texas water rights -- surface water: publicly owned by the state; riparian rights apply to adjacent owners
- Texas water rights -- groundwater: owned by the landowner under the rule of capture, subject to Texas Water Code and Groundwater Conservation Districts

CHAPTER 2 QUIZ:
BASICS OF TEXAS REAL ESTATE LAW

1. Which level of government is the primary regulator of the real estate licensing business in Texas?
   a. Federal government
   b. State government
   c. County government
   d. Municipal government

2. Which of the following statements correctly describes federal regulation of real estate?
   a. The federal government levies real estate taxes on all residential properties
   b. The federal government sets zoning requirements for every city in the United States
   c. The federal government directly licenses real estate brokers and sales agents
   d. The federal government establishes broad standards for property usage, fair housing, and environmental protection

3. Under the legal concept of land, which of the following is included in a parcel of land?
   a. The surface, everything beneath it to the earth's core, natural attachments, and air above to infinity
   b. Only the surface of the earth and the structures built upon it
   c. The surface and subsurface only, excluding all air space
   d. The surface and any structures permanently attached to it

4. Which of the following best describes the legal concept of real estate?
   a. Land only, with no improvements
   b. The bundle of rights held by a property owner
   c. Land plus all man-made improvements permanently attached to that land
   d. All personal property owned by an individual

5. The bundle of rights associated with real property ownership includes which of the following rights?
   a. Possession, taxation, inheritance, and zoning
   b. Use, distribution, annexation, and appropriation
   c. Encumbrance, condemnation, severance, and accretion
   d. Possession, use, transfer, encumbrance, and exclusion

6. In Texas, oil, gas, and other mineral rights are recognized as which of the following?
   a. Separate estates that may be sold independently from surface ownership
   b. A government-owned resource that requires a state permit to access
   c. Personal property belonging to the surface owner
   d. Rights that automatically transfer to a buyer whenever the surface is sold

7. Who publicly owns all surface water in Texas, including rivers, streams, and bays?
   a. The adjacent landowner
   b. The federal government
   c. The State of Texas
   d. The municipality in which the water is located

8. Which of the following describes groundwater within a ranch in Texas?
   a. It is publicly owned by the state and requires a permit to use
   b. It belongs to the landowner above it
   c. It is jointly owned by all adjacent landowners
   d. It belongs to the federal government and is regulated by the EPA

9. Which of the following tests is the primary method for distinguishing real property from personal property?
   a. Whether the item was purchased by the current owner
   b. Whether the item is listed in the county tax records
   c. Whether the item is permanently attached to the land or to structures on the land
   d. Whether the item has a market value greater than the land itself

10. Severance converts property from one classification to another. Which of the following correctly describes severance?
    a. Personal property is converted to real property by attaching it to the land
    b. A co-ownership arrangement is terminated through a court order
    c. A lease is converted to a freehold estate by a written agreement
    d. Real property is converted to personal property by detaching it from the land

11. A grocer installs refrigeration units in a leased retail space for use in the grocery business. How are those refrigeration units classified?
    a. Trade fixtures, which remain the tenant's personal property
    b. Real property, because they are attached to the building
    c. Fixtures that automatically pass to the landlord at the end of the lease
    d. Emblements, because they support a food-related business

12. Which of the following is the most important economic characteristic of real property?
    a. Scarcity
    b. Area preference
    c. Permanence of investment
    d. Indestructibility

13. Which of the following is a physical characteristic of real property?
    a. Scarcity
    b. Area preference
    c. Permanence of investment
    d. Immobility

14. Which form of co-ownership is the default in Texas when a deed does not specify otherwise?
    a. Tenancy in common
    b. Joint tenancy
    c. Community property
    d. Ownership in severalty

15. Which of the following is a key characteristic of joint tenancy in Texas?
    a. It is the default form of co-ownership when a deed does not state otherwise
    b. Joint tenants may hold unequal shares of the property
    c. It must be created by a written agreement that expressly states the intent to create a joint tenancy
    d. Each joint tenant's interest passes to that joint tenant's heirs upon death

16. In a joint tenancy, which of the following occurs when one joint tenant dies?
    a. The deceased tenant's interest passes to his or her heirs through probate
    b. The deceased tenant's interest passes automatically to the surviving joint tenants
    c. The property is partitioned equally among all remaining tenants
    d. The surviving tenants must purchase the deceased tenant's interest from the estate

17. Texas is a community property state. Which of the following correctly describes community property?
    a. All property earned or acquired by either spouse during the marriage, owned equally by both
    b. Property owned by one spouse before the marriage
    c. Property received by one spouse as a gift or inheritance during the marriage
    d. Property held in a trust for the benefit of a surviving spouse

18. When a married person holds separate property in Texas, which of the following applies to a conveyance of that property?
    a. Only the owning spouse needs to sign the deed
    b. The property must first be converted to community property before it can be sold
    c. A court order is required before either spouse can convey the property
    d. Both spouses must sign the deed to eliminate any question about community property interest

19. Which of the following describes a condominium as defined under Texas law?
    a. A form of ownership in which a shareholder holds stock in a corporation that owns an apartment building
    b. A hybrid ownership combining fee simple title to a unit's airspace with a tenancy-in-common interest in common elements
    c. A leasehold interest in a property shared by multiple owners on a periodic basis
    d. A form of ownership in which the developer retains title to all units and leases them to residents

20. How does a cooperative differ from a condominium?
    a. In a cooperative, each unit owner holds fee simple title to the unit's airspace
    b. In a cooperative, unit owners pay individual property taxes on each unit separately
    c. In a cooperative, the owner holds stock in a corporation and a proprietary lease, not real property
    d. In a cooperative, the common elements are owned by the municipal government

21. Before a developer may sell a time-share interest in Texas, what must the developer do?
   a. Obtain approval from the Texas Department of Housing and Community Affairs
   b. Register the time-share plan with the Texas Real Estate Commission
   c. File a certificate of limited partnership with the Secretary of State
   d. Record the time-share agreement with the county clerk in every county where buyers reside

22. Which of the following best describes a limited liability company as a form of property ownership?
   a. A form of co-ownership that has no legal distinction from a general partnership
   b. A nonprofit entity that holds title for the benefit of its shareholders
   c. A hybrid business entity combining limited liability protection with flexible management structure
   d. A form of ownership reserved exclusively for licensed real estate brokers

23. Which of the following federal laws prohibits discrimination in housing based on race, color, religion, national origin, sex, disability, and familial status?
   a. The Americans with Disabilities Act
   b. The Equal Credit Opportunity Act
   c. The Community Reinvestment Act
   d. The Federal Fair Housing Act of 1968

24. A person who plants and cultivates crops on rented farmland holds which type of interest in those crops?
   a. A personal property interest in emblements that the tenant retains the right to harvest
   b. A real property interest, because the crops are attached to the land
   c. A fixture interest that passes to the landlord when the lease expires
   d. A subsurface interest governed by the rule of capture

Chapter 2 Case Study:

Basics of Texas Real Estate Law

The Situation

Kevin and Laura Mettling have been married for twelve years and own a home in the Hill Country outside Kerrville, Texas. Kevin inherited the property from his father before the marriage. The deed from that inheritance is recorded in Kevin's name only, and Kevin has always regarded the home as his separate property. The Mettlings also purchased a residential lot adjacent to the property together during the marriage using funds from a joint bank account.

An oil and gas company, Performance Energy Programs, recently approached both Kevin and an unrelated neighboring landowner, Dale Crosby, about leasing subsurface mineral rights beneath their respective properties. Kevin signed a mineral lease with Performance Energy Programs without consulting Laura. Dale Crosby, who had purchased his property years ago from a seller who reserved the mineral rights at the time of sale, declined the approach on the grounds that he believed he already owned all rights to his land.

Meanwhile, the Mettlings decided to sell the family home and move to San Antonio. Their listing agent, Tricia Vance, researched the property and told Kevin that because the home was his separate property, Laura did not need to sign the listing agreement or the eventual sales contract. Tricia also told Kevin that the adjacent lot, which the couple owned together, could be listed and sold by Kevin alone since both parcels would be selling to the same buyer and it would simplify the paperwork.

Before the listing went live, Dale Crosby discovered that a portion of his fence had been built approximately four feet over the property line onto the Mettlings' land. The encroachment had existed for at least twelve years without any objection from the Mettlings or Kevin's father before them.

Discussion Questions

Question 1

Kevin signed the mineral lease with Performance Energy Programs without Laura's involvement. Analyze whether Kevin had the authority to do so. In your answer, address whether the home qualifies as separate property, whether mineral rights in Texas are a severable estate, and whether Laura has any interest in the transaction.

____

____

____

____

____

Question 2

Tricia Vance told Kevin that Laura did not need to sign the listing agreement or the sales contract for either property. Evaluate whether Tricia's advice was correct for the family home and for the adjacent lot separately, explaining the legal basis for each conclusion.

Question 3

Dale Crosby's fence has encroached on the Mettlings' property for at least twelve years. Identify the legal doctrine that may be relevant to this situation, explain the requirements that must be met and the steps Dale would need to take if he wanted to assert a legal claim, and describe what the Mettlings or Kevin's father could have done at any point to prevent this outcome.

CHAPTER 3:

INTRODUCTION TO CONTRACTS

Chapter Overview

Learning Objectives

Upon completing Chapter 3, the student will be able to:

1. Define performance, forbearance, default, and breach, and explain the legal consequences of failing to perform under a valid Texas real estate contract.
2. Identify and explain each of the six elements required for a valid contract, and describe what happens when any element is missing.
3. Distinguish between express and implied contracts, and explain the practical importance of putting real estate agreements in writing.
4. Compare bilateral and unilateral contracts, identify real estate examples of each, and explain how each may be breached and enforced.
5. Identify the four legal statuses of a contract and explain the circumstances that produce each status.
6. Explain the conditions that render an otherwise valid contract unenforceable, including lack of consideration, the Statute of Frauds, absence of mutual assent, and impossibility.
7. Define executed and executory contracts, distinguish between them, and apply the distinction to common real estate scenarios.
8. Describe Texas Property Code requirements for executory contracts, including contracts for deed, lease-purchases, and lease-options exceeding 180 days.

Contents

- Performance, Forbearance, Default, and Breach
- The Six Elements of a Valid Contract
- Express and Implied Contracts
- Bilateral and Unilateral Contracts
- Legal Status of Contracts
- Valid but Unenforceable Contracts
- Void and Voidable Contracts
- Unenforceable Contracts
- Executed Contracts
- Executory Contracts
- Texas Requirements for Executory Contracts
- From Executory to Executed

Performance, Forbearance, Default, and Breach

To be enforceable in a court of law, a contract must meet the requirements defined by Texas statute. Parties who enter into an agreement that does not satisfy those requirements carry significant legal risk. A valid contract is legally binding on all parties who sign it.

Performance

In contract language, performance means doing what one agreed to do. A homeowner who contracts with a flooring company to have wood floors installed must pay the agreed price at the agreed stages, and the company must install the specified materials within the agreed timeframe. Both parties are performing according to the contract.

Forbearance

Some contracts require a party to refrain from doing something rather than to act. That obligation is called forbearance. A tenant who signs a lease agreeing not to redecorate without management approval, not to park in driveways, and not to leave trash on the sidewalk is bound by a forbearance obligation. The landlord's agreement not to enter the unit without proper notice is likewise a forbearance obligation. A single contract may include both performance and forbearance requirements.

Default and Breach

Default means failing to do something required by law or duty. Texas law protects the rights of parties who have entered into valid contracts. A party who fails to perform is in default and may be sued by the other party for damages or specific performance.

A breach is the breaking of a contractual obligation. Breach of contract means that a party has failed to fulfill a term of the contract without a legally justifiable excuse. The non-breaching party may seek legal remedies including damages or, in real estate, specific performance compelling the breaching party to close the transaction.

The Six Elements of a Valid Real Estate Contract

Without all six of the following elements, a contract may not provide legal recourse when a party fails to perform. A real estate contract must clearly and specifically state what each party is expected to do and when.

1. Competent parties
2. Consideration
3. Mutual agreement
4. Lawful objective
5. In writing and signed by the parties
6. Legal description

Competent Parties

A competent party has the legal capacity to enter into a contract and may be held to the promises made in the agreement. An incompetent party may not be bound by a contract's terms.

In Texas, a competent party must have reached the age of majority, which is 18 years of age. A person under 18 is a minor, and a contract signed by a minor is voidable at the minor's election. If the minor chooses to proceed, the contract is binding. A minor may be legally emancipated and declared an adult with contractual capacity only by a court of competent jurisdiction.

A party may appoint an attorney-in-fact to act as a fiduciary under a power of attorney. For a transfer of title to real estate, the power of attorney must specifically identify the property involved. The attorney-in-fact's signature binds the authorizing party as though the party had signed personally.

Consideration

Consideration is the exchange of something of value that separates a contractual obligation from a gift. In a real estate sales contract, the consideration is the mutual exchange of promises: the seller promises to convey a specific property, and the buyer promises to pay a mutually agreed price. The property and the money are the things of value being exchanged.

A common misunderstanding is that earnest money is the consideration or that it is required to form a valid contract. Earnest money demonstrates the buyer's serious intent and may serve as liquidated damages if the buyer defaults, but it is not the consideration that creates the contract. The mutual exchange of promises is the consideration.

One contract type that does require payment to be binding is the option contract. In an option, the seller promises to sell under agreed terms, but the buyer is not obligated to purchase. Because only the seller is bound, the buyer must pay something of value to the seller in exchange for keeping that promise open. Without that payment, the seller's promise lacks consideration and the option is unenforceable.

Mutual Agreement

Mutual agreement, also called mutual assent or a meeting of the minds, means that all parties have freely and voluntarily agreed to the same terms based on full and truthful information. Every detail of the contract must be agreed upon by every party.

If a party relied on inaccurate or incomplete information, the contract may not hold up. If deliberate deception, fraud, or false information was present, the agreement is not enforceable. Deception may take the form of an affirmative lie (an act of commission) or the concealment of a material fact about the property (an act of omission).

When all parties agree to voluntarily cancel a contract, that act is called mutual rescission.

Lawful Objective

A contract is not valid if it requires performance that is unlawful. A contract calling for discriminatory terms in the sale of property is void because discrimination violates both state and federal law. A residential lease may not violate the federal Fair Housing Act. For example, a lease provision stating that no resident may be under 18 years of age discriminates against families with children in violation of the familial status protections of the Fair Housing Act. A lease entered into for the purpose of any unlawful activity is similarly void.

In Writing and Signed by the Parties

Most states, including Texas, require certain contracts to be in writing and signed by all parties charged under the agreement in order to be enforceable. This requirement traces back to the English Statute for Prevention of Frauds and Perjuries of 1677, commonly known as the Statute of Frauds.

In Texas, the Statute of Frauds requires that all contracts affecting title to or any interest in real estate be in writing and signed by the parties. An oral agreement to sell real estate is void and unenforceable. The most reliable way to conduct real estate transactions is to put everything in writing.

There is one limited exception: a lease for one year or less may be oral and is enforceable. The Texas Business and Commerce Code states that the Statute of Frauds applies to a contract for the sale of real estate and to a lease of real estate for a term longer than one year.

A contract may be signed by the contracting party directly, by a guardian, by an authorized corporate officer, or by an attorney-in-fact. Under TRELA, a person may not bring a court action to recover a real estate commission unless the agreement on which the action is based is in writing and signed by the party to be charged or by a person authorized to sign on that party's behalf. Properties may be listed under an oral agreement, but if the seller refuses to pay an orally agreed commission, the broker has no legal remedy to compel payment.

Legal Description

The sixth element is unique to real estate. Because real estate is non-homogeneous -- no two parcels are exactly alike -- a precise description of the property is required so the parties know exactly what is being transferred. A property address is not sufficient. The contract must include a legal description complete enough for an independent surveyor to locate and identify the specific parcel.

A legal description is required in every instrument that transfers real property or any interest in it, including sales contracts, leases, easements, rights-of-way, mortgages, and time-share arrangements.

The two commonly used types of legal description in Texas are:

- Metes and bounds -- a description using compass directions and distances to trace the boundary of the parcel
- Reference to a platted subdivision -- lot number, block number, section, and subdivision name as shown on a recorded plat

Express and Implied Contracts

Express Contracts

An express contract is one in which all terms and covenants of the agreement have been clearly stated and agreed to by all parties, whether verbally or in writing. The parties explicitly communicate the terms of the agreement, leaving nothing to be inferred from conduct.

Some express contracts may not be made orally and must be in writing to be enforceable. Under the Texas Statute of Frauds and related provisions, contracts that must be in writing include:

- A contract for the sale of real estate
- A lease of real estate for a term longer than one year
- A promise or agreement to pay a commission for the sale or purchase of an oil or gas lease, royalty, minerals, or mineral interest
- An agreement that cannot be fully performed within one year from the date it is made
- A loan agreement in excess of $50,000 made by a financial institution
- A promise by an executor or administrator to pay a debt out of the executor's or administrator's own estate

Even when a listing agreement may technically exist as an oral contract, TRELA is clear: a broker cannot enforce a commission claim in court unless the agreement is in writing and signed by the party against whom the action is brought. The six required elements apply equally to written and oral express contracts.

The basic rule is that parties must perform as specified in the contract unless the parties mutually agree to a change in its terms, or unless the deviating party's actions are implicitly accepted (ratified) by the other party's conduct.

Implied Contracts

An implied contract is an unstated or unintentional agreement considered to exist when the actions of the parties suggest that an agreement has been reached. Implied contracts arise from conduct rather than from explicit words. A contract implied in fact is a true contract; what differs is how it is established.

To prove an implied contract exists, the following must be shown: an unambiguous offer, unambiguous acceptance, mutual intent to be bound, and consideration. However, these elements may be demonstrated through the conduct of the parties rather than through express written or oral statements.

A common real estate example is implied agency. When a licensee who has no written agreement with a buyer performs acts on the buyer's behalf -- such as negotiating a price below the listing price -- the licensee may have created an implied agency relationship even without intending to. If the buyer then compensates the agent for those efforts, the existence of the implied agreement becomes difficult to dispute.

Implied agency may also arise from a prior relationship. A licensee who represented a buyer in acquiring a home and then informally helps that same person sell another property may be found to have an ongoing agency relationship even without a signed listing agreement. Prior clients who continue to work with a broker on subsequent transactions may remain clients in the eyes of the law.

Practical note: when involved in any oral agreement, a party should keep thorough documentation -- notes of conversations, times and dates of discussions, names of witnesses, and all emails and written correspondence. Even handwritten notes can be decisive in litigation over whether an implied contract existed.

Bilateral and Unilateral Contracts

Bilateral Contracts

A bilateral contract is one in which both parties promise to perform their respective parts of an agreement in exchange for performance by the other party. The exchange of mutual promises is what creates the obligation. Most business and personal contracts, and most real estate contracts, are bilateral.

Common examples of bilateral contracts in real estate include:

- Independent contractor agreement -- a bilateral agreement between a sales agent and a sponsoring broker, in which each party promises specific performance
- Listing agreement -- typically bilateral; the broker promises to perform marketing and representation services, and the seller promises to pay a commission and cooperate
- Buyer representation agreement -- defines the mutual obligations and responsibilities of both the buyer and the broker
- Lease -- the landlord promises to provide the leased premises, and the tenant promises to pay rent and comply with the lease terms
- Purchase agreement -- always bilateral; both the buyer and seller promise to perform at closing

Unilateral Contracts

In a unilateral contract, only one party makes a promise. That promise is made in exchange for an act or forbearance by the other party. The other party is not obligated to perform, but if that party does perform, the promisor is legally bound to fulfill the promise. The offeree cannot be forced to act because no return promise has been made to the promisor.

A reward is the classic example of a unilateral contract. The person offering a reward for a lost item promises to pay if anyone returns it. No one is obligated to search, but whoever does return the item is entitled to the reward. The promisor is bound only if and when the requested act is completed.

Unilateral contracts in real estate include:

- Open listing -- the seller promises to pay a commission to whichever broker produces a ready, willing, and able buyer; no broker is obligated to produce a buyer
- Option to purchase -- binds the seller and prevents sale to another party during the option period, but the prospective buyer is not obligated to purchase
- Option to terminate -- the seller is bound not to sell to another party during the option period, but the buyer is not obligated to proceed with the purchase

A useful rule to remember: options are always unilateral contracts.

Breach of Bilateral and Unilateral Contracts

Both types of contracts can be breached. To enforce either in court, the party seeking enforcement must establish four things:

- The contract existed
- The contract was broken
- A loss was suffered
- The person being challenged was responsible for the breach

The key distinction is when each type becomes enforceable. A bilateral contract is enforceable from the moment it is formed because both parties are bound by mutual promises. A unilateral contract becomes enforceable only when the party receiving the promise begins or completes the requested performance.

Regardless of whether a contract is bilateral or unilateral, all six elements of a valid contract must be present.

Legal Status of Contracts

A court may assess the legal status of a contract in one of four ways: valid, valid but unenforceable, void, or voidable.

Valid

A valid contract is one that meets all legal requirements for enforceability. It satisfies all six essential elements, is in writing where required, and has been signed by the parties. A valid written contract is enforceable within the applicable statutory period. If a party fails to perform as required, that party is in default and may be compelled to perform or to pay damages.

Under Texas law, a person is obligated to read a contract before signing. Unless fraud is involved, a signer is not excused from the consequences of failing to read. A person who signs without knowing the contents is presumed to have consented to the terms, and claims that the provisions differed from what was plainly written are generally not admissible.

Valid but Unenforceable Contracts

A contract may be technically valid yet still be unenforceable in court. This happens when a condition exists at the time the contract is signed, or develops during its term, that prevents a court from compelling performance. The contract retains its validity in the sense that if the parties choose to perform fully, the outcome is final, but neither party can use the courts to force the other to act. Several conditions produce this result.

Lack of Consideration

A real estate contract is unenforceable if the parties have not exchanged something of value. In most real estate transactions, the buyer's earnest money deposit constitutes consideration at the outset, and the seller's delivery of a deed constitutes consideration at closing. A contract in which the buyer never makes a required deposit or the seller refuses to convey title lacks consideration and is unenforceable.

Statute of Frauds

Real estate contracts must be in writing and signed to be enforceable. An oral agreement to buy or sell real estate is unenforceable regardless of how clearly both parties understood the terms. This applies to sales contracts, long-term leases, commission agreements, and other real estate instruments covered by the Texas Statute of Frauds.

Absence of Mutual Assent

A meeting of the minds means that all parties freely agreed to the exact terms written in the contract. If a mistake, misrepresentation, failure to disclose a material fact, or fraud affected any party's decision, mutual assent may be absent and the contract may be unenforceable. For example, if a seller honestly but incorrectly states that the roof was replaced five years ago when it was actually replaced ten years ago, the buyer may have grounds to challenge the contract because the seller's statement was inaccurate. Duress and undue influence also defeat mutual assent.

Impossibility

A condition beyond the parties' control that makes closing impossible or impractical may excuse performance. If a home under contract is destroyed by a tornado before closing, neither party is at fault, but the subject matter of the contract no longer exists. Courts may find the contract unenforceable on grounds of impossibility.

Void and Voidable Contracts

Void Contracts

A void contract is one that fails to meet the tests for validity and is therefore no contract at all. It has no legal effect. Neither party can enforce it, and no act of disaffirmation is necessary to nullify it. A void contract is sometimes described as null and void.

Examples of void contracts include a contract that lacks any consideration, a contract calling for an illegal act such as extortion or discrimination in housing, and a contract entered into for the purpose of unlawful activity.

Voidable Contracts

A voidable contract initially appears valid but may be cancelled by one of the parties on the basis of a legal disability or defect in how the contract was formed. Only the party who claims the disability has the right to disaffirm the contract. The other party cannot disaffirm.

A party who was the victim of duress, coercion, or fraud in the formation of the contract may disaffirm it. The disaffirmation must occur within the applicable legal time frame. If the party with the right to disaffirm instead chooses to perform, the contract is no longer voidable and becomes binding.

The critical distinction between void and voidable contracts: a void contract requires no action to be unenforceable because it never existed as a valid agreement. A voidable contract is binding unless and until the party entitled to rescind takes affirmative action to cancel it.

Unenforceable Contracts

An unenforceable contract is one that cannot be enforced in a court of law, even if it would otherwise qualify as valid. Unenforceability may result from ambiguous terms, from one party's right to void the contract, or from the expiration of the Statute of Limitations.

Statute of Limitations

The Statute of Limitations requires that lawsuits be filed within a specific period following a breach. In Texas, the statute of limitations for written contracts is four years. After that period expires, the right to sue on the contract is lost regardless of the merits of the claim. For example, if a seller attempts to challenge a written real estate contract seven years after closing, the claim is time-barred and the court will not hear it.

Doctrine of Laches

Even before the statute of limitations expires, a court may find a contract unenforceable under the Doctrine of Laches. This doctrine holds that a party who unreasonably delays in asserting a claim, to the detriment of the other party, may be barred from enforcing it. For example, if a buyer discovers a defect after taking possession of a home but waits three years before pursuing a claim, a court may rule that the delay was unreasonable and bar the action, even though the statute of limitations had not yet run.

Executed Contracts

An executed contract is one that has been fully performed by all parties. Neither party bears any further obligation under the agreement. A completed and expired lease is an executed contract: the landlord may repossess the premises, and the tenant has no further obligation to pay rent.

The word execute also has a narrower meaning in the context of documents. To execute a document means to sign it. When practitioners refer to an executed real estate contract, they typically mean that all parties have signed the document. In that sense, the date of execution is the date on which all required signatures appear, which is also the contract's effective date.

In a real estate sales transaction, the contract is not truly executed in the performance sense until closing, when payment and title change hands. Until that milestone is reached, the contract is executory.

Practical Steps for Properly Executed Documents

A license holder plays an important role in ensuring that contracts are properly executed. The following practices reduce errors and prevent future disputes.

- Verify the final version -- after multiple rounds of negotiation, confirm that every party is signing the same, current version of the contract; never assume a prior draft is the final one
- Date the contract -- a contract need not be dated to be valid, but dating it creates a clear chronological record and aids identification years later
- Obtain all signatures -- a contract is not binding until signed by all parties
- Initial handwritten changes -- any last-minute change made by hand must be initialed by all parties; a revised document or signed amendment is preferable to a handwritten change
- Verify authority to sign -- if a party is a corporation, confirm that the entity exists and that the person signing is authorized; in larger transactions, confirm board or shareholder approval
- Retain original copies -- each party should receive an original executed copy; the listing broker should also retain an office copy

Executory Contracts

An executory contract is one in which performance has not yet been completed. A sales contract signed before closing is executory: the parties have agreed to buy and sell, but the buyer has not yet paid the seller and the seller has not yet delivered the deed. The most important obligation in the transaction -- the transfer of title -- remains to be performed.

Executory contracts include any transaction that defers material action relating to ownership or possession of real property into the future. The classic executory contract in real estate is the contract for deed (also called a land sales contract), in which the buyer takes possession and makes payments over time but does not receive a deed until the payments are complete.

Under Texas law, contracts for deed, lease-purchases, and lease-options for periods longer than 180 days are all defined as executory contracts and are subject to the requirements of Texas Property Code sections 5.061 and following. The 180-day threshold exists partly as an accommodation to real estate brokers: without it, the standard one-to-four-family residential contract combined with a TREC temporary residential lease could technically be treated as an executory contract. Options that are not combined with a residential lease and options on commercial property are not subject to these provisions.

Texas Property Code Requirements for Executory Contracts

Texas Property Code sections 5.069 and 5.070 impose requirements that must be satisfied before the purchaser signs an executory contract -- that is, before and not at closing.

Under section 5.069:

- The seller must provide the purchaser with a survey no older than one year or a current plat, and must disclose that no restrictive covenants, easements, or other title exceptions prohibit construction of a house on the property
- The seller must provide copies of all liens, restrictive covenants, and easements affecting the property
- The seller must provide a Seller's Disclosure of Property Condition, as required in an outright sale
- If the property is not in a recorded subdivision, the seller must provide a separate written disclosure that utilities may not be available until the subdivision is recorded

Under section 5.070:

- The seller must provide a tax certificate from the collector for each taxing unit that levies taxes on the property
- The seller must provide a copy of any insurance policy, binder, or evidence of coverage identifying the insurer, the insured, the property, and the policy amount

These requirements are designed to protect buyers who are acquiring property under deferred ownership arrangements where full title will not pass immediately. Sellers who fail to comply face significant penalty provisions under the Property Code.

From Executory to Executed

Most real estate contracts begin as executory agreements and become executed contracts when all conditions are fulfilled and all obligations are performed. In a standard sales transaction, the contract becomes executed at closing when the buyer pays and the seller delivers the deed. At that point, both parties have fully performed and neither owes the other anything further under the agreement.

In some transactions, a contract may move from executory to executed in stages. A construction contract in which a builder completes the project in phases, with payment due at the completion of each phase, provides a clear example. Each completed and paid phase represents an executed portion of the overall contract. Until the final phase is completed and the final payment is made, the remaining obligations are executory.

A contract can also transition to an executed state almost immediately after signing if the only conditions remaining are the formality of completing the written agreement itself. This sometimes occurs in simultaneous delivery-and-payment transactions. Even in those cases, a signed executed contract is valuable because it serves as a record of both the delivery and the payment.

Chapter 3 Snapshot Review

The following review summarizes the key rules and concepts from Chapter 3.

The Six Essential Elements of a Valid Contract

- All six elements must be present for a real estate contract to be valid; the absence of any one element may defeat enforceability
- Competent parties -- both must be at least 18, mentally capable, and legally authorized to contract
- Consideration -- mutual exchange of something of value; in a sales contract, the mutual promises to convey property and pay the price (not earnest money)
- Mutual agreement -- all terms agreed to freely, voluntarily, and based on accurate information; every detail must be agreed upon by every party
- Lawful objective -- the contract's purpose and required performance must not violate any law
- In writing and signed -- required in Texas for all real estate contracts under the Statute of Frauds; oral agreements are void; the one exception is a lease of one year or less
- Legal description -- must be precise enough for an independent surveyor to locate and identify the specific parcel; a street address is never sufficient

Key Rules

- In Texas, all contracts affecting title to or any interest in real estate must be in writing and signed by the parties; oral real estate sales contracts are void and unenforceable
- A broker cannot sue to recover a real estate commission unless the agreement is in writing and signed by the party to be charged
- Earnest money is not the consideration that forms the contract; it is evidence of good faith and may serve as liquidated damages if the buyer defaults
- Options are always unilateral; the seller is bound, the buyer is not; payment from buyer to seller is required to create an enforceable option
- A bilateral contract is enforceable from formation; a unilateral contract becomes enforceable when the party receiving the promise performs
- The statute of limitations for written contracts in Texas is four years; the Doctrine of Laches may bar a claim even earlier if the delay was unreasonable
- A party is obligated to read a contract before signing; signing without reading generally creates a presumption of consent
- Contracts for deed, lease-purchases, and lease-options for more than 180 days are executory contracts subject to Texas Property Code sections 5.061 and following

Contract Types

- Express: all terms clearly stated verbally or in writing
- Implied: created by conduct of the parties rather than explicit words; may arise unintentionally from actions suggesting an agreement
- Bilateral: mutual promises; both parties are bound from formation; purchase agreements, leases, listing agreements, buyer representation agreements
- Unilateral: one party's promise in exchange for an act; the other party is not obligated to perform; options and open listings
- Executed: fully performed by all parties; no remaining obligations

- Executory: performance not yet complete; a signed sales contract before closing is executory

Legal Status of Contracts

- Valid: meets all six elements; enforceable within the statutory period
- Valid but unenforceable: meets elements but cannot be enforced due to Statute of Frauds, lack of mutual assent, or impossibility
- Void: fails validity requirements; not a contract at all; requires no action to nullify
- Voidable: appears valid but may be cancelled by one eligible party due to duress, fraud, coercion, or minority; binding until disaffirmed

Discharge and Breach

- Discharge by performance: full performance by all parties; also by partial performance, sufficient performance, or defective performance
- Discharge by infeasibility: subjective (promisor's death or disability) or objective (subject matter destroyed or purpose frustrated)
- Discharge by mutual agreement: rescission; replacement by a new contract is novation
- Discharge by operation of law: statute of limitations, bankruptcy
- Breach remedies: rescission, forfeiture of earnest money, suit for damages, suit for specific performance
- Four-year statute of limitations for breach of written real estate contracts in Texas

CHAPTER 3 QUIZ:
INTRODUCTION TO CONTRACTS

1. In contract law, the term performance refers to which of the following?
   a. Paying earnest money into an escrow account
   b. Doing what a party agreed to do under the terms of the contract
   c. Filing a lawsuit when the other party fails to act
   d. Signing a contract in the presence of a notary

2. A lease provision that requires a tenant to refrain from redecorating without management approval is an example of which contractual obligation?
   a. Performance
   b. Consideration
   c. Mutual assent
   d. Forbearance

3. How many criterion elements must be present for a real estate contract to be valid in Texas?
   a. Six
   b. Four
   c. Five
   d. Seven

4. In Texas, which of the following correctly states the minimum age requirement for a party to be considered competent to enter into a contract?
   a. 16 years of age
   b. 17 years of age
   c. 18 years of age
   d. 21 years of age

5. What is the consideration in a standard Texas real estate sales contract?
   a. The earnest money deposited by the buyer
   b. The option fee paid to the seller during the termination option period
   c. The commission paid to the listing broker at closing
   d. The mutual exchange of promises between buyer and seller

6. For a sales contract to be enforceable, the Texas Statute of Frauds requires that the contract meet which of the following requirements?
   a. It must be in writing and signed by the parties
   b. It must be witnessed by a notary public
   c. It must be recorded in the county clerk's office before it is enforceable
   d. It must include a minimum earnest money deposit of one percent of the sales price

7. Under the Texas Statute of Frauds, which of the following types of real estate agreements may legally be made as an oral agreement?
   a. A sales contract for a residential property
   b. A commercial lease for any term
   c. A lease for a term of one year or less
   d. A commission agreement between a seller and a listing broker

8. Which of the following best describes an express contract?
   a. A contract that arises from the conduct of the parties rather than from explicit words
   b. A contract in which all terms are clearly stated by the parties, whether verbally or in writing
   c. A contract that becomes binding only when one party completes a requested act
   d. A contract that is formed automatically when two parties exchange earnest money

9. A licensee who has no written agreement with a buyer begins negotiating on that buyer's behalf and eventually receives payment for the effort. What type of relationship may exist?
   a. An express bilateral agency relationship
   b. A principal-to-principal relationship with no agency duties
   c. An implied agency relationship
   d. A subagency relationship with the listing broker

10. In a bilateral contract, when does the agreement become enforceable?
    a. Only after one party has fully completed all required performance
    b. Only after a judge has approved the terms of the agreement
    c. After the earnest money has been deposited into escrow
    d. From the moment the contract is formed, because both parties are bound by mutual promises

11. Which of the following is the best example of a unilateral contract in real estate?
    a. An option to purchase in which the seller is bound but the buyer is not obligated to buy
    b. A purchase agreement in which buyer and seller both promise to perform at closing
    c. A listing agreement in which the seller and broker each promise specific performance
    d. A buyer representation agreement defining the obligations of buyer and broker

12. A court determines that a contract is void. What does this mean for the parties?
    a. Either party may choose to enforce the contract or cancel it
    b. The contract has no legal effect and neither party can enforce it
    c. The contract is valid but cannot be enforced until a court approves the terms
    d. The innocent party may enforce the contract but the breaching party cannot

13. A buyer who was induced to sign a real estate contract through fraud later decides to cancel the agreement. What is the correct legal classification for that contract before the buyer takes action?
    a. Void
    b. Executed
    c. Unenforceable due to impossibility
    d. Voidable

14. In Texas, what is the statute of limitations for filing a lawsuit based on a written contract?
    a. Four years from the date of the breach
    b. One year from the date of the breach
    c. Seven years from the date the contract was signed
    d. Two years from the date of discovery

15. A real estate sales contract is signed by buyer and seller before closing. How is this contract correctly classified at that point?
    a. Void, because title has not yet transferred
    b. Voidable, because either party may cancel before closing
    c. Executory, because the most important obligations have not yet been performed
    d. Executed, because both parties have signed the document

16. Under Texas Property Code sections 5.069 and 5.070, a seller who enters into an executory contract must provide certain disclosures to the buyer. When must those disclosures be delivered?
    a. At closing, along with the deed
    b. Before the purchaser signs the executory contract
    c. Within three business days after the contract is signed
    d. Within 20 days after the effective date of the contract

Chapter 3 Case Study:
Introduction to Contracts

The Situation

Bryan Mettling is a 17-year-old who has been saving money from part-time work for two years. He approaches Performance Property Programs, a residential real estate firm, and signs a buyer representation agreement and a purchase contract on a small investment property without telling anyone his age. The seller, Carol Nguyen, believes she is dealing with an adult and accepts the offer in good faith. Bryan pays earnest money out of his savings and the contract is executed.

Two weeks later, Bryan's parents learn what he has done and tell him to get out of the deal. Bryan notifies the firm that he wants to cancel the contract. Carol Nguyen objects, arguing that the contract was properly formed and that Bryan should be held to it since he misrepresented his age and acted like an adult throughout the negotiations.

Separately, a sales agent at Performance Property Programs named Gail Tanner is working with a commercial landlord who verbally agreed to lease a retail space to a business tenant for a period of 18 months. Both parties shook hands and the tenant began preparing to move in. No written lease was ever signed. When the landlord later received a higher offer from another tenant, he told Gail the deal was off. The prospective tenant, who had already paid for renovations in anticipation of the lease, demanded that the agreement be honored.

Discussion Questions

Question 1

Bryan is 17 years old. How does his age affect the legal status of the purchase contract he signed? Who has the right to cancel the contract, and under what circumstances would that right be lost?

____

____

____

____

____

Question 2

Carol Nguyen argues that Bryan should be bound by the contract because he misrepresented his age. Evaluate this argument. Does Bryan's misrepresentation eliminate his right to disaffirm, and does Carol have any legal recourse against Bryan as a result of his conduct?

____

____

Question 3

The landlord and the prospective tenant had a verbal agreement for an 18-month commercial lease. No written lease was signed. Identify the legal doctrine that governs this situation, explain whether the verbal agreement is enforceable, and describe what the tenant's options are after the landlord walked away.

CHAPTER 4:

OWNERSHIP RIGHTS AND LIMITATIONS

Chapter Overview

Learning Objectives

Upon completing Chapter 4, the student will be able to:

1. Explain the concept of interests in real estate, distinguish between possessory and non-possessory interests, and describe the role of encumbrances and public interests in limiting private ownership.
2. Describe the governmental powers that affect real property, including police power, taxation, eminent domain, and escheat, and explain the Texas limitations on eminent domain.
3. Identify the types of freehold estates, explain the differences between fee simple absolute and fee simple defeasible, and describe how life estates and their associated future interests operate.
4. Define encumbrances, distinguish between easements appurtenant and easements in gross, and explain how encroachments and licenses differ from easements.
5. Describe the legal features of liens and explain how liens attach, transfer, and terminate.
6. Explain Texas water rights including the Doctrine of Prior Appropriation, littoral rights, riparian rights, and groundwater rights, and identify the key regulatory bodies involved.
7. Describe Texas homestead rights, dower and curtesy, elective share, and mineral rights, and explain how each affects property ownership and transfer.
8. Identify the principal environmental hazards affecting real property in Texas, including asbestos, lead-based paint, radon, PCBs, mold, electromagnetic fields, and carbon monoxide, and describe the disclosure obligations associated with each.

Contents

Interests in Real Estate

An interest in real estate is ownership of any combination of the bundle of rights in real property: the rights to possess, use, transfer, encumber, and exclude. Interests in real estate range from complete ownership of all rights to narrow, limited rights held by non-owners.

Undivided Interest

An undivided interest is an ownership interest in a property shared by two or more parties. The terms undivided and indivisible mean that the owner's interest is in a fractional share of the entire estate, not in any specific physical portion of the land. For example, if two co-owners each hold an equal undivided interest, neither may claim exclusive use of the northern half or any other physical section of the property.

Types of Interests

Interests in real estate are distinguished primarily by whether they include the right of possession. The three general categories are estates, encumbrances, and public interests.

An estate in land exists when the interest holder enjoys the right of possession. Ownership of a freehold estate or a leasehold estate gives the holder the right to occupy and control the property.

An encumbrance exists when a private party holds an interest in the property but does not have the right to possess it. Encumbrances allow a non-owning party to restrict or otherwise affect the owner's full enjoyment of the property. Tax liens, mortgages, easements, and encroachments are common examples of encumbrances.

A public interest exists when a government entity holds a non-possessory interest in real estate for the benefit of the public. Government interests supersede the rights of individual property owners. The clearest examples are police power and eminent domain.

The characteristics that further define any given interest include how long the interest endures, what portion of the land the interest affects, whether the interest is public or private, and whether the interest includes legal ownership.

Governmental Powers

Private land use controls affect only limited and specific areas. Public land use controls cast a much wider net and encompass large areas within a government's jurisdiction.

Police Power

Police power gives a government entity the authority to regulate private property in order to protect the health, safety, and welfare of the public. The exercise of police power must always be in the public interest, although it may restrict certain freedoms of property owners. Property owners affected by police power regulations are generally not compensated for the resulting restrictions or losses of use. Common exercises of police power include:

- Zoning ordinances
- Building codes and subdivision regulations
- Environmental restrictions
- Eminent domain proceedings

Taxation

Property taxes are a specific lien on real property and represent an inherent encumbrance on private ownership. Property tax liens typically take priority over all other liens. Property owned by government entities, government agencies, and qualifying nonprofit organizations is generally exempt from property taxes.

Special assessments are a related form of taxation imposed on property in specific areas to fund particular improvements such as sidewalks, street lamps, or drainage systems. Special assessments are not permanent; they run for a defined number of years until the cost of the improvement is recovered.

Escheat

Escheat is the legal process by which the state acquires ownership of property when no private party has a valid claim to it. If a property owner dies with a valid will, the property is distributed according to the will. If the owner dies without a will, the property passes to heirs under state law. If the owner dies with no will and no qualifying heirs, the state uses its power of escheat to claim the property.

In Texas, if a property owner has been missing and cannot be located for a period of seven years, the property may also escheat to the state. Management of escheated property falls to the Texas General Land Office. Proceeds from the sale or lease of escheated property are deposited into the Foundation School Fund.

Eminent Domain and the Texas Landowner's Bill of Rights

Eminent domain is the legal authority granted to government entities and certain private entities, such as public utilities, to take private property for public use. Examples include road widening, the creation of easements, and highway construction. In exchange for the taking, the property owner must receive just compensation at market value.

If the owner and the condemning entity cannot agree on compensation, the condemnor may file a condemnation suit and ask a court to determine the appropriate amount. A property owner may also initiate an inverse condemnation proceeding when government action reduces the property's value by 25 percent or more without formally acquiring it.

Texas Limitations on Eminent Domain

The Texas Legislature amended the eminent domain statute in Government Code Chapter 2206. Under this amendment, the government may not take private property if the taking confers a private benefit on a particular private party, if the public use claimed is merely a pretext to benefit a private party, or if the sole purpose is economic development, unless that development is a secondary purpose resulting from municipal community development or urban renewal activities aimed at eliminating slum or blighted areas.

Condemnation Process

To initiate a taking, the public entity must first adopt a formal resolution of necessity at a public hearing where the owner may speak. The condemnor must demonstrate that the project is necessary, that the specific property is required for the project, and that the chosen location offers the greatest public benefit with the least detriment. Transfer of title extinguishes all existing leases, liens, and encumbrances on the property.

Public entities that hold the power of eminent domain include all levels of government, school districts, public utilities, public service corporations, public housing and redevelopment agencies, and railroads.

The Fifth Amendment and Just Compensation

The taking clause of the Fifth Amendment states that private property may not be taken for public use without just compensation. If government regulation restricts an owner's right to develop land to the point where the land becomes essentially valueless, a court may find that an unconstitutional regulatory taking has occurred and order compensation.

Texas Landowner's Bill of Rights

The Texas Legislature has codified landowner protections in Texas Government Code Section 402.031 and Chapter 21 of the Texas Property Code. Every property owner facing a potential condemnation has the following rights:

- The right to receive adequate compensation when property is taken for public use
- Property may only be taken for a public use
- Only a governmental entity or a private entity authorized by law may take property
- The condemning entity must provide written notice of its intent to take the property
- The condemning entity must provide the owner with a written appraisal of the property's value
- The condemning entity must make a bona fide offer to purchase before filing a condemnation lawsuit
- The owner may hire an independent appraiser or other professional to assess value
- The owner may hire an attorney to negotiate and represent the owner in any condemnation proceeding
- Before condemnation, the owner is entitled to a hearing before a panel of three court-appointed special commissioners who determine just compensation and any damages to remaining property
- If unsatisfied with the commissioners' award, the owner has the right to a trial before a judge or jury and may appeal any adverse judgment

Building Codes, Permits, and Certificates of Occupancy

Building codes allow counties and municipalities to protect the public against the hazards of unregulated construction. They establish minimum standards for virtually every aspect of a construction project, including offsite infrastructure such as streets, curbs, gutters, and drainage systems, and onsite work including the structure itself. Building codes typically address:

- Architectural and engineering standards
- Construction materials standards
- Building support systems including life safety, electrical, mechanical, and utility systems

Building Permits

Owners, contractors, and developers must obtain a building permit before beginning any construction or renovation project. Building permits are required for both residential and commercial properties and allow the local building department to monitor compliance with applicable codes throughout the project. Local inspectors conduct regular inspections during construction.

Some minor repair projects that do not materially affect structural features may be exempt from permit requirements, but the exemptions vary by jurisdiction. It is always wise to confirm with the local building department before beginning any renovation. Any violation of building codes, even an unintentional one, can render a property's title unmarketable.

Certificate of Occupancy

After a project is complete, local building inspectors examine the work for code compliance. If the improvements comply with all applicable standards, the municipality or county issues a certificate of occupancy, which officially clears the property for occupation and use. No property may be lawfully occupied as a residence or business after new construction or certain renovations until a certificate of occupancy has been issued.

Estates in Land

An estate in land is any interest in real property that includes the right of possession. Estates are broadly divided into freehold estates and leasehold estates based on the duration of the ownership interest.

In a freehold estate, the duration of the owner's rights cannot be determined in advance: the rights may endure for a lifetime, for less than a lifetime, or for generations beyond the owner's lifetime. A leasehold estate is distinguished by its specific duration as expressed in the lease term. Both types are referred to as tenancies.

Freehold Estates

Freehold estates differ primarily in their duration and in what happens to the estate when the owner dies. A freehold estate of potentially unlimited duration is a fee simple estate. A freehold estate limited to the life of an individual is a life estate.

Fee Simple Estate

The fee simple freehold estate is the highest form of ownership interest available in real estate. It includes the complete bundle of rights, and the tenancy is of unlimited duration. The fee simple interest is also called the fee interest or simply the fee, and its holder is called the fee tenant. In Texas, a transfer of title or an interest in real property is presumed to convey a fee simple estate unless the instrument specifically states otherwise.

Fee simple estates remain subject to governmental restrictions and private interests. There are two forms of fee simple estate: fee simple absolute and fee simple defeasible.

Fee Simple Absolute

The fee simple absolute estate is a perpetual estate that is not conditioned by any stipulated restrictions on use. It may be freely passed to heirs through a will or by intestate succession. Because it carries no conditions and no possibility of automatic termination, the fee simple absolute is the most desirable form of residential real estate ownership and the most common.

Fee Simple Defeasible

The fee simple defeasible estate is perpetual provided the owner uses the property in conformity with stated conditions. If those conditions are violated, the estate may revert to the grantor or the grantor's heirs. Two types exist.

Determinable fee The deed states specific usage limitations. If the restrictions are violated, the estate automatically reverts to the grantor or heirs without any additional action required.

Fee simple subject to condition subsequent If any stated condition is violated, the grantor has the right to repossess the property. Unlike the determinable fee, reversion is not automatic; the grantor must affirmatively re-take possession within a legally prescribed timeframe.

Life Estates

A life estate is a freehold estate limited in duration to the life of the owner or of some other named individual. Upon the death of the measuring life, the estate passes either to the original owner or to a third party named in the creating instrument. The holder of a life estate is called the life tenant.

Key characteristics of a life estate:

- The life tenant enjoys full ownership rights during the estate period
- Other parties hold a future interest in the property as either a remainder or a reversionary interest
- The estate may be created by private agreement between the parties or by operation of state law

Remainder A future interest held by a third party who will receive title upon termination of the life estate. The holder of this interest is called the remainderman.

Reversion If no remainderman is designated, the estate returns to the original grantor or the grantor's heirs at the termination of the life estate. The original owner retains a reversionary interest.

Conventional Life Estates

A conventional life estate is created by grant from a fee simple owner to a grantee, who becomes the life tenant. The life tenant enjoys all ownership rights during the estate period but may not damage the property or impair its value, since doing so would harm the future interest holders. Holders of remainder or reversionary interests may bring legal action if the life tenant commits waste.

Ordinary life estate An estate that ends with the death of the life tenant. The property then passes to the remainderman or reverts to the grantor. Example: John grants a life estate to Mary, with the property reverting to John upon Mary's death.

Pur autre vie A life estate measured by the life of a third person rather than the life tenant. The estate ends when that third person dies, after which the property passes to the remainderman or reverts to the grantor. Example: Yvonne grants a life estate to Ryan measured by the life of Yvonne's husband Steve; upon Steve's death, the property passes to Yvonne's mother Rose.

Legal Life Estates

A legal life estate is created by state law rather than by a private agreement between parties. Legal life estates exist to protect the property rights of surviving family members after the death of a spouse. The major forms in Texas are the homestead, dower and curtesy, and elective share, which are discussed in detail later in this chapter.

Encumbrances

An encumbrance is an interest in and right to real property that limits the legal owner's freehold interest. In effect, an encumbrance is another party's right to use the property, restrict its use, or prevent the owner from enjoying the full bundle of rights. An encumbrance does not include the right of possession and is therefore a lesser interest than an estate.

Encumbrances fall into two general categories: those that affect the property's use, such as easements and encroachments, and those that affect ownership, value, and transfer, such as liens and deed restrictions. An encumbrance can ultimately lead to the owner's loss of the property if, for example, a lien results in foreclosure.

Easements

An easement is an interest in real property that gives the holder the right to use a defined portion of the legal owner's property in a specific way. Easement rights may apply to the surface, subsurface, or airspace of a property, but the affected area must be clearly defined.

The party who receives the benefit of the easement is the benefited party. The party whose property is burdened by the easement is the burdened party. Key characteristics of easements include:

- An easement must involve the owner of the land over which it runs and a separate non-owning party; one cannot hold an easement over one's own property
- An easement applies to a specified physical area within the property boundaries
- An easement may be affirmative (permitting a use such as a right-of-way) or negative (prohibiting a use, such as an airspace easement preventing obstruction of a neighbor's view)

Easement Appurtenant

An easement appurtenant gives the owner of one property the right to use a defined portion of an adjoining property owned by another party. The property that benefits from the easement is the dominant tenement or dominant estate. The property that contains and must accommodate the easement is the servient tenement.

The word appurtenant means attaching to. An easement appurtenant attaches to both estates: it becomes a beneficial interest that runs with the dominant estate and a burden that runs with the servient estate. Both the rights and the obligations of the easement automatically transfer with the properties when either the dominant or servient estate is sold, whether or not the easement is mentioned in the deed.

While the servient tenement must allow the dominant tenement's use, both parties may use the easement area, provided the servient owner's use does not unreasonably obstruct the dominant use.

Easement in Gross

An easement in gross benefits a person or entity rather than an adjacent parcel of land. There is no dominant tenement. The most common examples are utility company easements allowing power, gas, and telephone companies to run lines across private property. Easements in gross generally do not transfer with the property and are non-exclusive unless specifically stated otherwise.

Creation of Easements

Easements may be created in several ways: by express grant in a deed or separate instrument, by express reservation in a deed, by implication arising from the circumstances of a property's use, by necessity when a parcel would otherwise be landlocked, or by prescription through open, continuous, and adverse use over a statutory period.

Encroachments and Licenses

Encroachments

An encroachment is the unauthorized physical intrusion of one owner's real property onto the property of another. Common examples include a tree limb extending over a boundary into a neighbor's airspace, a driveway extending beyond the lot line onto adjacent land, and a fence built outside the property boundary.

Encroachments can diminish property value and create title problems, particularly during a sale. They frequently do not appear in title records. A survey is typically needed to detect or document an encroachment. An affected owner may sue for removal of the encroachment or for damages. If the burdened owner takes no action for the period prescribed by law, the encroachment may ripen into an easement by prescription, giving the encroacher a permanent legal right to continue the use.

Licenses

A license is a personal, revocable permission granted by a property owner to another party to use the property for a specific purpose. Licenses are informal and are often given verbally. Unlike easements, licenses are not transferable, do not attach to the land, and terminate automatically upon the death of either party or upon the sale of the property. A license may be revoked by the grantor at any time.

A common example is a farmer granting a neighbor permission to cross the farm to fish in a pond. That permission is a license and gives the neighbor no permanent or transferable right.

Texas law allows property owners to post no trespassing signs or to use purple paint marks on trees and posts to indicate that entry is forbidden. Purple marks must meet specific size and placement requirements prescribed by law. Purple marks alone do not constitute legally effective no-trespassing notice unless they are accompanied by a sign at each vehicle entrance that meets the statutory lettering and size requirements and states that purple marks indicate entry is forbidden.

Legal Features of Liens

A lien is a legal claim against real property that secures payment of a debt or obligation. Liens are one of the most common forms of encumbrance. The legal features of liens are:

> **A lien does not convey ownership** A lienholder generally holds only an equitable interest in the property, not legal ownership. The exception is a mortgage lien in a title-theory state, where the lender holds legal title during the loan period. Texas is a lien-theory state, meaning the borrower retains legal title and the lender holds only a lien secured by the deed of trust.
>
> **A lien attaches to the property** When the property is transferred, the new owner takes title subject to the lien. The lienholder may pursue foreclosure against the new owner if the underlying debt is not satisfied.

A property may be subject to multiple liens Multiple liens can exist against the same property simultaneously. The more liens recorded, the less secure the collateral for any one creditor, since the total lien value may approach or exceed the property's market value.

A lien terminates on payment and recording Payment of the underlying debt and recording of the appropriate release or satisfaction document extinguishes the lien. If the debtor defaults, the lienholder may file a judgment action or initiate foreclosure to force a sale and satisfy the debt.

Texas Water Rights

Water rights govern the right to own, use, and access water found in lakes, streams, rivers, the ocean, and below the earth's surface. They also determine property boundaries where a parcel adjoins a body of water. Three variables determine what water rights a Texas landowner holds: whether the state controls the water, whether the water is moving, and whether the water is navigable.

Doctrine of Prior Appropriation

In states where water is scarce, the state may take the legal position that it owns and controls all bodies of water. Under the Doctrine of Prior Appropriation, property owners must obtain permits to use water. If a proposed use is reasonable and beneficial, the state grants a permit. Over time, that permit may attach to the property. Texas operates under prior appropriation for water rights acquired after July 1, 1895.

The Texas Commission on Environmental Quality (TCEQ) issues water rights permits to parties who demonstrate a beneficial use for the water, such as crop irrigation. Priority among competing permit holders is determined by the date the permit was issued. If a water right is unused for ten years, the TCEQ may revoke the permit unless the non-use resulted from a conservation program or other authorized restriction.

Texas Open Beach Law

Because Texas is a Gulf state, state law gives the public the right to use public beaches. The area between the high tide line and the low tide line is considered a public beach subject to a public access easement. The Texas Open Beaches Act (Chapter 61 of the Texas Natural Resources Code) prohibits any person from constructing a structure on this easement. Hurricane erosion can shift the easement landward, potentially placing an existing home within the easement boundary; in such cases, the owner may be required to remove the structure.

Littoral Rights

Littoral rights apply to properties abutting non-moving bodies of water such as lakes, seas, and bays. Owners of property abutting a navigable non-moving body of water have the right to use the water but do not own the water or the land beneath it. Ownership of the land extends to the high-water mark. Because a navigable lake or sea is considered public property owned by the state, private ownership of the water itself is not recognized. However, a body of water entirely contained within a single owner's property and not navigable is the owner's private property.

Littoral rights attach to the property and transfer automatically to a new owner upon sale.

Riparian Rights

Riparian rights apply to properties abutting moving water such as streams and rivers. The extent of these rights depends on whether the waterway is navigable.

If a property abuts a non-navigable stream, the owner has unrestricted use of the water and owns the land beneath the stream to its midpoint. If the waterway is navigable, it is treated as a public easement. The owner's property extends only to the water's edge, and the state owns the land beneath the water. Regardless of navigability, a riparian owner has the right to all accretions, meaning land formed by the natural deposit of soil by the river or stream.

In Texas, land granted into private ownership from the Republic of Texas or the State of Texas before July 1, 1895, carries riparian rights. Land granted after that date is subject to the prior appropriation doctrine. Since 1969, a riparian owner's right to use water has required a state permit for the maximum amount of water put to beneficial use without waste. Riparian rights attach to the property and transfer with it.

One's riparian rights are subject to three conditions: the use must be reasonable and must not infringe on the riparian rights of downstream owners; the use must not pollute the water; and the use must not impede or alter the course of water flow.

Texas Groundwater Rights

Groundwater is water located beneath the earth's surface at or below the saturation point, stored in underground geological formations called aquifers. Unlike surface water, which is publicly owned by the state, groundwater in Texas is the property of the landowner. A landowner has the right to capture, use, sell, lease, and transport water pumped from beneath his or her property.

Historically, groundwater has been governed by the rule of capture, which allows a landowner with legal rights to groundwater to pump whatever is available regardless of the effect on neighboring wells. Texas courts have limited the rule of capture to prohibit a landowner from pumping groundwater to maliciously harm a neighbor, pumping water wastefully, causing land subsidence on adjacent land through negligent pumping, or drilling a slant well that crosses a property line.

Texas law further restricts groundwater pumping in three circumstances: pumping from the underflow of a river, pumping from an aquifer within the jurisdiction of a Groundwater Conservation District, and pumping from the Edwards Aquifer within the jurisdiction of the Edwards Aquifer Authority.

Legal Life Estates and Homestead

A legal life estate is created by state law to protect the property rights of surviving family members upon the death of a spouse. Unlike conventional life estates, legal life estates arise by operation of law rather than by private agreement. The major forms in Texas are the homestead, dower and curtesy, and elective share.

Homestead

A homestead is an owner's principal residence. Texas homestead law is constitutional, meaning its protections cannot be waived by any contract or statute. Texas has one of the broadest homestead exemptions in the United States.

Homesteads in Texas may be urban or rural. A rural homestead may not exceed 200 acres for a family or 100 acres for a single person. An urban homestead may not exceed 10 acres and may include a business, provided the total does not exceed the 10-acre limit.

General principles of Texas homestead law:

- All or portions of the homestead are exempt from forced sale to satisfy most general debts and judgment liens
- Tax debts, seller financing, home improvement debts, mortgage debt, and home equity loans are not exempt
- The family must occupy the homestead, or the owner must intend to occupy it
- Both spouses must sign any deed conveying homestead property; one spouse cannot alone convey the homestead interest even if it is that spouse's separate property
- The homestead exemption endures over the life of the head of household and passes to minor children
- Homestead rights are extinguished if the property is sold or abandoned
- A homestead can be held by any head of household and by any single person
- An owner must have lived in the Texas homestead for 1,215 days to use the homestead exemption against bankruptcy claims

Liens not subject to the homestead exemption include purchase money liens, property tax liens, mechanic's liens for work performed on the homestead, home equity loans, certain reverse mortgages, federal government debts, encumbrances that existed before the property became a homestead, owelty of partition liens related to divorce or death proceedings, refinancing of existing homestead liens, and manufactured home refinancing liens.

The homestead exemption from certain debts is distinct from the homestead tax exemption, which exempts a portion of the property's appraised value from taxation. Homestead protections are available only to individuals, not to corporations, partnerships, or LLCs.

Dower and Curtesy

Dower is a wife's life estate interest in her husband's real property upon his death. Curtesy is the equivalent right of a husband in a deceased wife's property. Property acquired through dower or curtesy is owned by the surviving spouse for the duration of that spouse's life. To transfer property in states that recognize dower and curtesy, the non-title-holding spouse must release the dower or curtesy interest by signing the deed. If both spouses sign, the dower right is automatically extinguished. These rights have been largely supplanted in Texas by community property law and elective share statutes.

Elective Share

Elective share is a state-level statute that allows a surviving spouse to claim a minimum share of a deceased spouse's real and personal property regardless of what the will provides. For example, if a husband's will leaves nothing to his wife, she may elect to claim her statutory share instead.

Elective share laws generally provide that the surviving spouse is entitled to a defined percentage of the deceased spouse's property, excluding homestead and exclusively held property; the surviving spouse must file the claim within a limited period; if the spouse fails to file, the estate is distributed according to the will or state intestacy law; and the elective share right belongs only to the surviving spouse and is not transferable.

Mineral Rights in Texas

Private title to all land in Texas traces back to a grant by the sovereign authority, which has successively been Spain, Mexico, the Republic of Texas, and the State of Texas. Under Spanish and Mexican law, mineral rights did not pass with a land grant unless the instrument expressly conveyed them. Texas adopted this rule in one of its earliest legislative acts.

The Texas Constitution of 1866, carried forward in the constitutions of 1869 and 1876, released all minerals in land that had already passed from the sovereign to the private landowner. Since 1876, a grant of land from the sovereign is presumed to include all minerals unless they are expressly reserved. Since 1895, the state has frequently conveyed public domain land with a retention of mineral rights.

Under the Relinquishment Act of 1919 and its subsequent amendments, the surface owner acts as the state's agent for leasing mineral rights in state-retained mineral tracts, and both the surface owner and the state receive a fractional interest in leasing proceeds and production royalties.

To the extent a landowner also owns the minerals in a tract, the landowner may mine or sell those minerals. The more common arrangement is for the mineral owner to execute a mineral lease to an operator who develops the minerals at the operator's expense in exchange for a conveyance of seven-eighths of the mineral interest. The landowner retains one-eighth of all production free and clear of development costs. This one-eighth retained interest is called royalty, although the term is sometimes used more broadly to refer to any undivided interest in minerals created by an instrument other than a mineral lease.

Environmental Issues

Environmental issues can make or break a real estate transaction. If a buyer is concerned about potential environmental problems, the purchase contract should include a contingency requiring appropriate inspections and the resolution of any identified problems before closing. TREC's Environmental Assessment, Threatened or Endangered Species, and Wetlands Addendum (Form 28-2) is the appropriate vehicle for addressing these concerns in a Texas residential transaction.

Asbestos

Asbestos refers to a group of naturally occurring fibrous silicate minerals prized for their heat resistance, electrical insulation, and durability. Asbestos was widely used in building materials for much of the twentieth century. Locations where asbestos may be found in older homes include roofing and siding shingles, insulation in homes built between 1930 and 1950, textured paints and patching compounds used before 1977, artificial fireplace ashes and embers, vinyl floor tiles and sheet flooring backing, hot water and steam pipe insulation, and furnace door gaskets.

In its undisturbed condition, asbestos generally poses little risk. It becomes dangerous when it deteriorates or is disturbed during remodeling, releasing fibers into the air. The term friable describes any asbestos-containing material that can be crumbled or powdered by hand when dry. Inhaling asbestos fibers can cause asbestosis, a chronic inflammatory lung disease associated with long-term heavy exposure, and mesothelioma, a rare and aggressive cancer of the tissue surrounding the lungs. Asbestos is the leading cause of mesothelioma in the United States.

Lead-Based Paint

Lead is a heavy metal found in small amounts throughout the environment. Lead-based paint cannot be absorbed through the skin but is hazardous when it enters the bloodstream through ingestion or inhalation of paint chips or dust. The Environmental Protection Agency and the Department of Housing and Urban Development estimate that approximately 75 percent of homes built before 1978 contain some lead-based paint. Health effects of lead exposure include developmental problems in children, reproductive issues, high blood pressure, memory impairment, seizures, kidney failure, and severe abdominal pain. Children are particularly vulnerable because lead disrupts developing brain cells.

Texas real estate agents listing homes built before 1978 must have sellers complete the TREC Lead-Based Paint Addendum (Form 56-0) disclosing their knowledge of lead-based paint in the home. Buyers must acknowledge receipt of required disclosures and the EPA pamphlet Protect Your Family from Lead in Your Home, and must acknowledge whether they are exercising or waiving their right to a 10-day risk assessment period. The broker must confirm compliance in the broker's acknowledgment section of the form.

Radon

Radon is a colorless, odorless, tasteless, and radioactive gas produced naturally in the ground wherever uranium and radium are present. Uranium decays into radium, which decays into radon gas. The gas migrates upward through soil and generally disperses harmlessly into the atmosphere. Problems arise when radon enters a building and accumulates to hazardous levels.

Buildings draw radon inward because interior air pressure is typically lower than the soil pressure outside. Radon can enter through cracks in concrete floors or foundations, joints in construction materials, gaps around utility pipes, openings around sump pumps, cavities in walls, and crawl spaces open to the building interior.

The Surgeon General has identified radon as the second leading cause of lung cancer in the United States. Health risk increases with both the concentration of radon and the duration of exposure. Radon levels are measured in picocuries per liter of air (pCi/L). Testing is simple, inexpensive, and can be done by the homeowner using a charcoal canister or electret ion chamber, or by a professional using continuous electronic monitors.

Polychlorinated Biphenyls (PCBs)

PCBs are synthetic organic chemicals formerly used in hundreds of industrial and commercial applications including electrical transformers, hydraulic equipment, paints, plastics, rubber products, and carbonless copy paper. More than 1.5 billion pounds of PCBs were manufactured in the United States before their production was prohibited under the Toxic Substances Control Act in 1976. PCBs are persistent in the environment and have been shown to cause cancer in animals and a range of serious non-cancer health effects involving the immune, reproductive, nervous, and endocrine systems. If PCBs are suspected, the EPA takes soil and groundwater samples. Contaminated soil is removed to licensed incinerators or landfills.

Mold

Mold is a fungus that grows in moist conditions and can cause allergic reactions and other health problems. When mold spores land on a damp indoor surface, they may begin growing and digesting whatever material they contact, including wood, paper, carpet, and other building materials. The primary factor controlling indoor mold growth is moisture. When excess moisture accumulates indoors and is not addressed promptly, mold growth almost always follows.

Health effects of mold exposure include hay fever-like allergic reactions (sneezing, runny nose, red eyes, and skin rash), asthma attacks in susceptible individuals, and, in cases involving certain toxic mold species, more serious systemic effects. Mold testing kits are available for homeowner use, and professional remediation services are available for more serious infestations. Because mold often grows inside walls or ductwork where it may not be visible, it may not be detected during a standard inspection.

A licensee who is aware of mold, flooding, or water damage in a property is obligated to disclose that information as a latent defect. Disclosure is required even when the mold is not currently visible.

Electromagnetic Fields (EMFs)

Electromagnetic fields are invisible lines of force surrounding any electrical device. They are generated by power lines, electrical wiring, and appliances. Electric fields are partially shielded by grounded conducting objects such as buildings and trees. Magnetic fields are not shielded and cannot be felt.

Scientific research into the health effects of EMFs continues. Some studies suggest a possible association with increased cancer risk, but no regulatory threshold for safe EMF exposure has been established. No federal laws currently regulate EMF emissions. The recommended approach is prudent avoidance, meaning that low-cost or no-cost steps to reduce unnecessary exposure are sensible, while major financial investment in minimization measures is generally not warranted given the current state of research.

Carbon Monoxide (CO)

Carbon monoxide is a colorless, odorless, and poisonous gas produced by the incomplete combustion of fuels including coal, wood, charcoal, oil, kerosene, propane, and natural gas. Common sources include malfunctioning furnaces, ranges, water heaters, room heaters, portable generators, fireplaces, and vehicles left running in enclosed spaces. The Centers for Disease Control and Prevention estimates that several thousand people receive emergency treatment for CO poisoning each year in the United States.

Because CO is undetectable by the senses, people may not realize they are being exposed. Initial symptoms at low to moderate levels resemble the flu without fever: headache, shortness of breath, fatigue, nausea, and dizziness. High-level exposure causes mental confusion, vomiting, loss of muscular coordination, loss of consciousness, and death. Symptom severity depends on both CO concentration and duration of exposure.

CO concentration is measured in parts per million (ppm). Prolonged exposure to levels of approximately 1 to 70 ppm causes few symptoms in most healthy individuals, though some heart patients may experience chest pain. Levels above 70 ppm produce noticeable symptoms. Levels above 150 to 200 ppm sustained over time can result in disorientation, unconsciousness, and death.

Texas requires CO detectors in certain day-care centers, group day-care homes, and family homes under the Texas Health and Safety Code. The state is also required to prepare public information on CO detector availability and the proper maintenance of fossil fuel-burning appliances.

Chapter 4 Snapshot Review

The following review summarizes the key rules and concepts from Chapter 4.

Governmental Powers

- Police power: government regulates property for public health, safety, and welfare through zoning, building codes, environmental rules; no compensation to owner
- Taxation: property tax is a specific lien with priority over all other liens; special assessments fund specific improvements benefiting specific properties
- Eminent domain: taking of private property for public use; just compensation required; Texas Government Code Chapter 2206 restricts takings that primarily benefit private parties
- Texas Landowner's Bill of Rights: 10 constitutional protections for property owners facing condemnation
- Inverse condemnation: owner may claim compensation when government action reduces property value by 25 percent or more without a formal taking
- Escheat: property with no valid private claimant reverts to the state; in Texas also applies after seven years of an owner's unexplained absence

Freehold Estates

- A private party holding a possessory interest has an estate in land; a non-possessory interest is an encumbrance; a government non-possessory interest is a public interest and supersedes private rights
- Fee simple absolute: perpetual, unconditional, fully inheritable; most common and most desirable residential ownership form
- Determinable fee: reverts automatically to grantor when stipulated use conditions are violated
- Fee simple subject to condition subsequent: grantor must take affirmative action to repossess upon violation
- Life estate: duration tied to a measuring life; life tenant has full ownership rights but may not commit waste or impair the rights of remainder or reversionary interest holders
- Ordinary life estate: measured by the life tenant's life; pur autre vie: measured by a third person's life
- Remainder: future interest in a named third party; reversion: future interest retained by the original grantor

Encumbrances, Easements, and Liens

- Encumbrance: any non-possessory interest that limits the owner's full bundle of rights; does not include a right of possession
- Easement appurtenant: benefits the dominant estate, burdens the servient estate; runs automatically with both properties upon transfer whether mentioned in the deed or not
- Easement in gross: benefits a person or entity, not an adjacent parcel; most utility easements are easements in gross
- Easement by prescription: created by open, continuous, hostile, and adverse use over the statutory period
- Encroachment: unauthorized physical intrusion; may ripen into an easement by prescription if the burdened owner fails to act within the statutory period

- License: personal, revocable, non-transferable use permission; terminates upon death of either party or sale of the property
- Lien: creditor's claim against property securing a debt; attaches to and transfers with the property; Texas is a lien-theory state -- the borrower retains legal title
- Property tax liens take priority over all other liens regardless of recording date

Texas Water Rights

- Surface water: publicly owned by the state; the TCEQ issues permits; priority by permit date; unused for 10 years may be revoked
- Groundwater: owned by the landowner under the rule of capture, subject to Texas Water Code and Groundwater Conservation Districts
- Edwards Aquifer Authority imposes additional pumping restrictions in Central Texas
- Littoral rights: property abutting non-moving water; ownership to the high-water mark
- Riparian rights: property abutting moving water; non-navigable stream -- ownership to midpoint; navigable -- ownership to water's edge; state owns the bed
- Texas Open Beach Act: area between high and low tide is a perpetual public easement; no private structures permitted

Texas Homestead and Mineral Rights

- Texas homestead protections are constitutional and cannot be waived; both spouses must sign any deed conveying homestead property
- Homestead exemption protects against most judgment liens but not tax liens, purchase money liens, home improvement liens, or equity loans
- Mineral rights in Texas are severable from surface rights and may be separately owned, leased, and transferred
- Standard mineral lease: operator receives seven-eighths of production; mineral owner retains one-eighth as royalty

Environmental Disclosure

- Environmental hazards must be disclosed as latent defects when known to the licensee
- Lead-based paint disclosure using Form 56-0 is mandatory for all homes built before 1978
- Environmental concerns should be addressed through a contingency and the TREC Environmental Assessment, Threatened or Endangered Species, and Wetlands Addendum (Form 28-2)
- Common environmental hazards requiring disclosure: asbestos, radon, carbon monoxide, lead-based paint, mold, PCBs, underground storage tanks, urea formaldehyde, groundwater contamination, waste disposal sites

CHAPTER 4 QUIZ:

OWNERSHIP RIGHTS AND LIMITATIONS

1. Which governmental power allows a government entity to regulate private property use in order to protect public health, safety, and welfare, generally without compensating the affected owner?
   a. Eminent domain
   b. Escheat
   c. Police power
   d. Inverse condemnation

2. Under Texas law, if a property owner has been missing and cannot be located for how many years may the property escheat to the state?
   a. Three years
   b. Seven years
   c. Five years
   d. Ten years

3. When the government takes private property for public use through eminent domain, what must the property owner receive?
   a. A tax credit equal to the property's assessed value
   b. A replacement property of equal size and use
   c. A right of first refusal to repurchase the property if it is ever resold
   d. Just compensation at market value

4. Under Texas Government Code Chapter 2206, which of the following is a prohibited basis for a government entity to take private property through eminent domain?
   a. Economic development that solely benefits a private party
   b. Construction of a new public highway
   c. Creation of a utility easement for a water line
   d. Elimination of a designated blighted area within a city

5. Which form of fee simple estate is perpetual and carries no conditions or restrictions on use?
   a. Fee simple defeasible
   b. Fee simple absolute
   c. Determinable fee
   d. Fee simple subject to condition subsequent

6. A deed conveys property to a school district with language stating that the property automatically reverts to the grantor if it is ever used for any purpose other than education. What type of estate does the school district hold?
   a. Fee simple absolute
   b. Fee simple subject to condition subsequent
   c. Life estate pur autre vie
   d. Determinable fee

7. A life tenant has the right to use and enjoy a property during the estate period, but which of the following actions is the life tenant prohibited from taking?
   a. Committing waste that impairs the value of future interest holders' rights
   b. Renting the property to a third party
   c. Paying property taxes from personal funds
   d. Making cosmetic improvements to the interior of the home

8. A property owner grants a life estate to a friend, with the property reverting to the owner upon the friend's death. What is the owner's interest called during the life estate period?
   a. Remainder
   b. Undivided interest
   c. Reversionary interest
   d. Dominant tenement

9. Which of the following best describes an encumbrance?
   a. A private party's interest in real property that includes the right of possession
   b. A government entity's interest in real property that supersedes all private rights
   c. A co-ownership arrangement that gives each party an equal and undivided interest in the whole property
   d. A private party's non-possessory interest in real property that limits the owner's full enjoyment of the bundle of rights

10. An owner of a landlocked parcel has a right-of-way over a neighbor's property to reach a public road. The landlocked parcel benefits from which type of easement?
   a. Easement appurtenant
   b. License
   c. Easement by adverse possession
   d. Easement in gross

11. A power company holds the right to run electrical lines across the back of a homeowner's lot. The homeowner's property is not adjacent to any property owned by the power company. What type of easement does the power company hold?
   a. Easement appurtenant
   b. Easement by necessity
   c. Easement in gross
   d. Prescriptive easement

12. A neighbor's driveway extends two feet beyond the property line onto an adjacent owner's land. The adjacent owner has done nothing about the intrusion for several years. If the adjacent owner continues to take no action for the full statutory period, what may result?
   a. The adjacent owner loses all property rights on that side of the lot
   b. The encroachment may mature into an easement by prescription
   c. The neighbor may acquire the overlapping strip of land by adverse possession
   d. The encroachment automatically becomes a valid easement appurtenant

13. A farmer verbally gives a neighbor permission to cross the farm each weekend to go fishing. How is that permission classified under Texas law?
   a. A license that the farmer may revoke at any time
   b. An easement appurtenant that runs with the neighbor's property
   c. An easement in gross held by the neighbor personally
   d. A deed restriction that binds future owners of the farm

14. Texas is described as a lien-theory state. What does this mean for a borrower who has given a deed of trust to secure a mortgage loan?
   a. The lender holds legal title to the property until the loan is repaid
   b. Both the borrower and the lender share legal title equally until the loan is satisfied
   c. The trustee holds permanent title and transfers it to the borrower only after the final payment
   d. The borrower retains legal title and the lender holds only a security interest

15. Who owns surface water, including rivers, streams, and bays, in Texas?
   a. The landowner whose property abuts the waterway
   b. The State of Texas
   c. The adjacent riparian landowners on a proportional basis
   d. The federal government through the Army Corps of Engineers

16. Under Texas homestead law, both spouses must sign any deed conveying homestead property. Which of the following situations also requires both spouses to sign the deed?
   a. Only when the homestead is community property
   b. Only when the outstanding mortgage balance exceeds the property's market value
   c. Even when the homestead is the separate property of one spouse
   d. Only when the sale price exceeds a threshold set by the Texas Finance Code

17. Under a standard Texas mineral lease, what fraction of mineral production does the landowner who retains the mineral rights receive?
   a. One-half
   b. One-fourth
   c. One-sixteenth
   d. One-eighth

18. Which federal law requires the disclosure of known or potential lead-based paint hazards in residential properties built before 1978?
   a. The Residential Lead-Based Paint Hazard Reduction Act
   b. The Environmental Protection Agency Disclosure Rule
   c. The Toxic Substances Control Act
   d. The National Flood Insurance Program

19. Radon gas is identified as the second leading cause of which serious health condition in the United States?
   a. Heart disease
   b. Lung cancer
   c. Mesothelioma
   d. Asbestosis

20. A licensee learns that a property the licensee is about to list has visible mold growth inside a bathroom wall cavity discovered during a recent plumbing repair. What is the licensee required to do with this information?

   a. Repair the mold problem at the licensee's own expense before listing the property
   b. Include the mold information only if the buyer specifically asks about water damage
   c. Disclose the mold as a latent defect, even if it is no longer visible after repair work was performed
   d. Report the mold to the Texas Department of State Health Services before disclosing it to any buyer

Chapter 4 Case Study: Ownership Rights and Limitations

The Situation

Helen and George Mettling own a five-acre rural property outside of Waco, Texas, where they have lived as their primary residence for nine years. The property borders a small creek at its eastern edge. Several years ago, without asking the Mettlings, a neighboring landowner named Frank Pryor installed a water pump at the creek and began drawing water for his cattle operation. He has done so openly and continuously ever since.

The Mettlings recently received a letter from the city stating that a planned road-widening project will require the city to take a 30-foot strip along the front of their property. The letter stated that the city intends to pay the Mettlings the tax-assessed value of the strip, which is considerably below what the Mettlings believe the strip is worth at market value.

Around the same time, a home inspector hired by a prospective buyer discovered visible mold growth inside a wall cavity near the master bathroom. The Mettlings had noticed a musty smell in that area for over a year but had not disclosed it on their Seller's Disclosure Notice. The listing agent, Dana Voss of Performance Property Programs, was aware that the Mettlings had mentioned the smell to her during the listing appointment but had not followed up on it.

The prospective buyer, once informed of the mold, demanded that the Mettlings remediate the problem and reduce the price. George Mettling argued that the mold was inside the wall and therefore invisible and that neither he nor Dana had any obligation to disclose something they could not see.

Discussion Questions

Question 1

The city intends to pay the Mettlings only the tax-assessed value for the strip of land it is taking. Explain the legal basis for the city's right to take the property, identify the constitutional protection available to the Mettlings, and describe what options the Mettlings have if they believe the offered compensation is inadequate.

____

____

____

____

____

Question 2

Frank Pryor has been drawing water from the creek at the edge of the Mettlings' property for several years without their permission. Identify what type of water is involved, explain who owns it under Texas law, and analyze whether Frank's use of the water is lawful.

____

____

____

____

____

Question 3

George Mettling argues that neither he nor Dana Voss had an obligation to disclose the mold because it was hidden inside a wall. Evaluate this argument. Address the seller's disclosure obligation under Texas law, the licensee's independent duty to disclose, and whether the musty smell the Mettlings noticed for over a year affects the analysis.

____

____

____

____

____

CHAPTER 5:

CONTRACTS USED IN TEXAS REAL ESTATE

Chapter Overview

Learning Objectives

Upon completing Chapter 5, the student will be able to:

1. Define the principal types of real estate contracts including express, implied, bilateral, unilateral, executed, and executory, and explain how each arises in Texas real estate practice.
2. Identify and apply the six essential elements of a valid contract and explain the four legal statuses a court may assign to a contract.
3. Explain how offers and mutual agreement are reached, describe the licensee's duty to present offers promptly, and identify the consequences of failing to do so.
4. Identify the ways a contract may be discharged, describe the legal remedies available for breach of contract, and explain assignment in Texas real estate.
5. Describe the contracts most commonly used in Texas real estate brokerage, including listing agreements, buyer representation agreements, sales contracts, leases, and escrow agreements.
6. Compare the four types of listing agreements used in Texas and explain the fiduciary responsibilities of both listing and buyer's agents.
7. Identify the laws that apply to leasing real estate in Texas, describe the four types of leasehold estates, and explain the major provisions found in TREC's promulgated temporary lease forms.
8. Describe options, contracts for deed, and lease purchase agreements, including the rights and obligations of each party, the risks involved, and best practices for Texas transactions.

Contents

- Real Estate Contracts Defined
- The Six Essential Elements of a Valid Contract
- Offers, Mutual Agreement, and the Duty to Present
- Discharge of Contracts
- Breach of Contract and Legal Remedies
- Contracts Used in the Real Estate Business
- Listing Agreements
- Buyer Representation Agreements
- Leasing Real Estate in Texas
- Laws Applicable to Leases
- Leasehold Estates
- TREC Temporary Lease Forms
- Lease Provisions and Types of Leases
- Lease Termination and Default
- Options

- Contracts for Deed
- Lease Purchase Agreements

Real Estate Contracts Defined

Real estate contracts are the legal agreements that underlie the transfer and financing of real estate and the real estate brokerage business. Sales contracts, leases, and option agreements transfer real estate interests. Mortgage contracts and promissory notes facilitate financing. Listing and representation agreements establish client relationships and provide for compensation.

A contract is an agreement between two or more parties who, in a meeting of the minds, have pledged to perform or refrain from performing some act. A valid contract is legally enforceable because it meets specific requirements of contract law. If those requirements are not met, the parties cannot use a court to enforce the agreement. A contract is not a legal form or a prescribed set of words; it is the intangible agreement reached in the minds of the parties.

Express Contracts

An express contract is one in which all terms and covenants have been clearly stated and agreed to by all parties, verbally or in writing. A listing agreement signed by both the seller and the licensee is the most common written express contract in residential real estate. Some express contracts must be in writing under Texas law. Those include a contract for the sale of real estate, a lease for more than one year, a promise to pay a commission on oil and gas interests, an agreement that cannot be performed within one year, and a loan agreement over $50,000 made by a financial institution. A listing agreement may be oral, but TRELA prohibits a broker from suing to recover a commission unless the agreement is in writing and signed by the party against whom the action is brought.

Implied Contracts

An implied contract is an unstated or unintentional agreement considered to exist when the conduct of the parties suggests that an agreement has been reached. An implied contract cannot arise when an enforceable express contract already exists on the same subject matter. To establish an implied contract, a party must demonstrate an unambiguous offer, unambiguous acceptance, mutual intent to be bound, and consideration, all through conduct rather than explicit words.

Implied agency is a common real estate example. When a licensee without a signed buyer representation agreement acts on a buyer's behalf -- such as negotiating a lower price -- an implied agency relationship may arise even though unintended. If the buyer compensates the agent, the existence of the implied agreement becomes difficult to refute. Prior relationships between a licensee and a former client can also create implied agency in subsequent transactions.

Bilateral Contracts

A bilateral contract is one in which both parties exchange mutual promises. Each party's promise is both an offer and consideration for the other's promise. Most real estate contracts are bilateral. An exclusive listing is bilateral: the broker promises to market diligently and the seller promises to pay a commission if the property sells. A bilateral contract is enforceable from the moment it is formed.

Unilateral Contracts

In a unilateral contract, only one party makes a promise, offered in exchange for an act by the other party. The other party is not obligated to act, but if the party does perform, the promisor must fulfill the promise. The contract is accepted by performance, not by a return promise. An option to purchase is the primary real estate example: the seller is bound to sell if the buyer exercises the option, but the buyer is free to let the option expire. Open listings are also unilateral.

Executed and Executory Contracts

An executed contract has been fully performed by all parties with no remaining obligations. An executory contract has performance that is not yet complete. A signed residential sales contract before closing is executory. Contracts for deed, lease-purchases, and lease-options for periods longer than 180 days are executory contracts under Texas law subject to Texas Property Code sections 5.061 and following.

The steps from offer to executed contract: the buyers sign and initial the written offer; the offer is presented to the sellers; the sellers agree and sign and initial in all required places; the sellers notify the buyers of their acceptance; and the effective date is entered as the date of notification. The agreement is then a binding executory contract requiring performance by all parties.

The Six Essential Elements of a Valid Contract

Without all six elements a contract may not be enforceable. Every real estate contract must specify clearly what each party is to do and when.

1. Competent parties
2. Consideration
3. Mutual agreement
4. Lawful objective
5. In writing and signed by the parties
6. Legal description

Competent Parties

A competent party has legal age, mental capacity, and the authority to enter into a binding contract. In Texas, the age of majority is 18. A contract signed by a minor is voidable at the minor's election; if the minor chooses to proceed, the contract is binding. A court may emancipate a minor. Mental competency requires that the party understand the nature and consequences of the contract. When a court has declared a person incompetent, a court-appointed guardian may act with court approval. A party representing another person or entity must hold a valid power of attorney or appropriate corporate authorization.

Consideration

Consideration is the exchange of something of value that distinguishes a contractual obligation from a gift. In a sales contract, consideration is the mutual exchange of promises: the seller's promise to convey a specific property and the buyer's promise to pay. Earnest money is not the consideration; it demonstrates good faith and may serve as liquidated damages if the buyer defaults. An option requires the optionee to pay the optionor something of value to hold the option open; without that payment, the option lacks consideration and is unenforceable.

Mutual Agreement

Mutual agreement (mutual assent, meeting of the minds) means all parties have voluntarily agreed to the same terms based on full and accurate information. Every detail must be agreed upon by every party. Deliberate deception, fraud, or concealment of material facts about the property renders the agreement unenforceable. When parties agree to cancel a contract voluntarily, that is mutual rescission. A court may void a contract where one party's acceptance was partial, accidental, or vague.

Practical example: A purchase agreement covers a property at $575,000. Sellers John and Beth Sanders and buyer Maggie Wallace sign. During negotiations, the closing date is moved from February 15 to January 30. John Sanders and Maggie Wallace initial the change, but Beth Sanders is out of town and does not approve. When Beth learns of the change, she refuses to agree. At that point there is no mutual agreement on the closing date. The four possible outcomes are: the contract fails by mutual rescission; Maggie renegotiates her moving arrangements and agrees to the February date; the Sanders agree to cover Maggie's storage costs; or John persuades Beth to approve the earlier date and she initials it. Only when all three parties agree to the same terms is there a binding contract.

Lawful Objective

A contract requiring unlawful performance is void. A lease barring children violates the familial status protections of the federal Fair Housing Act. A listing directing the agent to refuse showings to minorities is discrimination, which immediately voids the agreement. A lease for an apartment that would exceed health and safety occupancy limits is invalid. Texas law prohibits common law dual agency; a broker representing both parties must comply with TRELA's intermediary requirements. Any contract requiring an illegal act is void ab initio (null and void).

In Writing and Signed by the Parties

The Texas Statute of Frauds requires all contracts affecting title to or any interest in real estate to be in writing and signed by the parties. An oral agreement to sell real estate is void. The one exception is a lease for one year or less, which may be oral and is enforceable. Written contracts provide a reliable record and allow courts to determine what the parties actually agreed to without relying on competing oral accounts.

Legal Description

A property street address is not sufficient to transfer title. Real estate is non-homogeneous; no two parcels are identical. A legal description sufficient for a competent surveyor to locate and identify the specific parcel is required in every real estate instrument, including sales contracts, leases, easements, rights-of-way, mortgages, and time-share arrangements. The two most common forms in Texas are metes and bounds, and reference to a platted subdivision by lot number, block number, section, and subdivision name.

The Four Legal Statuses of a Contract

Valid Meets all six essential elements and is legally enforceable.

Valid but unenforceable Meets the elements but cannot be enforced due to the Statute of Frauds, lack of consideration, absence of mutual assent, or impossibility.

Void Fails to meet the tests for validity; is no contract at all; cannot be enforced by either party.

Voidable Appears valid but may be cancelled by one party on the basis of a legal disability such as minority, fraud, duress, or coercion.

Offers, Mutual Agreement, and the Duty to Present

All offers must be in writing and presented to the property owner as soon as possible. TREC rules require immediate presentation. A licensee must never withhold an offer from the seller for any reason. Failure to present an offer promptly may constitute incompetent practice, grounds for TREC disciplinary action, and potential liability for a tort. A tort is a negligent or wrongful act constituting a breach of a legal duty that damages another person and may give rise to legal action. Withholding an offer that causes financial harm to the seller can constitute tortious interference with the transaction.

Example: A listing agent believes a buyer he is working with personally will make an offer within a few days. Meanwhile, a cooperating broker submits an offer close to the asking price. The listing agent must present that offer immediately. Delaying creates the risk that the cooperating buyer withdraws, the agent's own buyer never makes an offer, and the seller -- perhaps facing financial pressure -- suffers a material loss.

Under TREC Canon of Ethics Rule 531.1 (Fidelity), the agent's primary duty is to the client's interests. The agent must be faithful to that trust, meticulous in performance, and must place no personal interest above the client's. Unless a seller provides written instructions to the contrary, all offers must be presented without delay.

Discharge of Contracts

Discharge (cancellation or termination) of a contract releases the parties from their obligations. Discharge may occur for the following reasons.

Performance

A contract terminates when fully performed. If only partial performance is delivered, the non-defaulting party may recover the cost of completion. Sufficient performance occurs when a court determines a party substantially fulfilled the contract even if not perfectly; damages are limited to the difference in value between what was promised and what was delivered. Defective performance entitles the other party to the cost of repairing the defect.

Infeasibility

A contract may be cancelled if performance becomes impossible. Subjective infeasibility results from the personal inability of the promisor to perform, as when a contract depends on a unique individual who dies or becomes disabled. Objective infeasibility means no one can perform, as when the subject matter of the contract is destroyed or supervening events make performance fundamentally different from what was contemplated.

Mutual Agreement

Parties may rescind a contract at any time by mutual agreement. If the parties replace the cancelled contract with a new one, the substitution is called novation, and the new contract must independently satisfy all validity requirements.

Operation of Law

The rights of contracting parties may change by operation of law. The Statute of Limitations limits the period for bringing suit; in Texas the statute of limitations for written contracts is four years. When a person files for bankruptcy, obligations under existing contracts generally terminate as of the filing date.

Assignment of a Contract

A real estate contract that does not involve unique personal services may be assigned to a third party unless expressly prohibited. Sales contracts are assignable because they concern the purchase of real property. Contractual rights are not freely assignable when the rights involve unique personal services, assignment would substantially increase the burden on the obligor, assignment is prohibited by law, or the contract forbids it.

Breach of Contract and Legal Remedies

A breach of contract is a failure to perform according to the contract's terms without lawful justification. Also called default, a breach gives the non-defaulting party the right to pursue legal action. In Texas, the statute of limitations to sue for breach of a written real estate contract is four years from the date of breach.

Available Remedies

Rescission Cancels the contract and returns both parties to their pre-contract condition, including return of any funds transferred.

Forfeiture Requires the breaching party to give up something specified in the contract. A buyer who defaults typically forfeits the earnest money deposit as liquidated damages.

Suit for damages The non-defaulting party sues in civil court. If the contract specifies a fixed amount of damages, that is the liquidated damages. Otherwise the court determines compensatory damages. The suit must be filed within the statutory period.

Suit for specific performance Asks the court to compel the defaulting party to perform. Most commonly used when a party wants the court to require completion of a real estate transaction rather than a money award.

Reformation A legal action to correct a contract that does not accurately reflect the parties' intentions due to a clerical or mechanical drafting error.

Measuring Damages

The standard measure of loss-of-bargain damages is the difference between the contract price and the market value of the property on the date of breach. If a property is under contract at $600,000 and the buyer defaults when the market value has dropped to $530,000, the seller may recover $70,000. If the seller defaults when the property has risen to $680,000, the buyer may recover $80,000.

Special damages are additional recoverable amounts if they were foreseeable at the time the contract was made. These may include survey fees, appraisal costs, title search expenses, financing costs, moving expenses, and broker commissions incurred in reliance on the contract. Buyers who intended to profit from the property through resale, rental, or development may also recover provable lost-profit damages, subject to foreseeability and reasonable certainty.

Contracts Used in the Real Estate Business

Texas license holders regularly work with the following categories of contract. Understanding the purpose, requirements, and limitations of each is essential to competent practice.

- Listing agreements -- authorize a broker to represent a seller or landlord
- Buyer representation agreements -- authorize a broker to represent a buyer or tenant
- Sales contracts -- document the mutual agreement to buy and sell real property
- Option agreements -- give a potential buyer the right but not the obligation to purchase
- Contracts for deed -- provide seller financing with deferred title transfer
- Leases -- convey a temporary right to possession in exchange for rent
- Escrow agreements -- govern the custody and disbursement of earnest money and other funds

Earnest Money and Escrow

An earnest money deposit typically accompanies a buyer's offer. It is not required to form a valid contract, but it signals serious intent, increases seller confidence, and provides potential liquidated damages if the buyer defaults. In Texas, earnest money is placed in a third-party trust account managed by a licensed escrow agent at a title company, financial institution, or brokerage. The escrow holder is an impartial fiduciary for both parties. If the buyer performs, the deposit is credited toward the purchase price at closing. If the buyer defaults, the contract governs distribution, often to the seller with a portion to the broker not exceeding the commission on the full listing price. Strict rules govern how brokers handle, account for, and segregate earnest money from their own funds.

Contingencies

A contingency is a condition that must be met before the contract is fully enforceable. The most common is a financing contingency, allowing the buyer to cancel and recover the deposit if a specified type of financing cannot be obtained by a defined date. A contingency should be specific about what it requires, carry an expiration date, and expressly require the party to exercise diligence in satisfying the condition. A vague, overly broad, or open-ended contingency may destroy mutual agreement and void the contract. Failure to meet a contingency is not a default; it entitles the parties to cancel without penalty.

Sale Contract Primary Provisions

A standard residential sales contract includes provisions for: identifying the parties, property, and consideration; the legal description; the purchase price, down payment, and financing type; title policy and survey; property condition, inspections, and seller's disclosure; settlement expenses and prorations; casualty loss; default and remedies; mediation; escrow; closing date and possession; and the termination option. Unless expressly excluded, all fixtures are included. Items of personal property are excluded unless expressly included.

Listing Agreements

A listing agreement is a contract between a property owner and a broker authorizing the broker to act as the owner's agent to find a buyer or tenant for compensation. Under TRELA, only brokers may list, sell, or rent property. A sales agent may list property but the listing must be held in the sponsoring broker's name. Listing agreements must be in writing to be enforceable; oral listings afford no legal protection for the broker's commission. Most listing agreements are bilateral employment contracts in which the owner promises compensation and the broker promises to find a ready, willing, and able buyer or tenant.

Exclusive Right to Sell

The exclusive right to sell is the most widely used listing. The broker earns the commission if the property sells during the listing period regardless of who found the buyer -- even the seller acting alone. This arrangement maximizes the broker's incentive to invest in marketing and typically produces the fastest, most profitable sale. All exclusive listings must contain a definite termination date; collecting a commission under an agreement without one is grounds for TREC disciplinary action.

Exclusive Agency

An exclusive agency listing gives one broker the marketing right while the owner retains the right to find a buyer independently without owing a commission. The seller pays a commission only if the broker or the broker's agents produce the buyer. This type is less common because it creates the potential for procuring cause disputes.

Open Listing

An open listing is non-exclusive, allowing the seller to engage multiple brokers simultaneously. Only the broker who produces the buyer earns the commission. If the seller finds the buyer independently, no commission is owed. Open listings are typically treated as unilateral contracts because the seller's promise to pay is conditioned on the broker's act of producing a buyer. They are rare because they offer brokers minimal protection and little incentive for substantial marketing investment.

Net Listing

In a net listing the seller sets a minimum net amount to receive from the sale, and the broker keeps everything above that minimum as commission. Net listings are legal in Texas but are viewed as unprofessional because they create a direct conflict between the broker's financial interest and the fiduciary duty to maximize the client's proceeds. TREC Rule 535.16(b) requires that the seller request the net listing arrangement, appear to be familiar with current market values, and be guaranteed no less than the desired net amount, while the broker is limited to a specified maximum commission. Licensees should decline net listings unless all of these conditions are met.

Procuring Cause

The procuring cause agent is the one whose efforts were the proximate, efficient, and producing cause of the completed transaction. This is not necessarily the agent who first showed the property but generally the agent whose negotiations led to the buyer's decision to purchase. Procuring cause disputes may arise when multiple agents work with the same buyer and are sometimes resolved by arbitration. A clearly written exclusive buyer representation agreement substantially eliminates procuring cause disputes.

Buyer Representation Agreements

A buyer representation agreement is the contract a prospective buyer signs to establish an agency relationship with a broker. Under post-2024 NAR settlement rules adopted in Texas, licensees must have a signed buyer agreement before showing property to a buyer. A buyer's agent owes fiduciary duties to the buyer-client comparable to what a listing broker owes a seller: care, skill, diligence, full disclosure, and loyalty.

The buyer's agent has an affirmative duty to investigate thoroughly and to disclose all facts relevant to the buyer's decision to purchase. At the same time, the buyer's agent must deal fairly with sellers, though the agent owes sellers no duty to advise or counsel them.

Exclusive Right to Purchase

Most experienced buyer's agents use an exclusive right to purchase agreement giving the broker the sole right to represent the buyer for a defined period. This protects the broker's compensation if the buyer purchases a property during the agreement period even if the broker did not show the property. Key provisions include the agent's role, conflicts of interest, termination date and conditions, exclusivity, and compensation. TREC does not promulgate a buyer representation agreement form. The Texas REALTORS and local associations provide such forms for member use. Brokers who draft their own agreements without legal review take unnecessary risks.

Advantages and Limitations of Exclusive Buyer Agency

Advantages include greater buyer confidence that all available properties will be shown, stronger buyer loyalty, reduced risk of unauthorized dual representation, and more precise negotiating strategy. Limitations include that the exclusive buyer's broker cannot list properties and therefore cannot earn both sides of a commission, a potential conflict of interest when two buyer-clients want the same property, and that buyers who also need to sell must find separate representation.

Leasing Real Estate in Texas

A lease is both an instrument of conveyance and a contract. As a conveyance, it transfers a leasehold estate -- the right to exclusively use and occupy a property for a defined period in exchange for rent and the return of the property at the end of the term. A leasehold is sometimes called a less-than-freehold estate because it does not convey legal title. In a lease, the owner is the landlord (lessor) and the occupant is the tenant (lessee). A lease becomes binding when the parties accept its terms and communicate acceptance to each other. Texas license holders are prohibited by TRELA from preparing lease agreements outside of sales transactions; for non-sales leasing, they must use forms from the Texas REALTORS or the Texas Apartment Association.

Laws Applicable to Leases

Statute of Frauds

In Texas, a lease for more than one year must be in writing and signed by both the landlord and the tenant. A lease for one year or less may be oral. The property description must be complete and thorough because the Texas Statute of Frauds requires that the leased property be accurately identified.

Lead-Based Paint Disclosure

Lead-based paint disclosure applies to all lease transactions involving properties built before 1978. Before a lease is signed, landlords must disclose all known lead-based paint hazards, provide copies of available inspection reports, and give the tenant the EPA pamphlet Protect Your Family from Lead in Your Home. Lead-based paint notification language must be included in the lease agreement. Landlords, lessors, and real estate agents share responsibility for compliance.

Agency Disclosure

When a tenant is entering into a lease for more than one year or is contemplating an option to purchase, the licensee must provide the TREC Information About Brokerage Services disclosure at the beginning of negotiations.

Fair Housing Laws

Federal, state, and local Fair Housing laws apply to landlords and tenants exactly as they apply to sellers and buyers. Landlords must comply in advertising, reviewing applications, setting screening criteria, and dealing with tenants throughout the tenancy. Violations can result in costly complaints and litigation.

Americans with Disabilities Act and Fair Housing Amendments

The Fair Housing Amendments Act of 1988 establishes design and construction requirements for covered multi-family dwellings first occupied after March 13, 1991. Covered multi-family dwellings include buildings with an elevator and four or more units, and all ground-floor units in buildings with four or more units. The ADA of 1990 addresses public accommodations and services operated by private entities.

Sex Offender Disclosure

Texas has no statute requiring landlords of single-family rental homes to disclose the presence of nearby registered sex offenders. The Texas Apartment Association recommends that owners of multiple-dwelling properties disclose this information to applicants based on common law disclosure principles.

Leasehold Estates

The four basic types of leasehold estate each have distinct characteristics governing how the tenancy is created, maintained, and terminated.

Estate for Years

An estate for years has a definite fixed beginning and ending date measured in any period of time. The tenancy ends automatically without notice on the stated date with no automatic renewal. This type is common for commercial leases and long-term apartment leases. The tenant often has a fixed rent for the term; the landlord has guaranteed occupancy and income. Neither party can easily exit the arrangement early.

Estate from Period to Period

A periodic tenancy (estate from period to period, or month-to-month lease) continues from one period to the next with no defined end date. It renews automatically until proper notice is given, typically 30 or 60 days as specified in the lease. If a property is sold while a periodic tenancy is in effect, the new owner takes title subject to the existing lease.

Estate at Will

An estate at will has no defined term and no agreed rent; the tenant occupies with the owner's informal permission. Common when a family member occupies a property or when a tenant must move in before a formal lease can be executed. Terminable by either party with proper notice. Once a written lease is executed, the estate at will ends.

Estate at Sufferance

An estate at sufferance arises when a tenant who lawfully held possession remains after the lease expires without the landlord's consent. This holdover tenant situation gives the landlord the choice to accept a new month-to-month tenancy or to pursue eviction.

TREC Temporary Lease Forms

TREC promulgates two temporary residential lease forms for sales transactions only. Both were updated effective January 5, 2026.

- Seller's Temporary Residential Lease (Form 15-7): used when the seller will remain in the property for up to 90 days after closing; the buyer becomes the landlord and the seller is the tenant
- Buyer's Temporary Residential Lease (Form 16-7): used when the buyer will occupy the property for up to 90 days before closing; the seller is the landlord and the buyer is the tenant

Both forms are addenda to a sales contract and may never be used as stand-alone lease agreements or for periods exceeding 90 days. If more than 90 days are needed, a standard residential lease form must be used instead.

Both temporary lease forms address: Parties (legal names of landlord and tenant); Lease (legal description and any included personal property); Term (start and end dates); Rent (daily rate); Deposit (refundable conditions); Utilities (allocation); Use of Property (residential only); Pets; Condition of Property; Alterations; Special Provisions; Inspections and Entry; Applicable Laws; Repairs and Maintenance; Indemnity; Insurance; Default; Termination; Holding Over; Attorney's Fees; Smoke Alarms; Security Devices; Consult Your Attorney; and Notices.

In the Seller's Temporary Residential Lease, the seller agrees the property will be in the condition required by the sales contract at the end of the lease. In the Buyer's Temporary Residential Lease, the tenant-buyer may not make holes in walls, paint, alter the property, or install fixtures without the landlord-seller's prior written consent; any improvements installed during the lease become part of the property. Texas Property Code security device requirements do not apply to leases of 90 days or less; leases over 90 days require the landlord to re-key locks from the previous tenant.

Lease Provisions and Types of Leases

Required Lease Covenants

The requirements for a valid lease are the same as for any valid contract. The following covenants are common to most leases:

- Capacity to contract -- parties must meet age, mental competency, and authority requirements
- Demising clause -- recites that the landlord leases and the tenant takes possession
- Description of the premises -- identifies the property by address, legal description, or any description making it identifiable
- Clear statement of term -- specifies the duration of the lease
- Rent amount and payment -- states amount, timing, method, grace period, and late fee
- In writing -- required for leases exceeding one year
- Signatures -- landlord must sign; tenant should sign to enforce the lease terms against the tenant
- Delivery -- each party should have a duplicate original

Types of Leases

Gross lease The landlord pays all property operating expenses; the tenant pays only rent. Common for office and industrial properties. Residential leases are typically gross leases with the tenant paying utilities.

Net lease The tenant pays rent plus some or all operating expenses. A net lease adds maintenance and taxes. A net-net lease adds insurance. A triple net (net-net-net) lease requires the tenant to pay taxes, insurance, and all maintenance and repairs. Common in commercial and industrial leases.

Graduated lease Rent starts fixed and increases as the term matures, often based on periodic property appraisals.

Ground lease Covers land only, not improvements; the owner grants the tenant a leasehold in the land in exchange for rent. Used for agriculture, development projects, or to separate land ownership from improvement ownership. Typically long-term, 30 to 50 years.

Index lease Rent adjusts periodically according to a price index, most commonly the consumer price index.

Percentage lease Rent is based on a percentage of the tenant's gross sales at the site with a minimum base rent. A recapture clause may allow lease termination if the tenant fails to reach a defined sales threshold. Common in retail shopping center leases.

Proprietary lease Conveys a leasehold interest to an owner in a cooperative; no stated rent or fixed term; the owner pays a pro rata share of the cooperative's operating expenses.

Commercial lease May be net, gross, or percentage; typically long-term (up to 25 years); involves significant tenant improvement costs; virtually all clauses are negotiable.

Lease Termination and Default

A lease may terminate for any of the following causes: term expiration, proper notice by either party (for periodic or at-will tenancies), voluntary agreement, destruction of the property, condemnation by eminent domain, foreclosure, or breach of contract.

Tenant Default

Tenant default most commonly arises from failure to pay rent or maintain the premises. Before filing a suit for possession, the landlord must give the tenant proper written notice to pay or vacate by a stated deadline. A successful eviction suit (filed in Justice of the Peace Court in Texas) allows the landlord to obtain a judgment for possession and an order directing the sheriff to complete the eviction. Texas law allows a landlord to change the locks when rent is delinquent, but only once per payment period, only when the tenant is not in the dwelling, and only after posting a notice stating the amount due and a 24-hour contact number.

Texas law allows active-duty military members and certain family violence victims to terminate a lease without liability for future rent. If the landlord fails to provide written notice of these rights, the tenant may also be relieved of delinquent rent. Abandonment does not release the tenant from rent obligations unless the landlord terminates the lease and re-lets the premises.

Landlord Default

The most common landlord default is failure to maintain the property or provide promised services. When a landlord's neglect or disruptive conduct renders the property uninhabitable, the tenant may vacate and declare the lease cancelled by default. This is called constructive eviction. To obtain a constructive eviction judgment the tenant must actually vacate. If successful, the tenant's lease obligations are nullified and the tenant may recover damages including relocation costs and property losses.

Death, Sale of Property, and Special Circumstances

Death or change in ownership does not terminate a lease. The new owner takes title subject to the existing lease. If the landlord dies, the estate remains obligated to provide occupancy. If the tenant dies, the lease becomes part of the estate, which is bound by its terms. A tenant 62 years of age or older may terminate with 30 days' written notice if admitted to an adult care facility, residential health care facility, senior housing receiving subsidies, or a relative's home for health care; documentation of admission must accompany the notice.

Options

An option to buy is an enforceable unilateral contract in which a property owner (the optionor) grants a potential buyer (the optionee) the right to purchase a property before a stated date, at a stated price, and under stated terms, in exchange for valuable consideration paid to the optionor. The optionee has no obligation to purchase. If the optionee exercises the option, the optionor must perform and a bilateral sales contract is created. An unused option terminates at its expiration date.

Practical Example

A buyer wants to purchase a property listed at $575,000 but needs two months to liquidate an investment account for the down payment. The seller offers a 60-day option. The buyer pays $3,000 for the option. If exercised, the $3,000 is credited toward the earnest money deposit. If the option expires unused, the seller keeps the $3,000. The parties complete a sales contract as an addendum to the option agreement and then execute the option.

Right of First Refusal

A right of first refusal gives a person the first opportunity to purchase or lease property when the owner decides to sell or lease. Unlike an option, no purchase right exists until the owner actually decides to sell or receives a qualifying third-party offer. At that point the holder can match the offer or decline, after which the owner may sell to the third party at that price or higher.

Options for Land Purchasing

Options are particularly valuable for developers acquiring land for future projects. A developer holding a land option incurs no taxes, insurance, interest, or maintenance costs until the option is exercised. During the option period, the developer investigates zoning, permits, environmental conditions, and project feasibility without committing to ownership. If the project is not viable, the developer loses only the option fee rather than the costs associated with outright ownership and resale. Experienced developers often negotiate a partial refund of the option fee if the option is dropped early in exchange for sharing feasibility study results with the owner.

Option Agreement Provisions and Legal Aspects

A well-drafted option agreement should include: the option price; the option period; the legal description; delivery requirements for exercising the option; forfeiture terms; property and title condition warranties; how the consideration will be credited at closing; and, if the seller will provide financing, the note and deed of trust. An option should be recorded to protect the optionee's equitable interest. An option is assignable unless the agreement expressly prohibits it.

Declining credit options allow progressively smaller portions of the option price to count toward the purchase price as the option period lengthens. Rolling options allow the optionee to add new parcels to the option as previously included parcels are purchased.

Contracts for Deed

A contract for deed -- also called an installment sales contract, land contract, conditional sales contract, or agreement for deed -- is a bilateral agreement in which a seller (the vendor) defers receipt of the purchase price while the buyer (the vendee) takes possession and makes periodic payments. The vendor retains legal title during the contract period; the vendee holds equitable title. When all payments are made, the vendor conveys legal title by deed. Under Texas Property Code section 5.081, a vendee may convert equitable interest to legal title by paying the full amount due or delivering a promissory note equal to the balance with the same terms as the contract. Contracts for deed are executory contracts subject to Texas Property Code sections 5.061 and following.

Benefits to the Buyer

A contract for deed enables a buyer who cannot qualify for conventional financing to acquire property. The seller acts as the lender. Benefits include: homeownership without meeting conventional income or down payment requirements; deductibility of interest paid on the tax return; the right to make improvements; an opportunity to rebuild credit; and time to qualify for conventional financing. Sellers typically allow pre-payment without penalty.

Benefits to the Seller

Benefits to the seller include: access to a larger pool of buyers who have stable income but imperfect credit; the potential for a rapid sale; the buyer's responsibility for maintenance and often for taxes and insurance; favorable installment sale tax treatment (capital gain is recognized as payments are received); the ability to sell above market value when no appraisal is required; and relatively simple cancellation if the buyer defaults.

Rights and Obligations of the Parties

During the contract period, the vendor may mortgage the property, assign interests, and incur liens, but must convey legal title to the vendee upon receipt of the full purchase price and remains liable for any existing underlying mortgage. The vendee may occupy, use, and improve the property subject to the agreement; must make periodic payments; and typically must pay property taxes and hazard insurance.

Default, Recourse, and Usage Guidelines

If the vendor defaults by failing to convey the deed, the vendee may sue for specific performance, cancellation, and damages. If the vendee defaults, remedies depend on the amount paid and Texas law; typical remedies include cancellation, retention of payments received, and eviction. Both parties should engage an attorney to draft the agreement, use professional escrow and title services, record the transaction, and understand enforcement under current Texas law. Texas has no standardized form for contracts for deed, creating risks for both parties that professional guidance can minimize.

Lease Purchase Agreements

A lease purchase agreement -- also called rent-to-own, lease-to-own, or lease option purchase -- combines a lease with the right or obligation to purchase the property within a specified period, typically one to three years, at an agreed price. The parties are landlord and tenant rather than buyer and seller until the purchase is completed. The terms lease purchase and lease option are now used interchangeably; reviewing the contract carefully for the exact obligations of each party is essential.

A portion of each monthly rent payment is typically designated as a rent credit toward the tenant-buyer's down payment. The agreement may specify that once sufficient credit accumulates, the tenant-buyer may convert the arrangement to an owner-financed purchase by receiving a warranty deed and giving the seller a note and deed of trust. Alternatively, the accumulated credit may be shown on a loan application to a third-party lender.

Consideration Fee and Rent Credit

At the start of the agreement, the tenant typically pays a non-refundable consideration fee for the right to purchase. The rent credit is the agreed portion of each monthly rent payment set aside for the eventual down payment and closing costs. If the tenant does not purchase, the landlord keeps both the consideration fee and the accumulated rent credit.

Example: A house could rent for $3,500 per month. Under a lease purchase arrangement the parties agree on $3,750 per month, with $250 per month designated as a rent credit. Over a three-year lease the tenant accumulates $9,000. If the tenant exercises the purchase, that $9,000 applies toward earnest money, the down payment, or closing costs. If the tenant does not purchase, the landlord retains the $9,000 and the consideration fee.

Benefits and Disadvantages

For the tenant-buyer: the tenant lives in the home before committing to purchase, builds credit and savings during the lease term, and may walk away losing only the consideration fee and accumulated rent credit if circumstances change. Lease purchase agreements suit buyers who have a meaningful down payment but whose credit is not yet sufficient for conventional financing.

For the landlord-seller: the seller can continue servicing an existing mortgage when the property is not selling, lock in a rent amount and purchase price in a declining market, and receive security through the consideration fee and rent premium. Even if the tenant does not purchase, the landlord keeps those funds.

Disadvantages for the tenant-buyer include the fact that a single late payment typically voids the rent credit for that month, and the tenant must trust the seller to continue paying the underlying mortgage. Disadvantages for the landlord-seller include the risk of choosing a dishonest tenant with no genuine intention to purchase, the inability to accept higher offers during the option period, and the possibility that the tenant still cannot qualify for financing at the end of the lease term.

Key Provisions and Texas Requirements

A lease purchase agreement includes all standard lease provisions plus: the purchase price and application of rent credits; the option term; the notice required to exercise the option; the non-refundable consideration fee; financing arrangements (the seller typically plays no role; the buyer must obtain institutional financing); default remedies; and closing and settlement details. In Texas, Chapter 5, Subchapter D of the Texas Property Code contains specific requirements for sellers in lease purchase transactions. Non-compliance can result in fines and loss of the transaction. Both parties should consult an attorney before signing. Other best practices include obtaining a home inspection, making transparent disclosures about the property and mortgage, setting a specific purchase price or defining the pricing formula precisely, and considering separate lease and option documents to provide the seller additional security.

Chapter 5 Snapshot Review

The following review summarizes the key rules and concepts from Chapter 5.

Contract Fundamentals

- All six elements must be present for a valid contract: competent parties, consideration, mutual agreement, lawful objective, in writing and signed, and legal description
- Earnest money is not the consideration in a sales contract; the consideration is the mutual exchange of promises
- Under TRELA, a broker cannot sue to recover a commission unless the agreement is in writing and signed by the party to be charged
- TREC rules require immediate presentation of all offers; withholding an offer is a breach of fiduciary duty, grounds for disciplinary action, and potential tortious interference
- Statute of limitations for breach of a written contract in Texas: four years from the date of breach
- Options are always unilateral; the optionor is bound, the optionee is not; exercising the option creates a bilateral sales contract
- All exclusive listing agreements must contain a definite termination date

Contract Types

- Express: all terms clearly stated verbally or in writing
- Implied: arises from conduct; may arise unintentionally; proven through offer, acceptance, mutual intent, and consideration through actions
- Bilateral: both parties promise; enforceable from formation; most real estate contracts
- Unilateral: one party promises; accepted by the other's performance; options and open listings
- Executed: fully performed; no remaining obligations
- Executory: performance not yet complete; signed sales contract before closing

Listing Types

- Exclusive right to sell: commission owed regardless of who produces the buyer; strongest broker protection; most widely used
- Exclusive agency: owner retains right to sell without commission; procuring cause disputes possible
- Open listing: multiple brokers; producing broker earns the commission; unilateral; owner may sell independently without commission
- Net listing broker keeps amount above seller's minimum net; legal in Texas but disfavored; strict conditions under TREC Rule 535.16(b)

Leasehold Estates

- Estate for years: definite term; terminates automatically; no automatic renewal, no notice required
- Estate from period to period: no defined end; renews each period; requires proper notice to terminate
- Estate at will: no defined term or rent; either party may terminate with proper notice
- Estate at sufferance: holdover after lease expires without landlord's consent; landlord may accept new tenancy or pursue eviction

TREC Temporary Lease Forms and Leasing Rules

- Seller's Temporary Residential Lease (Form 15-7, effective 01/05/2026): seller stays up to 90 days after closing; buyer is landlord; addendum to sales contract only
- Buyer's Temporary Residential Lease (Form 16-7, effective 01/05/2026): buyer occupies up to 90 days before closing; seller is landlord; addendum to sales contract only
- Leases for more than one year must be in writing and signed by both parties; leases of one year or less may be oral
- A landlord cannot physically remove a tenant, change locks (except under strict Texas rent delinquency law conditions), shut off utilities, or remove doors without a court order
- Death or sale of property does not terminate a lease; the new owner takes subject to it; the tenant's estate is bound by the lease if the tenant dies

Options, Contracts for Deed, and Lease Purchase

- Option: unilateral; optionor is bound; optionee is not; requires consideration; should be recorded; assignable unless prohibited
- Right of first refusal: no purchase right until the owner decides to sell; differs from an option
- Contract for deed: seller retains legal title; buyer holds equitable title; subject to Texas Property Code sections 5.061 et seq.; attorney and title company strongly recommended
- Contracts for deed, lease-purchases, and lease-options for more than 180 days are executory contracts subject to mandatory pre-signing disclosure requirements under Texas Property Code Chapter 5, Subchapter D
- Lease purchase: landlord-tenant relationship until purchase; consideration fee non-refundable; rent credit forfeited if tenant does not purchase

CHAPTER 5 QUIZ:
CONTRACTS USED IN TEXAS REAL ESTATE

1. Which of the following best describes a bilateral contract in real estate?
   a. A contract in which only one party makes a promise in exchange for an act by the other party
   b. A contract in which both parties exchange mutual promises and each is bound from the moment the contract is formed
   c. A contract that is accepted by the performance of a requested act rather than by a return promise
   d. A contract that involves unique personal services and therefore cannot be assigned to a third party

2. Under the Texas Statute of Frauds, which of the following lease arrangements must be in writing and signed by both parties to be enforceable?
   a. Any lease that includes a pet deposit
   b. Any lease for residential property regardless of the term
   c. Any lease for commercial property regardless of the term
   d. Any lease for a term exceeding one year

3. TREC rules require that a real estate licensee present all offers to a seller in what manner?
   a. Immediately, without delay, unless the seller has given specific written instructions to the contrary
   b. Within 24 hours of receipt, unless the offer is below the listed asking price
   c. Within three business days of receiving the offer from the buyer's agent
   d. Only after the licensee has reviewed the offer with the sponsoring broker

4. A listing agreement contains a provision directing the listing agent to refuse to show the property to buyers of a particular national origin. How is that agreement classified under Texas and federal law?
   a. Voidable at the listing broker's election
   b. Valid because the seller has the right to determine who enters the property
   c. Void, because it requires unlawful performance that violates fair housing law
   d. Unenforceable only if a buyer files a formal complaint with HUD

5. Which of the following statements correctly describes an option to purchase?
   a. It is a bilateral contract because both the buyer and seller must perform if the option is exercised
   b. It requires no payment from the buyer to the seller because it is merely a right to purchase
   c. It creates an immediate obligation for the buyer to close on the property within the option period
   d. It is a unilateral contract in which the seller is bound to sell but the buyer is not obligated to purchase

6. In an exclusive right to sell listing, who earns the commission if the seller independently finds a buyer during the listing period?
   a. The listing broker still earns the commission because the broker holds the exclusive right regardless of who produces the buyer
   b. Neither the broker nor the seller owes a commission because the seller found the buyer without the broker's help
   c. The commission is split equally between the broker and the seller for the effort each contributed
   d. The broker earns a reduced commission equal to half the agreed rate because the seller performed part of the work

7. A tenant's lease expires on June 30 and the tenant remains in the property without the landlord's consent on July 1. What type of leasehold estate does the tenant now hold?
   a. Estate at will
   b. Estate from period to period
   c. Estate at sufferance
   d. Estate for years

8. What is the primary purpose of earnest money in a Texas residential sales transaction?
   a. It comprises the legal consideration that creates a binding contract between buyer and seller
   b. It signals the buyer's serious intent and may serve as liquidated damages if the buyer defaults
   c. It is required by TREC rules as a condition of submitting a valid offer on any listed property
   d. It guarantees that the title company will issue a commitment within 20 days of the contract date

9. In a contract for deed, which of the following correctly describes the legal status of title during the contract period?
   a. The vendor retains legal title while the vendee holds equitable title
   b. The vendee receives legal title at the time of possession and loses it if payments are not made
   c. Title is held in escrow by a neutral third party until all payments are complete
   d. Both parties hold an undivided interest in legal title until the final payment is received

10. A net listing is legal in Texas but is generally considered unprofessional. Which of the following best explains why net listings are disfavored?
    a. They require the broker to split the commission with the seller rather than collecting a fixed percentage
    b. TREC has never promulgated a form for net listings, which means they cannot be used in residential transactions
    c. They are classified as unilateral contracts and therefore cannot be enforced if the seller changes the asking price
    d. They create a direct conflict between the broker's financial interest and the fiduciary duty to maximize the seller's proceeds

11. In a lease purchase agreement, what happens to the consideration fee paid by the tenant-buyer at the start of the arrangement if the tenant does not exercise the purchase option?
    a. It is refunded in full because the tenant completed the full term of the lease without defaulting
    b. It is credited toward the tenant's last month of rent as compensation for the inconvenience
    c. The landlord retains the consideration fee because it is non-refundable
    d. It is placed in escrow and returned to the tenant minus a penalty equal to one month's rent

12. Which of the following correctly describes an estate for years as a leasehold estate?
   a. It renews automatically each period unless either party provides proper advance notice to terminate
   b. It has a fixed beginning and ending date and terminates automatically without notice on the stated date
   c. It arises when a tenant remains in possession after a lease expires without the landlord's consent
   d. It has no defined term and no agreed rent and is terminable by either party at any time

13. Both of TREC's promulgated temporary residential lease forms may be used only as addenda to a sales contract and are subject to which maximum term?
   a. 30 days
   b. 45 days
   c. 60 days
   d. 90 days

14. In Texas, what is the statute of limitations for a lawsuit based on a breach of a written real estate contract?
   a. Four years from the date of the breach
   b. Two years from the date the injured party discovers the breach
   c. One year from the closing date of the transaction
   d. Seven years from the date the contract was signed

15. Which of the following correctly describes an exclusive agency listing?
   a. The broker earns a commission regardless of who produces the buyer, including the seller acting independently
   b. Multiple brokers may market the property simultaneously and only the producing broker earns a commission
   c. One broker has the marketing right but the seller may find a buyer independently without owing a commission
   d. The broker agrees to net the seller a specified amount and retains all proceeds above that amount

16. Under the 2024 NAR settlement rules adopted in Texas, a real estate licensee must have a signed buyer representation agreement in place before doing which of the following?
   a. Submitting an offer on behalf of a buyer to a listing agent
   b. Showing property to a buyer
   c. Disclosing information about the property's condition to a prospective buyer
   d. Providing a buyer with a list of comparable sales in a neighborhood

17. Which of the following best describes how an implied contract arises in real estate practice?
   a. It arises from the conduct of the parties when no express agreement exists, such as when a licensee acts on a buyer's behalf without a signed representation agreement
   b. It arises from a written agreement that both parties sign but choose not to record with the county clerk
   c. It arises when a listing agreement expires and the broker continues to market the property under the expired terms
   d. It arises when the seller instructs the broker to accept any offer above a specified minimum price

18. Which of the following best describes an open listing?
   a. A listing in which the seller sets a minimum net amount and the broker keeps all proceeds above that amount
   b. A listing in which one broker holds the exclusive right to sell for a defined period
   c. A non-exclusive listing that allows the seller to engage multiple brokers simultaneously, with only the producing broker earning a commission
   d. A listing in which the broker is paid only if the property sells above the original list price

19. Under Texas Property Code section 5.081, a vendee in a contract for deed who has been making payments may do which of the following to convert equitable interest to legal title?
   a. Record an affidavit of interest with the county clerk without the vendor's consent
   b. File a quiet title action if the vendor refuses to deliver a deed after the final payment
   c. Request that a court impose a constructive trust over the property in the vendee's favor
   d. Pay the full amount due or deliver a promissory note equal to the balance under the same contract terms

20. A landlord's sustained failure to provide heat and running water renders a rental unit uninhabitable. The tenant vacates the premises and claims the lease is cancelled. What legal doctrine supports the tenant's position?
   a. Adverse possession
   b. Constructive eviction
   c. Inverse condemnation
   d. The rule of capture

21. In a real estate transaction, the procuring cause agent is generally defined as which of the following?
   a. The agent whose efforts were the proximate, efficient, and producing cause of the completed transaction
   b. The agent who first showed the property to the buyer regardless of who the buyer ultimately used
   c. The listing broker because the listing broker controls access to the property
   d. The agent who submits the highest-priced offer on behalf of a buyer-client

22. When a buyer defaults on a residential sales contract and the seller wants the court to require the buyer to complete the transaction rather than simply pay money damages, which remedy does the seller seek?
   a. Rescission
   b. Reformation
   c. Forfeiture of earnest money
   d. Specific performance

23. A ground lease covers which of the following?
   a. Both the land and all improvements on the property, with the tenant responsible for all taxes
   b. The land only, not improvements; the tenant typically develops the land at the tenant's expense over a long term
   c. A residential property on which the tenant has the option to purchase the improvements but not the land
   d. Agricultural land on which the tenant pays a percentage of crop proceeds as rent

24. A commercial lease in a shopping center requires a tenant to pay a base rent plus a percentage of the tenant's gross sales above a specified threshold. What type of lease is this?

    a. Index lease
    b. Net-net lease
    c. Percentage lease
    d. Graduated lease

25. Under Texas Property Code sections 5.061 and following, which of the following arrangements is classified as an executory contract subject to mandatory pre-signing disclosure requirements?

    a. A lease purchase agreement with a term exceeding 180 days
    b. A standard residential sales contract with a 30-day option period
    c. A month-to-month rental agreement for a single-family home
    d. An exclusive right to sell listing agreement with a six-month term

Chapter 5 Case Study:

Contracts Used in Texas Real Estate

The Situation

Paula Mettling owns a small rental house in Corpus Christi that she has been trying to sell for several months. She signed an open listing agreement with three different brokers, including Marcus Webb of Performance Programs Realty. Marcus has been showing the property regularly and has developed a strong relationship with a prospective buyer named Tina Okafor.

Without a signed buyer representation agreement in place, Marcus showed Tina the property on four separate occasions, answered her questions about the neighborhood, and negotiated informally on her behalf by relaying her comments about price to Paula. Tina eventually submitted an offer through a different broker, Greg Salinas, who had shown her the property once after she found the listing online. Paula accepted Tina's offer and Greg Salinas claimed the commission. Marcus objected, arguing that his efforts produced the buyer.

Separately, Paula had also been approached by a neighbor, Tom Hendricks, who expressed strong interest in purchasing the property but said he could not qualify for conventional financing. Paula verbally agreed to let Tom move into the property and make monthly payments directly to her for two years, after which she would deed him the property. Tom moved in, began making payments, and spent $6,000 on repairs and improvements. After eight months, Paula changed her mind and told Tom the arrangement was off. Tom demanded that the agreement be honored.

Discussion Questions

Question 1

Marcus Webb worked extensively with Tina Okafor without a signed buyer representation agreement. Identify what type of agency relationship, if any, may have been created between Marcus and Tina, explain the legal basis for that conclusion, and describe what Marcus should have done differently from the outset of his work with Tina.

Question 2

Both Marcus Webb and Greg Salinas claim the right to the commission on the sale of Paula's property. Explain what type of listing agreement Paula signed and how commission is determined under that type of agreement. Then analyze which broker has the stronger claim to the commission and identify the legal doctrine that governs the dispute.

Question 3

Paula and Tom Hendricks had a verbal agreement for Tom to move in and make payments toward purchasing the property over two years. Tom has already moved in, made payments, and spent money on improvements. Classify the type of arrangement Paula and Tom entered into, identify the Texas law that governs it, and explain whether Tom has any basis to enforce the agreement or recover his losses.

CHAPTER 6:

THE TEXAS SALES CONTRACT

Chapter Overview

Learning Objectives

Upon completing Chapter 6, the student will be able to:

1. Describe the offer and acceptance process, identify the four options available to a seller upon receiving an offer, and explain what transforms an offer into a binding contract.
2. Explain a licensee's obligations under TREC rules regarding the presentation of offers and the legal and ethical consequences of failing to meet those obligations.
3. Identify and explain the primary and secondary provisions found in a Texas residential sales contract.
4. Describe the financing provisions in the One to Four Family Residential Contract (Form 20-19), explain the structure of Paragraphs 3 and 5, and identify the addenda required for each financing type.
5. Explain the purpose and provisions of Paragraph 4 (Leases) and Paragraph 5 (Earnest Money and Termination Option), including how the option fee and earnest money are delivered and how the Termination Option works.
6. Explain the seller's duty to disclose material defects, identify the environmental hazards that require disclosure, and list the statutory exemptions from the seller's disclosure requirement.
7. Define conveyance, explain the role of the deed, title company, and escrow agent, and describe how property conveyance is completed in a Texas residential transaction.
8. Explain the Statute of Frauds as it applies to Texas real estate contracts, describe the requirements for valid signatures, and identify the remedies available to each party when a breach of contract occurs.

Contents

- Title Company and Title Evidence
- Closing and Possession Under Form 20-19
- The Statute of Frauds
- Signature Requirements
- Breach of Contract and Default
- Remedies for Breach of Contract

Making an Offer

The buying process begins when a real estate licensee has found a buyer who wants to make an offer on a property. The licensee sits down with the buyer and reviews the guidelines for the offer. Together they go through every paragraph of the sales contract form, fill in all required blanks, and add any applicable addenda. A cover letter explaining the buyer's position, including loan approval status and genuine interest level, is helpful. Once the contract is complete, the licensee reviews it with the buyer one more time and then asks the buyer to sign. At this stage, the document is an offer, not yet a contract.

After the buyer decides on the offering price, closing date, and any other terms, the offer is delivered to the seller or the listing agent. Delivery transforms the buyer's signed document into a formal offer that the seller must consider.

The Seller's Options

When a seller receives an offer, the seller has four possible courses of action.

Accept the Offer

Acceptance must be absolute, meaning the seller agrees to every term of the offer exactly as written. The acceptance must then be communicated back to the buyer to create a binding contract. A call, text, or email to the buyer's representative constitutes notice, followed by delivery of the signed contract. Failing to communicate acceptance promptly can create confusion about whether the offer is still pending or has ripened into a contract. Resolving that ambiguity is the licensee's responsibility.

Reject the Offer

Rejection frees the seller to consider other offers and frees the buyer to look at other properties or make a new offer on the same property. Rejection of any single term of an offer constitutes a rejection of the entire offer. Even if the seller wants to change only one item, the proper response is a counteroffer rather than a partial acceptance. While sellers are not legally obligated to respond in writing, best practice is to give the buyer written notice that the offer is unacceptable and invite a revised offer.

Make a Counteroffer

A counteroffer is the seller's response to the buyer's offer in which one or more terms are changed. For example, the buyer asked the seller to pay for the survey and the seller believes that cost should fall on the buyer. The seller's modified response is a new offer from the seller to the buyer. The original buyer's offer is terminated the moment the counteroffer is made. If the buyer declines the counteroffer, the seller has no right to revert to and accept the buyer's original offer because it no longer exists.

Listing agents should encourage sellers to take offer presentations seriously and think strategically. Minor issues should not automatically generate a counteroffer. If the offer would accomplish the seller's primary goal of selling the home, the seller is paying the agent to get the home sold. Decent offers deserve the opportunity to be accepted rather than needlessly negotiated away.

Fail to Act

A seller is not legally obligated to respond to an offer within any specific timeframe. Failing to act simply means the seller is deferring a decision. The buyer retains the right to withdraw the offer at any time before the seller communicates acceptance. While this is the seller's prerogative, best practice is to respond in a timely manner so that the buyer's attention and commitment are maintained.

Counteroffers and Acceptance

When a counteroffer is presented to the buyer, the buyer faces the same four options the seller had: accept it, reject it, make another counteroffer, or fail to act. This process continues until the parties reach a meeting of the minds or arrive at an impasse that cannot be resolved. All offers and counteroffers should be in writing to avoid disputes about the specific terms agreed upon.

The offer-counteroffer process carries risk. While negotiations are ongoing, another buyer can emerge and compete for the same property. If the first buyer is the licensee's client, that client may find the property has gone under contract with someone else. For this reason, real estate professionals should coach buyers to lead with their strongest offer. A long, drawn-out negotiation benefits no one, especially in a residential transaction where buyers are emotionally invested in the property.

Acceptance is the final step before a document becomes a contract. Acceptance must be communicated as quickly as possible; waiting even an hour gives the buyer an opportunity to move on. The listing agent should contact the buyer's agent immediately by phone, text, and email, and deliver an executed original contract no later than the following day. An original contract is one with original handwritten or properly authenticated electronic signatures. Electronic signatures are valid in Texas provided both parties agree to their use.

When all required signatures and initials from both the buyer and the seller are in place, the other side must be notified. The contract is now effective. Once the buyer's agent is notified that acceptance has occurred, the effective date is entered on the contract and the process of preparing for closing begins.

TREC Regulations on Offer Presentation

TREC rules require immediate presentation of all offers. A real estate licensee must never withhold an offer from the seller. The only exception is when the seller has given specific written instructions directing the licensee not to present certain types of offers. For example, a seller may state in writing that offers contingent on seller financing need not be presented. Even then, the seller's instruction must be documented in writing.

Failure to present offers or counteroffers promptly may result in disciplinary action by TREC, including suspension or revocation of the license. Beyond TRELA violations, a licensee who delays or withholds an offer may face a lawsuit for tortious interference. A tort is a negligent or wrongful act that constitutes a breach of a legal duty and causes damages to another person. If the seller suffers financial harm because a good offer was not presented in a timely manner, the licensee could be held personally liable.

The TREC standard residential contract allows the seller to continue showing the property after entering into a contract in order to generate back-up offers. If the seller has specifically agreed not to continue showing the property, additional offers need not be presented. In any case, the licensee should obtain all such instructions from the seller in writing.

Primary Provisions of the Sales Contract

The current TREC One to Four Family Residential Contract is Form 20-19, effective July 1st, 2026. It is the form Texas licensees use for the resale of one- to four-family residential properties. The contract contains both primary and secondary provisions. Primary provisions address the core elements of the transaction.

Parties, Consideration, and Property

One or more provisions identify the parties, the property, and the basic consideration, which is the exchange of the property for the agreed purchase price. There must be at least two parties to a sales contract; one cannot convey property to oneself. All parties must be identified by full legal name, be of legal age, and have the capacity to contract. The property clause also identifies fixtures and personal property included in the sale. Unless expressly excluded, items commonly construed as fixtures pass with the property. Items commonly considered personal property are not included unless the contract expressly includes them.

Legal Description

The legal description must be sufficient for a competent surveyor to locate and identify the property. A property address is not legally sufficient to transfer real estate.

Price and Terms

A clause states the final agreed price and the details of how the purchase will be funded. Of particular interest to the seller is the buyer's down payment amount, since a larger equity contribution increases the buyer's ability to secure financing. The earnest money deposit, down payment, loan proceeds, and any other promised funds must together equal the stated purchase price. If seller financing is involved, this clause sets out the loan amount, type, interest rate, term, and repayment structure.

Loan Approval

A financing contingency clause specifies the conditions under which the buyer may cancel the contract without default and receive a refund of the earnest money. If the buyer cannot obtain the stated financing by the specified deadline, the parties may agree to extend the contingency period by initialing a date change on the contract or by executing an amendment.

Earnest Money and Termination Option

Paragraph 5 documents the buyer's earnest money deposit and the Termination Option together. Both the earnest money and the option fee must be delivered to the escrow agent within three days after the effective date. These amounts may be paid separately or combined in a single payment. The Termination Option gives the buyer the unrestricted right to cancel the contract for any reason during the agreed option period. The option fee is credited toward the sales price at closing if the transaction closes. If the buyer terminates during the option period, the option fee is not refunded but the earnest money is returned to the buyer.

Escrow

The escrow clause provides for the custody and disbursement of the earnest money deposit and releases the escrow agent from certain liabilities associated with the performance of escrow duties. The earnest money is held in a third-party trust account by a licensed escrow agent, typically a title company.

Closing and Possession Dates

The contract states the date by which the closing must occur and the date on which the buyer takes physical possession. Customarily, possession occurs when the deed is recorded and the seller receives closing proceeds, unless the parties have agreed to different arrangements through a temporary lease addendum. The closing clause describes the specific actions that must be completed to avoid default: the seller must provide clear and marketable title, and the buyer must produce all purchase funds in the agreed form.

Conveyed Interest and Type of Deed

The contract states what type of deed the seller will use to convey the property and what conditions will be reflected in the deed. Sellers in a standard residential resale typically convey a fee simple interest by general warranty deed. The deed will be subject to existing easements, association memberships, encumbrances, and any special assessments that have been disclosed in the contract.

Title Evidence

The seller covenants to provide the best available evidence of property ownership, most commonly in the form of a title insurance commitment from a licensed title company.

Closing Costs

The contract identifies which closing costs each party will pay. Customarily, the seller pays title-related and property-related costs, and the buyer pays financing-related costs. Annual costs such as property taxes and insurance premiums are prorated between the parties as of the closing date. The allocation of any specific closing cost item is always a matter for negotiation.

Damage and Destruction

This clause addresses the rights and obligations of the parties if the property is damaged or destroyed before closing. Under Paragraph 14 of Form 20-19, if a fire or other casualty loss occurs before closing, the seller has until closing to restore the property to its prior condition. If the seller cannot restore the property, the buyer may terminate and recover the earnest money, extend the time for performance by up to 15 days, or accept the property in its damaged condition with a credit from the seller for the deductible under the seller's insurance policy if the carrier permits assignment of proceeds.

Default

A default clause identifies the remedies available to each party. Generally, a buyer who defaults may face suit for damages, specific performance, or cancellation, and forfeiture of the earnest money as liquidated damages. A seller who defaults faces the same remedies from the buyer.

Broker Representation and Commission

The broker discloses the applicable agency relationships in the transaction and identifies the party responsible for paying the brokerage commission. Commission terms are governed by the separate listing agreement or buyer representation agreement.

Effective July 1, 2026, Form 20-19 reorganized how brokerage compensation is documented in the contract. Reflecting recent changes in industry practice surrounding compensation, the contract now addresses brokerage compensation within Paragraph 12, including a new Paragraph 12B. As part of the same revision, the former Paragraph 8B was removed, and the broker-to-broker compensation disclosure that previously appeared at the bottom of the broker information page was deleted to reduce confusion. Because these amounts now reside in Paragraph 12, the TREC Amendment to Contract (Form 39-11) modifies them through its Paragraph 12A(1)(b) and Paragraph 12B entries.

Seller's Representations

The seller warrants that no liens will remain on the property at closing that cannot be extinguished from the proceeds, and that all representations made in the contract are true. If any representation is found to be false at closing, the buyer has the right to cancel and recover the earnest money.

Residential Property Condition Disclosure

The seller's written summary of the property's condition is required by statute and must be delivered to the buyer no later than when the buyer makes an offer to purchase. If the seller fails to deliver the disclosure in a timely manner, the buyer may have the right to rescind the contract within seven days of receiving it. The buyer's right to cancel persists until closing or occupancy, whichever occurs first.

The listing agent must ensure that the disclosure is completed and delivered. If an agent is involved in the transaction, the agent must independently disclose any and all material facts the agent knows or should reasonably know about the property, regardless of what the seller disclosed on the form.

Completing the Disclosure Form

The standard Texas Seller's Disclosure Notice (Form 55-1, effective May 28, 2026) requires the seller to state whether problems exist in each listed feature or system of the property. Responding no means the seller has no knowledge of a defect. If a defect in fact exists, the seller can be held liable for intentional misrepresentation. A response of unknown means the seller makes no claim of knowledge about that particular feature; the seller is not liable for any defect that is genuinely unknown. Once the seller signs and delivers the form, the buyer must acknowledge receipt.

Secondary Provisions of the Sales Contract

In addition to the primary provisions, a sales contract typically contains secondary provisions that address specific circumstances of the transaction. The following are the most common.

Inspections The parties agree to what inspections will be conducted and what remedial action will be required based on findings.

Owner's association disclosure The seller discloses the existence of a mandatory owners' association and the obligations it imposes, including dues, assessments, and rules.

Survey The parties agree to a survey to satisfy financing requirements or to verify the property's boundaries.

Environmental hazards The seller notifies the buyer of any known environmental hazards that could affect the use or value of the property.

Groundwater and Surface Water Rights. The seller must disclose whether the buyer has received or will receive the Seller's Water Disclosure or that the seller is not required to provide the disclosure. Effective July 1, 2026, Form 20-19 added Paragraph 7(I) to direct prospective buyers to information about the groundwater and surface water rights associated with the property; that information is provided on the Seller's Disclosure about Groundwater and Surface Water Rights (Form 61-0, effective July 1, 2026).

Compliance with laws The seller warrants that there are no undisclosed building code or zoning violations affecting the property.

Due-on-sale clause The parties acknowledge that any loan surviving the closing may be called due by the lender, and each agrees to hold the other harmless for the consequences of any loan acceleration.

Seller financing disclosure The parties agree to comply with applicable state and local disclosure laws concerning seller financing. TREC promulgates a Seller Financing Addendum (Form 26-8) to be attached to the contract when the seller is providing financing.

Rental property and tenant rights The buyer acknowledges the rights of any existing tenants following closing.

FHA or VA financing condition A contingency allowing the buyer to cancel if the property does not appraise at the contract price for purposes of FHA or VA financing.

Flood plain and flood insurance The seller discloses that the property is located in a designated flood plain and that flood insurance will be required if the buyer uses certain federally-backed lenders.

Condominium assessments The seller discloses any current or pending special assessments the new owner will be obligated to pay.

Foreign seller withholding The seller acknowledges that the buyer is required to withhold 15 percent of the purchase price at closing if the seller is a foreign person or entity as defined by FIRPTA and remit it to the IRS. Certain exemptions and limitations apply.

Governmental reporting (FinCEN) Effective July 1, 2026, Form 20-19 added Paragraph 20B in response to federal Financial Crimes Enforcement Network (FinCEN) reporting requirements. It requires the parties to provide the escrow agent with the information needed to satisfy any governmental reporting requirements and requires the buyer to pay any charges associated with gathering and reporting that information.

Tax-deferred exchange For income properties, the buyer and seller disclose intentions to participate in a Section 1031 exchange and agree to cooperate in completing the required procedures. The TREC Addendum for Section 1031 Exchange (Form 60-0, effective January 3, 2025) is the appropriate vehicle.

Merger of agreements The buyer and seller state that there are no other agreements between them not expressed in the contract.

Notices The parties agree on how they will give notice to each other and what constitutes effective delivery of a notice.

Time is of the essence The parties agree that dates and deadlines may be extended only by mutual written agreement.

Electronic communications The parties agree to accept electronic transmission of documents, provided receipt is acknowledged and original copies are subsequently delivered if required.

Survival The parties remain liable for the truthfulness of their representations and warranties after closing.

Dispute resolution The parties agree to resolve disputes through mediation before resorting to court proceedings.

Addenda All addenda attached to and made part of the contract become binding components of the overall agreement.

Financing Provisions: Paragraphs 3 and 5

Two paragraphs in the One to Four Family Residential Contract (Form 20-19) address the price and financing structure of the transaction. These paragraphs must be completed carefully and consistently, as they form the financial foundation of the agreement.

Paragraph 3: Sales Price

Paragraph 3 is where the offer amount is stated. It contains three components that must always balance:

- Paragraph 3.A is the cash portion of the sales price payable by the buyer at closing, which is the down payment amount.
- Paragraph 3.B is the sum of all financing described in the attached addenda. Three checkboxes appear within this paragraph identifying which addenda are attached: the Third Party Financing Addendum, the Loan Assumption Addendum, and the Seller Financing Addendum. The buyer checks the appropriate box or boxes, and the total of all financing must equal the amount entered in Paragraph 3.B.
- Paragraph 3.C is the total sales price, which equals the sum of 3.A and 3.B.

The formula is: 3.A + 3.B = 3.C. All three blanks must use dollar amounts; percentages are never used in these fields. Any counteroffer that changes the sales price requires updating all three sub-paragraphs so that the numbers remain consistent throughout the contract.

Financing Addenda

The type of financing the buyer intends to use determines which addendum is attached and checked in Paragraph 3.B. Three options are addressed:

Third Party Financing Addendum (Form 40-11, effective January 3, 2025) used when the buyer is obtaining a loan from an institutional lender or other third party that is not one of the named parties in Paragraph 1 of the contract. This addendum details the loan specifications and the buyer's obligation to apply promptly and diligently pursue approval. If the property does not satisfy the lender's underwriting requirements or does not appraise for the loan amount, the buyer may terminate the contract by giving written notice to the seller within the timeframe specified in the addendum. Paragraph 3.B also provides a checkbox for an all-cash purchase with no financing, which does not require an addendum.

Loan Assumption Addendum (Form 41-3, effective February 1, 2023) used when the buyer will assume the seller's existing loan. The addendum addresses the buyer's credit qualification, assumption of the existing loan terms, the noteholder's consent, any transfer fees, and tax and insurance escrow arrangements. Loan assumptions are uncommon today but still occur.

Seller Financing Addendum (Form 26-8, effective February 1, 2023) used when the seller is financing all or part of the purchase price directly for the buyer. The addendum addresses the buyer's creditworthiness, the promissory note, the deed of trust, and escrow for taxes and insurance.

Paragraph 4: Leases

Paragraph 4 of Form 20-19 addresses leases affecting the property. Except as disclosed in the contract, the seller represents that no leases affect the property. After the effective date, the seller may not, without the buyer's written consent, create a new lease, amend any existing lease, or convey any interest in the property. Three categories of lease are addressed:

Paragraph 4.A -- Residential Leases If the property is subject to one or more residential leases, this box is checked and the Addendum Regarding Residential Leases is attached to the contract.

Paragraph 4.B -- Fixture Leases If fixtures on the property are subject to one or more fixture leases, such as solar panels, propane tanks, a water softener, or a security system, this box is checked and the Addendum Regarding Fixture Leases is attached.

Paragraph 4.C -- Natural Resource Leases A natural resource lease is an existing oil and gas, mineral, geothermal, water, wind, or other natural resource lease affecting the property to which the seller is a party. If such a lease exists, the seller must either deliver a copy to the buyer before the effective date or deliver it within three days after the effective date, giving the buyer an agreed number of days to terminate the contract after receiving it if the terms are unacceptable.

License holders should review Paragraph 4 carefully with sellers at the time of listing. An undisclosed lease, whether a month-to-month tenant arrangement or a long-term solar panel lease, can create significant complications at closing and give the buyer grounds to terminate.

Paragraph 5: Earnest Money and Termination Option

Paragraph 5 of Form 20-19 combines the earnest money deposit and the Termination Option into a single paragraph. Both the earnest money and the option fee are due within three days after the effective date of the contract. They may be paid separately or combined in a single payment to the escrow agent.

Paragraph 5.A -- Delivery of Earnest Money and Option Fee

Within three days after the effective date, the buyer must deliver both the earnest money and the option fee to the escrow agent. The escrow agent is typically the title company that will facilitate the closing. Each blank in this section requires an entry:

- The escrow agent's name and address
- The earnest money amount. There is no mandatory minimum, but earnest money is typically between one and three percent of the offer price with a practical minimum of $500.
- The option fee amount. There is no mandatory minimum, but the fee must represent something of value in order for the Termination Option to be enforceable.
- Any additional earnest money amount to be deposited at a later date, such as after the inspection period ends.
- The number of days after the effective date by which the additional earnest money must be deposited. If the buyer fails to deposit the additional amount by the deadline, the buyer is in default under the contract.

Paragraph 5.A(3) provides that amounts received are applied first to the option fee, then to the earnest money, and then to the additional earnest money. Paragraph 5.A(4) authorizes the escrow agent to release and deliver the option fee to the seller at any time without further notice to or consent from the buyer. The option fee will be credited to the sales price at closing if the transaction closes.

If the last day to deliver the earnest money, option fee, or additional earnest money falls on a Saturday, Sunday, or legal holiday (defined by the Texas Government Code), the time to deliver is extended until the end of the next business day.

Paragraph 5.B -- Termination Option

The Termination Option gives the buyer the unrestricted right to terminate the contract for any reason during the agreed option period by giving notice of termination to the seller by 5:00 p.m. local time on the last day of the option period. The option period is entered as a number of days after the effective date.

If the buyer gives timely notice of termination: the option fee is not refunded to the buyer and the escrow agent will release any remaining option fee to the seller; and the earnest money is refunded to the buyer. If the buyer does not terminate during the option period, the right to terminate lapses and the buyer is bound by the contract.

In practice, buyers use the Termination Option period to complete inspections, review the title commitment, negotiate repairs, and assess all aspects of the property. An option period of at least 10 to 15 days is advisable to allow sufficient time to schedule and review all inspections, including any specialized follow-up inspections.

Paragraphs 5.C, 5.D, and 5.E

Paragraph 5.C addresses the consequence of a buyer's failure to deliver earnest money on time: the seller may terminate the contract or exercise remedies under the default paragraph, or both, by providing notice before the buyer delivers the earnest money.

Paragraph 5.D addresses the consequence of a buyer's failure to deliver the option fee: if no dollar amount is stated or if the buyer fails to deliver the option fee within the time required, the buyer does not have the unrestricted right to terminate under Paragraph 5.

Paragraph 5.E states that time is of the essence for Paragraph 5, meaning strict compliance with all deadlines is required.

Seller's Disclosure Requirements

Duty to Disclose

A seller of real property in Texas, a real estate broker, and all licensed associates must disclose to prospective buyers any known material defect in the property. The licensee's duty to disclose known defects applies regardless of who the broker represents in the transaction. Only defects that are actually known must be disclosed; a party cannot be held responsible for disclosing what is genuinely unknown.

A material defect is any defect in the property that could affect a buyer's decision to purchase it or affect the property's value, such as a leaking roof, the presence of termites, or a malfunctioning HVAC system. TRELA identifies failure to make required disclosures as grounds for revocation or suspension of a license.

TRELA also specifies certain information that a licensee is not required to disclose because it relates to the occupants of the property rather than to material defects in the real estate itself. A licensee does not need to disclose that a previous or current occupant has, or had, AIDS or any HIV-related illness, or that a death occurred on the property by natural causes, suicide, or an accident unrelated to the condition of the property.

Certain causes of death do require disclosure. A death caused by faulty electrical wiring, a gas leak, or another defect in the property must be disclosed along with the corrective action taken to eliminate the hazard. Any murder that occurred on the property must be disclosed. Texas has no time limit on how far back disclosure must reach, but only information that is actually known to the disclosing party must be shared.

Mandatory Seller's Disclosure

In 1993, the Texas Legislature enacted a mandatory seller disclosure law, effective in 1994. The current form is the Seller's Disclosure Notice (Form 55-1, effective May 28, 2026). The seller is required to complete and sign the form. The buyer must receive it, sign it, and acknowledge receipt.

The disclosure notice must be delivered to the buyer on or before the effective date of the contract binding the buyer to purchase. If a contract is entered into without the required disclosure, the buyer may terminate the contract for any reason within seven days after receiving the notice. Failure by the seller to deliver the disclosure creates a voidable contract at the buyer's option.

Only the property owner should complete the Seller's Disclosure Notice. A real estate licensee must never fill it out on the seller's behalf, including a property manager acting on behalf of the owner. When a property is exempt from the disclosure requirement, the listing agent should inform prospective buyers and their agents of that exemption and strongly encourage thorough inspections.

Seller's Disclosure Exemptions

There are eleven statutory exemptions from the seller's disclosure requirement:

- Court-ordered or actual court foreclosures
- Bankruptcy trustee sales

- Deeds in lieu of foreclosure
- Resale of property acquired by a lender through foreclosure
- Probate sales, guardian sales, conservatorship sales, and trust sales
- Sales from one co-owner to another co-owner
- Sales to a relative or a spouse
- Divorce sales between two spouses
- Government sales
- Homebuilder sales of homes that have never been occupied as a residence
- Sales of land with a house valued at five percent or less of the total property value

Environmental Disclosure Obligations

In addition to the standard property condition disclosure, the seller has an obligation to disclose any known environmental hazards that may affect future occupants. Environmental conditions that require disclosure when known include asbestos, carbon monoxide sources, electromagnetic fields from nearby infrastructure, groundwater contamination, lead-based paint, mold, polychlorinated biphenyls (PCBs), radon gas, underground storage tanks, urea formaldehyde, and waste disposal sites. The seller should also disclose the known presence of any endangered species of animals or plants on the property.

Lead-Based Paint Disclosure

The federal Lead-Based Paint Hazard Reduction Act, effective in 1996, requires disclosure of any tests for lead and of the known or potential presence of lead-based paint or lead-based paint hazards. The law applies to the sale and leasing of homes and apartments built before 1978. It does not require testing, removal, or abatement; it requires disclosure of what is known.

Before entering into a contract for a targeted residential property, the buyer must receive the EPA pamphlet titled Protect Your Family from Lead in Your Home. The TREC Addendum for Seller's Disclosure of Information on Lead-Based Paint and Lead-Based Paint Hazards as Required by Federal Law (Form 56-0) must be attached to the contract for any pre-1978 property. The addendum includes the seller's disclosure of known lead paint, the buyer's acknowledgment of receipt of required information, and the broker's acknowledgment of compliance responsibilities.

Real estate brokers are responsible for ensuring seller compliance with lead-based paint disclosure. Failure to comply can result in federal fines of up to $11,000 per violation. Brokers in areas near the Texas-Mexico border are advised to include lead-based paint disclosure on all residential properties regardless of age because paint manufactured in Mexico is not subject to the same regulatory standards.

Property Conveyance

Conveyance is the transfer of legal title to real property from one person to another, or the granting of an encumbrance such as a mortgage or lien. A typical conveyance transaction has two major milestones: the exchange of contracts, at which point equitable title passes to the buyer, and completion or closing, at which point legal title passes.

Conveyance occurs across three stages: before contract (the negotiation and due diligence phase), before completion (satisfying conditions such as inspection, title clearance, appraisal, and financing approval), and after completion (the post-closing recording and delivery of documents). Once all conditions have been met or waived, the buyer holds equitable title and the closing may proceed, or may be compelled by court order if a party refuses to perform.

A buyer must obtain good and marketable title to the property, meaning the seller is the owner, has the right to sell, and no undisclosed factor would impede a future mortgage or resale. Words of conveyance used in deeds include grant, devise, give, and sell.

Documents typically exchanged at a residential closing include the deed, certified or wire-transfer funds, the promissory note and deed of trust, a certificate of no liens, prorated property tax statements, the title insurance commitment and policy, and evidence of hazard insurance. The parties may also execute side agreements relating to holdover tenants, escrow arrangements for unresolved repairs, or post-closing obligations.

The Deed, Closing Date, and Escrow Agent

The Deed

A deed is a legal instrument in writing that passes, affirms, or confirms an interest, right, or title in property and that is signed, delivered, and in some jurisdictions sealed. A deed is the vehicle through which legal title transfers from seller to buyer at closing. In a standard Texas residential resale, the seller delivers a general warranty deed conveying fee simple title to the buyer. The deed is then recorded in the county real property records, giving constructive notice to the world of the ownership change.

Date of Closing

The sales contract specifies the date by which closing must occur. Closing is the event at which the buyer delivers the purchase funds and the seller delivers the executed deed. The closing date is normally also the date on which possession transfers, unless the contract specifies otherwise through a temporary lease arrangement. Transfer of physical possession is accomplished by delivering the keys to the property.

Escrow Agent

The escrow agent is a fiduciary responsible for securing and disbursing funds and documents in the transfer of property from one party to another. In a Texas residential transaction, the escrow agent is typically a title company. The escrow agent acts impartially for both buyer and seller, holds the earnest money in a trust account, coordinates the collection and review of all closing documents, and disburses funds in accordance with the closing instructions and the terms of the sales contract.

Title Company and Title Evidence

Role of the Title Company

The title company conducts an abstract of title by searching the real estate records in the county where the property is located. The abstract search accomplishes three objectives: it determines the legal owner of the property; reveals any mortgages, liens, judgments, or unpaid taxes that must be satisfied before title can be conveyed; and identifies any existing easements, restrictions, or leases that affect the property.

After the abstract is complete, the title company issues a Commitment for Title Insurance to the lender and the prospective buyer. The title company then prepares all necessary closing documents and undertakes to correct any title problems identified in the commitment. Once all title issues are resolved, the parties are ready to close.

Types of Title Evidence

Evidence of title is the means by which ownership of land is satisfactorily demonstrated. The four recognized types of title evidence are:

> **Abstract and opinion** A complete summary of every recorded document affecting the title, accompanied by a written opinion from a licensed attorney as to the state of the title.
>
> **Certificate of title** A written statement by a title examiner or attorney certifying that the title is valid based on a review of the public records.
>
> **Title insurance** A policy issued by a title insurance company insuring the owner and/or lender against losses arising from defects in title that existed before the policy date. Title insurance is the most common form of title evidence in Texas.
>
> **Torrens certificate** A government-issued certificate of title based on a judicial proceeding that conclusively establishes ownership. Rarely used in Texas.

Closing and Possession Under Form 20-19

Paragraph 9: Closing

Under the current Form 20-19, the closing date may be extended by up to seven days when necessary to cure objections to the title commitment or the survey. At closing:

- The seller delivers a general warranty deed conveying title to the property
- The buyer delivers good funds, meaning certified funds or wire transfer, in the amount required to close
- Both seller and buyer deliver all documents needed to issue the title policy
- No liens or undisclosed charges will remain against the property
- If the property is leased, the seller transfers any lease deposits and assignments to the buyer at closing

Paragraph 10: Possession

Paragraph 10.A requires the seller to deliver possession of the property in its present or required condition, ordinary wear and tear excepted. The parties must elect one of two options: possession upon closing and funding, or possession according to a temporary residential lease form promulgated by TREC or other written lease required by the parties.

Any possession by the buyer before closing or by the seller after closing that is not authorized by a written lease establishes a tenancy at sufferance relationship between the parties. The form includes a prominent notice reminding the parties to consult their insurance agents before any change in ownership or possession, because existing insurance coverage may be limited or terminated at that point. The absence of a written lease or appropriate insurance coverage can expose both parties to economic loss.

Paragraph 10.B addresses Smart Devices. A Smart Device is defined as any device that connects to the internet to enable remote use, monitoring, and management of the property, items identified in any Non-

Realty Items Addendum, or items in a fixture lease assigned to the buyer. At the time the seller delivers possession, the seller must deliver to the buyer written information containing all access codes, usernames, passwords, and applications the buyer will need to operate and control the Smart Devices, and must terminate and remove all of the seller's own access and connections from personal devices including phones and computers.

The Statute of Frauds

The Statute of Frauds in Texas requires that all contracts affecting title to or any interest in real estate be in writing and signed by the parties to be enforceable. An oral agreement to sell real estate is void and unenforceable. The legal origin of this requirement traces to English law enacted in 1677 to prevent fraud through false claims of oral agreements.

There is one exception: a lease for one year or less may be oral and is enforceable. The Texas Business and Commerce Code states that a promise or agreement affecting real estate is not enforceable unless it is in writing and signed by the person to be charged or by someone lawfully authorized to sign on that person's behalf. The two specific categories covered are a contract for the sale of real estate and a lease of real estate for a term longer than one year.

The most prudent approach in real estate transactions is to put everything in writing, including negotiations. Even oral negotiations can lead to serious misunderstandings. Following up any verbal discussion with a written confirmation, whether by email, fax, or letter, creates a record of what was understood and agreed. Conducting the entire negotiation in writing is the safest practice.

Part Performance

A defendant in a Statute of Frauds dispute who wishes to use the Statute as a defense must raise it in a timely manner. Part performance is a doctrine that, in some circumstances, may allow enforcement of an oral agreement to convey land. In most jurisdictions, part performance is established when the purchaser has paid the purchase price, taken possession of the land, and made improvements on the land, all with the seller's permission. Payment of price alone is not sufficient in any jurisdiction.

In an action for specific performance, an oral agreement to convey may be enforced if part performance is proven. However, only the executed portion of a partially performed contract is outside the Statute of Frauds; any unexecuted portion remains within the Statute and is unenforceable.

Statute of Frauds and Contract Modifications

The Statute of Frauds applies not only to original real estate contracts but also to modifications. Under common law, if an oral agreement modifies a written contract in a way that brings the total term within the Statute's requirements, the modification must itself be in writing. In practice, virtually all real estate contract modifications in Texas should be made in writing and signed by the parties.

Signature Requirements

Contracts may be signed by handwriting, stamped impression, engraving, electronic pen, or any other form generally accepted as a valid signature. Electronic signatures are valid in Texas provided both parties agree to their use. The key question is whether all parties intended to be bound by the signed document. Under the Electronic Signatures in Global and National Commerce Act (ESIGN) and the Uniform Electronic Transactions Act (UETA), electronic signatures are legally equivalent to handwritten signatures for real estate contracts.

A person other than the named party may sign a real estate contract on the party's behalf if properly authorized. Authorization may arise through a power of attorney, through corporate authority granted to an officer, or through a contractual provision granting a designated person signing authority. A contract signed by someone who lacked authority to sign does not bind the party whose name appears on the document.

Signature Requirements Under Form 20-19

The One to Four Family Residential Contract (Form 20-19) requires specific signatures and initials as follows:

- Pages 1 through 7 require buyer and seller initials at the bottom of each page
- All notices from one party to another must be in writing per Paragraph 21, even where formal signatures on that paragraph are not required
- Page 8 requires buyers and sellers to provide attorney contact information if applicable and to sign the contract, with the effective date entered by the listing broker
- Page 9 requires only identifying information for the listing and selling brokers and associates; no buyer or seller signatures are needed on this page
- The Option Fee Receipt and the Contract and Earnest Money Receipt on page 9 identify the escrow agent
- All amendments and addenda to the contract must be signed by the appropriate parties and attached to the original contract

Breach of Contract and Default

A breach of contract is a failure to perform according to the terms of the agreement, also called default. Breach of contract gives the non-defaulting party the right to take legal action. In Texas, the statute of limitations to sue for breach of contract in real estate is four years from the date the breach occurred.

Nonperformance by one party constitutes breach of contract. That party is in default. The non-defaulting party is released from further performance obligations under the contract and may pursue available remedies. It is not a crime to default on a real estate contract, but the defaulting party may be sued in civil court for failure to perform and for resulting damages.

Common Causes of Default

The most frequent causes of default in real estate contracts include:

- Signing the contract without reading it -- a party who signs without understanding every term is still bound by all provisions; claiming ignorance of contract terms is not a defense
- Ignoring the contract -- failing to take any of the required actions under the contract automatically puts the inactive party in default; real estate contracts depend on the performance of specific tasks by each party by specified deadlines

- Missing critical dates -- contracts contain expiration dates for offers, closing deadlines, option exercise periods, and contingency deadlines; missing any of these without an agreed extension can constitute default

Types of Breach

Actual breach Occurs when one party refuses to perform its obligations on the due date or performs incompletely.

Anticipatory breach Occurs when one party announces in advance of the performance date that it will not perform. The innocent party may treat the contract as discharged and sue for damages immediately upon the announcement.

Remedies for Breach of Contract

When a party defaults on a real estate contract, the non-defaulting party may elect among the following remedies.

Rescission The non-defaulting party may rescind the contract. Rescission cancels the agreement and returns both parties to their pre-contract positions. Any earnest money or other funds deposited are refunded.

Forfeiture The contract may provide that the buyer forfeits the earnest money deposit as liquidated damages if the buyer defaults. This remedy is generally enforceable provided the deposit is not grossly disproportionate to the seller's actual damages. Many contracts provide for the seller and the listing broker to share the forfeited earnest money, but the broker may not receive more than would have been earned as a commission at the full listing price.

Suit for Damages Either party may sue the defaulting party for compensatory money damages. The lawsuit must be filed within the applicable statute of limitations, which is four years in Texas for written contracts. The standard measure of damages for a total breach is the difference between the contract price and the fair market value of the property on the date of breach. Special damages may also be recoverable for expenses incurred in reliance on the contract, provided they satisfy the foreseeability test.

Suit for Specific Performance A suit for specific performance asks the court to compel the defaulting party to perform the contract obligation rather than pay money damages. This remedy is most common in real estate transactions where the buyer wants the court to order the seller to convey title, or the seller wants the court to order the buyer to close. Because every parcel of real estate is unique, courts recognize specific performance as an appropriate remedy for real estate contract breaches.

Mediation

The One to Four Family Residential Contract includes a mediation provision under Paragraph 16. Mediation is a dispute resolution process in which a neutral third party, the mediator, facilitates communication between the parties to help them reach a mutually acceptable resolution. Mediation is non-binding, meaning the mediator cannot impose an outcome; the parties must voluntarily agree to any settlement. Mediation is less formal and typically less expensive than litigation. If both parties agree to mediate, the costs are split equally. If mediation fails to resolve the dispute, the parties retain all of their legal remedies.

Chapter 6 Snapshot Review

The following review summarizes the key rules and concepts from Chapter 6.

Offer and Acceptance

- An offer exists when a signed contract is completed and delivered to the seller or listing agent
- Seller's four options: accept, reject, counteroffer, or fail to act
- A counteroffer terminates the buyer's original offer and creates a new offer from the seller; if the buyer rejects it, the seller cannot revive the original offer
- Acceptance must be absolute and must be communicated to the other party
- The contract is effective when the last required signature is obtained and acceptance is communicated; the effective date is entered at that point
- TREC rules require immediate presentation of all offers; withholding or delaying an offer can result in disciplinary action and civil liability for tortious interference

Key Rules

- In Paragraph 3 of Form 20-19, 3.A + 3.B = 3.C; dollar amounts only, never percentages; the financing type is selected by checkboxes within Paragraph 3.B
- Third-party financing requires Form 40-11; loan assumption requires Form 41-3; seller financing requires Form 26-8; the total in each addendum must match Paragraph 3.B
- Paragraph 4 addresses Leases, not financing; residential leases use the Addendum Regarding Residential Leases; fixture leases use the Addendum Regarding Fixture Leases; natural resource leases must be disclosed and delivered to the buyer
- Earnest money and option fee are both delivered within three days of the effective date and may be combined in one payment; the option fee is non-refundable if the buyer terminates; the earnest money is refunded if the buyer terminates during the option period
- The Termination Option is Paragraph 5.B; notice of termination must be delivered by 5:00 p.m. local time on the last day of the option period
- The Seller's Disclosure Notice (Form 55-1) must be delivered by the contract effective date; late delivery gives the buyer seven days to terminate; only the property owner may complete the form
- A licensee must disclose all known material defects regardless of who the broker represents; HIV/AIDS and deaths by natural causes, suicide, or accident unrelated to property condition need not be disclosed; deaths from property defects and all murders must be disclosed
- Lead-based paint disclosure (Form 56-0) is mandatory for all pre-1978 properties; EPA pamphlet must be delivered before contracting; broker non-compliance can result in federal fines up to $11,000 per violation
- All Texas real estate contracts must be in writing under the Statute of Frauds; the only exception is a lease of one year or less
- Statute of limitations for breach of a written real estate contract in Texas: four years
- Mediation under Paragraph 16 of Form 20-19 is non-binding; costs split equally; mediation does not waive other legal remedies
- Eleven statutory exemptions from the seller's disclosure requirement include foreclosure, probate, government, co-owner, divorce, and homebuilder sales

Primary Provisions of Form 20-19

- Parties, consideration, property: identifies all parties, the property, and the exchange
- Legal description (Paragraph 2): must be sufficient for a surveyor to locate the parcel; street address alone is never adequate
- Sales price (Paragraph 3): down payment (3.A) plus financing (3.B) equals total sales price (3.C); dollar amounts only; financing type selected by checkboxes in 3.B
- Leases (Paragraph 4): seller discloses residential leases, fixture leases, and natural resource leases; appropriate addendum required for each
- Earnest money and Termination Option (Paragraph 5): both due within three days of effective date; option fee non-refundable on termination; earnest money refunded on termination
- Closing and possession (Paragraphs 9 and 10): general warranty deed; good funds required; Smart Devices access information must be delivered at possession
- Property condition disclosure (Paragraph 7.B): Seller's Disclosure Notice Form 55-1; seven-day termination right after late delivery
- Default and remedies (Paragraph 15): rescission, forfeiture of earnest money, suit for damages, suit for specific performance

Seller's Disclosure

- Mandatory since 1994 under Texas law; current form is Seller's Disclosure Notice (Form 55-1, effective May 28, 2026)
- Must be delivered on or before the contract effective date; failure creates a voidable contract at the buyer's option
- Only the property owner may complete the form; licensees must never fill it out on the seller's behalf
- Eleven statutory exemptions including foreclosure, bankruptcy trustee, probate, government, and homebuilder sales

Conveyance and Title

- Conveyance occurs in three stages: before contract, before completion, and after completion
- General warranty deed is standard in Texas residential sales; warrants title against all claims past and present
- Title company issues commitment identifying the property, insured parties, and any exceptions before issuing the policy
- Four types of title evidence: abstract and opinion, certificate of title, title insurance, and Torrens certificate; title insurance is standard in Texas
- Texas title insurance rates are set by the Texas Department of Insurance; same rate from all companies; loan policy and owner policy typically issued together

Breach and Remedies

- Statute of limitations for breach of written real estate contract in Texas: four years
- Actual breach: failure to perform on the due date
- Anticipatory breach: advance declaration of non-performance; innocent party may sue immediately
- Buyer's remedies against defaulting seller: specific performance, damages, cancellation

- Seller's remedies against defaulting buyer: forfeiture of earnest money as liquidated damages, specific performance, suit for damages
- Reformation: court action to correct a contract that does not reflect the parties' actual intentions
- Mediation: non-binding; required under Paragraph 16 of Form 20-19 before litigation; costs split equally

CHAPTER 6 QUIZ:

THE TEXAS SALES CONTRACT

1. When a seller receives an offer, the seller has four available courses of action. Which of the following is one of those four options?
   a. Counter only after the listing broker reviews the offer for compliance with TREC rules
   b. Accept the offer only if it is at or above the original listing price
   c. Reject the offer, which frees both parties and terminates the offer
   d. Request that TREC arbitrate the terms of the offer before responding

2. Under TREC rules, when must a real estate licensee present an offer received from a buyer to the seller?
   a. Immediately, unless the seller has given specific written instructions directing otherwise
   b. Within 24 hours, provided the offer meets the minimum price threshold set in the listing agreement
   c. Within three business days of receiving the offer from the buyer's agent
   d. Only after reviewing the offer with the sponsoring broker to check for compliance errors

3. A seller receives an offer and responds with a counteroffer that changes the closing date. The buyer then rejects the counteroffer. Which of the following correctly describes the status of the buyer's original offer at that point?
   a. The original offer is still pending and the seller may accept it within the next 24 hours
   b. The original offer is suspended during negotiations and is automatically revived if the counteroffer fails
   c. The original offer becomes binding at the original terms because the counteroffer was rejected
   d. The original offer no longer exists because a counteroffer terminated it the moment the seller made it

4. What is the primary purpose of an earnest money deposit in a Texas residential sales transaction?
   a. To signal the buyer's serious intent and to serve as potential liquidated damages if the buyer defaults
   b. To serve as the legal consideration that creates a binding contract between buyer and seller
   c. To cover the title company's costs of searching and insuring the title before closing
   d. To guarantee that the seller will not accept any additional offers after the contract is signed

5. When a buyer in a Texas residential transaction intends to obtain conventional financing from a bank, which addendum must be attached to the One to Four Family Residential Contract?
   a. Seller Financing Addendum (Form 26-8)
   b. Loan Assumption Addendum (Form 41-3)
   c. Third Party Financing Addendum (Form 40-11)
   d. Addendum Concerning Right to Terminate Due to Lender's Appraisal (Form 49-1)

6. Under Texas law, by what deadline must the seller deliver the Seller's Disclosure Notice to the buyer?
   a. At least ten days before the closing date
   b. Within seven days after the effective date of the contract
   c. At the time of the final walkthrough inspection
   d. On or before the effective date of the contract binding the buyer to purchase

7. A property is being sold through a court-ordered foreclosure proceeding. Which of the following applies to the seller's disclosure requirement for that transaction?
   a. The seller must still deliver the Seller's Disclosure Notice because the buyer has a right to know about property conditions
   b. The seller is exempt from the disclosure requirement because court-ordered foreclosures are among the eleven statutory exemptions
   c. The seller must provide a limited disclosure covering only structural defects and environmental hazards
   d. The exemption applies only if the lender, not a court, initiates the foreclosure action

8. The federal Lead-Based Paint Hazard Reduction Act requires disclosure of lead-based paint hazards in residential properties built before which year?
   a. 1968
   b. 1972
   c. 1978
   d. 1985

9. When the seller of a Texas residential property is a foreign person or entity as defined by FIRPTA, what percentage of the purchase price must the buyer withhold at closing and remit to the IRS?
   a. 15 percent
   b. 10 percent
   c. 20 percent
   d. 28 percent

10. In a standard Texas residential resale, which type of deed does the seller typically use to convey fee simple title to the buyer?
   a. Quitclaim deed
   b. Special warranty deed
   c. Limited warranty deed
   d. General warranty deed

11. Which of the following is the most common form of title evidence used in Texas residential transactions?
   a. Abstract and attorney's opinion
   b. Title insurance policy
   c. Torrens certificate
   d. Certificate of title issued by the county clerk

12. The Texas Statute of Frauds requires that all contracts affecting title to real estate be in writing. Which of the following is the one exception permitted by Texas law?
   a. A lease for a term of one year or less, which may be oral and is still enforceable
   b. A listing agreement between a seller and a broker, which may be oral if both parties are licensed
   c. A sales contract where earnest money has already been deposited with the title company
   d. An option agreement where the option fee has been received by the seller

13. In Texas, what is the statute of limitations for filing a lawsuit based on a breach of a written real estate sales contract?
   a. One year from the date of the breach
   b. Two years from the date of discovery of the breach
   c. Four years from the date of the breach
   d. Seven years from the date the contract was signed

14. A seller informs the buyer three weeks before the closing date that the seller will not go through with the transaction. Under which legal doctrine may the buyer immediately sue for damages without waiting for the closing date to pass?
   a. Constructive eviction
   b. Inverse condemnation
   c. The Doctrine of Laches
   d. Anticipatory breach

15. A buyer defaults on a residential sales contract and the seller wants the court to compel the buyer to complete the purchase rather than simply pay money damages. Which legal remedy does the seller seek?
   a. Rescission
   b. Specific performance
   c. Reformation
   d. Forfeiture

16. Under the mediation provision included in the One to Four Family Residential Contract (Form 20-19), which of the following correctly describes how costs are handled and what outcome the mediator may impose?
   a. The losing party pays all mediation costs, and the mediator's decision is binding on both parties
   b. The seller pays all mediation costs because the seller signed the listing agreement first
   c. Costs are split equally between the parties, and the mediator cannot impose an outcome because mediation is non-binding
   d. TREC covers the cost of mediation and the mediator files a report with TREC after the session

17. Which party is authorized to complete the Seller's Disclosure Notice (Form 55-1) for a Texas residential property?
   a. Only the property owner
   b. The listing agent, provided the agent has inspected the property within the past 90 days
   c. Any licensed Texas real estate agent who is familiar with the property
   d. The title company, as part of the title commitment process

18. In a Texas residential transaction, which party typically serves as the escrow agent who holds the earnest money and coordinates the closing?

  a. The buyer's lender
  b. The listing broker
  c. The buyer's attorney
  d. The title company

19. In the One to Four Family Residential Contract (Form 20-19), who is responsible for entering the effective date on the contract?

  a. The buyer, as the party who initiates the offer
  b. The listing broker, upon receiving notification that the seller has accepted
  c. The title company, after confirming that earnest money has been deposited
  d. The cooperating broker, as the party representing the buyer in the transaction

20. Which TREC form must be attached to a residential sales contract when the property was built before 1978 in order to comply with the federal lead-based paint disclosure requirements?

  a. Seller's Disclosure Notice (Form 55-1)
  b. Environmental Assessment, Threatened or Endangered Species, and Wetlands Addendum (Form 28-2)
  c. Addendum for Seller's Disclosure of Information on Lead-Based Paint and Lead-Based Paint Hazards (Form 56-0)
  d. Notice to Prospective Buyer (Form 58-0)

21. When a buyer defaults on a Texas residential sales contract and the contract provides for forfeiture of the earnest money as liquidated damages, what limitation applies to the amount the listing broker may receive from those forfeited funds?

  a. The broker may not receive any portion of the forfeited earnest money under any circumstances
  b. The broker may receive up to 50 percent of the forfeited funds regardless of the agreed commission rate
  c. The broker may receive the full forfeited amount if the listing agreement specifically authorizes it
  d. The broker may not receive more than the commission that would have been earned at the full listing price

Chapter 6 Case Study:
The Texas Sales Contract

The Situation

Carl and Donna Mettling are selling their home in Plano through Performance Programs Realty. Their listing agent, Sandra Voss, has been managing an active negotiation with buyer Hector Reyes. After several rounds of back and forth, Hector submitted a written offer that Sandra considered strong. Before presenting it to the Mettlings, Sandra spent two days trying to negotiate a higher offer price directly with Hector's agent, believing she could squeeze out an additional $5,000 for her clients. Hector withdrew the offer before Sandra presented it.

A second buyer, Lisa Park, then submitted a full-price offer. The Mettlings accepted and the contract was executed. The property was built in 1971. Sandra knew this but did not attach Form 56-0 to the contract and did not provide Lisa with the EPA pamphlet about lead-based paint hazards. Sandra assumed the disclosure was the seller's responsibility and that she had no personal obligation to ensure it was completed.

Shortly before closing, the Mettlings informed Sandra that the seller's net proceeds would be less than the amount owed on their mortgage. Their lender had verbally indicated it might accept a payoff short of the full balance, but nothing had been confirmed in writing. Sandra told Lisa's agent that the transaction would close on schedule. Three days before the closing date the lender formally declined the short payoff, and the closing could not occur. Lisa, who had already given notice at her apartment and hired movers, suffered significant out-of-pocket losses.

Discussion Questions

Question 1

Sandra Voss held Hector Reyes's offer for two days without presenting it while she attempted to negotiate a better price. Identify the TREC rule Sandra violated, explain what consequences she may face, and describe the only circumstance under which a listing agent may permissibly delay presenting an offer.

_____

_____

_____

_____

_____

Question 2

Sandra did not attach Form 56-0 or provide Lisa Park with the required EPA pamphlet, believing lead-based paint disclosure was solely the seller's responsibility. Explain the federal law that requires this disclosure, identify who is responsible for ensuring compliance, and describe the consequences of failing to meet the requirement.

_____

_____

_____

Question 3

Sandra told Lisa's agent the transaction would close on schedule despite knowing the lender had not confirmed a short payoff. The closing failed and Lisa suffered financial losses. Identify any legal exposure Sandra and the Mettlings may have as a result of the failed closing, and explain what steps should have been taken before the contract was executed to address the short payoff situation properly.

CHAPTER 7

CONTINGENCIES, ADDENDA, AND AMENDMENTS

Chapter Overview

Learning Objectives

Upon completing Chapter 7, the student will be able to:

1. Define a contract contingency, explain how contingencies affect contract enforceability, and describe the consequences of missing a contingency deadline.
2. Identify and explain the most common types of contract contingencies used in Texas residential transactions, including appraisal, financing, house sale, inspection, title, insurance, HOA documents, and home business contingencies.
3. Distinguish between an amendment and an addendum, explain when each is used, and describe the ten permissible uses of the TREC Amendment to Contract (Form 39-11).
4. Explain the purpose and key provisions of the Third Party Financing Addendum (Form 40-11), including how it addresses conventional, Texas Veterans, FHA, VA, USDA, reverse mortgage, and other financing types.
5. Describe the Loan Assumption Addendum (Form 41-3) and the circumstances under which a buyer might choose to assume an existing loan.
6. Explain the Seller Financing Addendum (Form 26-8) and the Addendum for Release of Liability on Assumed Loan (Form 12-3), including the protections each provides to buyer and seller.

Contents

- Contract Contingencies
- Appraisal Contingency
- Financing Contingency
- House Sale Contingency and Kick-Out Clause
- Inspection Contingency
- Title Contingency
- Insurance Contingency
- HOA Documents Contingency
- Home Business Contingency
- General Contingency Guidelines
- Amendments vs. Addenda
- Amendment to Contract (Form 39-11)
- Third Party Financing Addendum (Form 40-11)
- Loan Assumption Addendum (Form 41-3)
- Seller Financing Addendum (Form 26-8)
- Addendum for Release of Liability on Assumed Loan (Form 12-3)

Contract Contingencies

A contingency clause is a condition attached to an offer to purchase real property that is included in the sales contract and must be satisfied before the purchase becomes binding on the buyer. A contingency becomes part of a binding sales contract when both parties agree to the terms and sign the agreement. Common contingencies include financing approval, a satisfactory property inspection, and the sale of the buyer's existing home.

A contingency gives the affected party the right to exit the contract without default if the specified condition is not met. For example, if a buyer has 30 days to secure a mortgage loan and fails to do so, the contract may become null and void, and the buyer is entitled to recover the earnest money. Once a contingency is satisfied, however, the party who benefited from it can no longer use it as an exit. If the buyer backs out after all contingencies have been met, that party is in breach of contract and the consequences range from forfeiture of the earnest money to a lawsuit for specific performance.

Most contingencies carry specific release dates. On or before that date, the buyer must notify the seller in writing whether the contingency has been satisfied or whether the buyer is exercising the right to terminate. If the deadline passes without notice, the contingency is typically deemed waived, and the buyer becomes obligated to proceed with the purchase even if the condition was not technically met. License holders must track all contingency deadlines carefully and keep their clients informed.

Appraisal Contingency

An appraisal contingency protects the buyer by ensuring that the property is independently valued at or near the offering price. Because most home purchases are financed, the lender will not advance more than a specified percentage of the appraised value. If the property does not appraise at or above a minimum stated amount, the buyer may be unable to obtain the necessary financing to complete the purchase. When that condition is present, the contract may be terminated and the earnest money is typically returned to the buyer.

An appraisal contingency may include provisions that allow the transaction to proceed even if the appraised value falls short of the contract price. Common remedies when an appraisal comes in low include the seller reducing the sales price to the appraised value, the buyer making a larger cash down payment to bridge the gap, the cooperating licensees agreeing to reduce their compensation so that the transaction can close, or some combination of those approaches.

The TREC Addendum Concerning Right to Terminate Due to Lender's Appraisal (Form 49-1, effective March 1, 2019) is the promulgated vehicle for addressing appraisal contingency rights in a Texas residential transaction. When this addendum is attached, the buyer's right to terminate based on an appraisal shortfall is clearly defined and must be exercised within the timeframe specified.

Financing Contingency

A financing contingency gives the buyer a specified number of days to apply for and obtain loan approval for the purchase of the property. This contingency is one of the most important protections a buyer can have, because it allows the buyer to exit the contract without default and recover the earnest money if financing cannot be secured within the agreed timeframe.

If the buyer cannot obtain financing by the specified deadline, the buyer must notify the seller in writing. Failure to provide timely written notice automatically waives the contingency and the buyer becomes obligated to purchase the property even without an approved loan. This is a significant risk that license holders must explain clearly to their clients.

Buyers should be pre-qualified by a lender before making any offer on a property. Pre-qualification reduces the risk that a financing contingency will fail and gives the seller greater confidence in the offer. In Texas, financing contingency rights are implemented through the Third Party Financing Addendum (Form 40-11), discussed in detail later in this chapter.

House Sale Contingency and Kick-Out Clause

House Sale Contingency

A house sale contingency gives a buyer a specified amount of time to sell an existing home in order to generate the down payment or otherwise qualify financially for the new purchase. A house sale contingency can be difficult for the seller, who may pass up other offers while waiting for the buyer's contingency to be satisfied. For that reason, the seller should retain the contractual right to cancel if the buyer's home is not sold within the stated period.

There are two ways to structure a house sale contingency. A settlement contingency is used when the buyer has already accepted an offer on the existing home but has not yet closed. The seller is typically prohibited from accepting other offers for a specified period. A sale and settlement contingency with right to continue marketing allows the seller to continue showing and marketing the property to other potential buyers. If the seller receives another acceptable offer, the original buyer is given a defined period, typically 24 to 72 hours, to remove the sale contingency and proceed. If the buyer does not remove the contingency in time, the seller may accept the competing offer and the original contract terminates with the earnest money returned to the buyer.

Kick-Out Clause

A kick-out clause is the informal name for a sale and settlement contingency with the right to continue marketing. It gives the seller a measure of protection against being held off the market indefinitely while the buyer attempts to sell an existing home. When a kick-out clause is present, the MLS listing must reflect the contingent status. Settlement contingencies are written far more often than sale and settlement contingencies because the seller's risk is lower when the buyer's prior home is already under contract.

Inspection Contingency

An inspection contingency gives the buyer the right to have the property professionally inspected within a specified number of days. This contingency protects the buyer who can, depending on the findings, cancel the contract without default, negotiate repairs or a price reduction, or accept the property in its current condition.

In Texas, the inspection contingency is most commonly managed through the Termination Option in Paragraph 5.B of the standard residential contract (Form 20-19). The buyer pays an option fee to the seller for the unrestricted right to terminate the contract for any reason during the agreed option period. During this period, the buyer typically schedules inspections and reviews reports. If the buyer is uncomfortable with the findings, the Termination Option can be exercised. If the option period expires without the buyer terminating, the right to terminate is waived and the buyer is bound by the contract.

Buyers should request an option period of at least 10 to 15 days to allow sufficient time to schedule and review all inspections, including any follow-up specialized inspections triggered by the general inspector's findings.

Title Contingency

As part of the home purchase process, the buyer's title company researches the property's title history and generates a title commitment summarizing previous title transfers, liens, encumbrances, judgments, easements, and any other matters of record affecting the property. The buyer reviews this report and has the right to raise objections within a timeframe specified in the contract.

Many title issues are minor clerical problems that the title agent can resolve quickly. Others require the seller to take action, such as paying off an unknown lien, correcting a break in the chain of title, or addressing a boundary dispute. Not every title issue will halt a sale outright, but some may give the buyer a legitimate reason to reconsider the purchase. The standard TREC residential contract (Form 20-19) addresses title objection procedures in Paragraph 6 and provides the buyer with defined rights and deadlines for raising and resolving title objections.

Insurance Contingency

Mortgage lenders routinely require the buyer to obtain hazard insurance before or at closing and to provide proof of coverage. Some buyers include an insurance contingency in the contract, making the purchase contingent on their ability to obtain adequate homeowner's insurance at a reasonable cost. This contingency is particularly relevant for older homes, properties in high-risk areas, homes with aluminum electrical wiring, and properties with prior claims history that may affect insurability. License holders should proactively raise the issue of insurability when dealing with older homes, historic properties, and properties being acquired for renovation.

HOA Documents Contingency

Any buyer planning to purchase property subject to a mandatory homeowners association should include a contingency making the sale dependent on receipt and review of all HOA documents, rules, bylaws, and fee schedules. The buyer should identify key financial obligations including monthly or annual dues, any special assessments currently approved or under consideration, reserve fund status, and restrictions on how the property may be used. Buyers should also check whether any pending litigation has been filed against or by the association, as this can affect both value and insurability.

In Texas, the TREC Addendum for Property Subject to Mandatory Membership in a Property Owners Association (Form 36-11, effective July 1, 2026) is the promulgated vehicle for managing this contingency. When this addendum is attached, it specifies the documents the seller must deliver to the buyer, the timeframe for delivery, and the buyer's right to terminate if the documents reveal unacceptable conditions.

Home Business Contingency

The ability to operate a business from a residential property has become an important consideration for a growing number of buyers. Zoning laws, subdivision restrictions, and HOA rules can all prohibit or restrict home-based business activity. A buyer who needs to operate a business from the property should include a contingency specifically addressing that requirement.

A verbal assurance from a neighbor or even from a local government official is not sufficient protection. To be properly protected, the closing documents should include a written letter from the appropriate zoning authority confirming that a business of the specified type may legally be operated from the property's address. Without that documentation, the buyer cannot be certain that the approval will be honored after closing.

General Contingency Guidelines

License holders should keep the following principles in mind when advising clients on the use of contingencies. The fewer contingencies in an offer, the more attractive that offer will appear to a seller, particularly in a competitive market. When possible, limit the offer to a single essential contingency. Include a contingency only when it is genuinely necessary to protect the buyer's interests. Always specify an exact calendar date for each contingency release; writing a vague deadline such as within a reasonable time is insufficient and can lead to disputes and TREC disciplinary action. Track all contingency deadlines carefully and notify clients well in advance of each deadline.

Amendments vs. Addenda

Addendum A document attached to and made part of the original contract at the time of execution. An addendum may be explanatory, informational, or may set out requirements of the parties that are not fully addressed in the main contract form. An addendum is executed simultaneously with, and becomes part of, the original contract.

Amendment A document that makes a change to a contract that has already been fully ratified and signed by all parties. An amendment is used when circumstances after execution require a modification to one or more agreed terms. Each amendment must be signed by all parties and has its own effective date.

To illustrate the difference: if a buyer wants to make the purchase contingent on verifying mineral rights before signing the contract, that provision is added as an addendum to the original offer. If after the contract is signed the closing date needs to be extended because an inspector discovered a structural issue requiring engineering review, the closing date is changed through an amendment to the ratified contract.

If an agent neglects to list a required addendum on the contract or fails to attach it, the intentions of the parties may be unclear and the agent could be held legally responsible for resulting damages. All addenda must include the names of all parties and the legal address of the property to which they pertain.

Amendment to Contract (Form 39-11)

The TREC Amendment to Contract (Form 39-11, effective July 1, 2026) is a one-page promulgated form that provides ten defined categories of permissible changes to a ratified residential contract. Rather than rewriting an entire contract when a term needs to change, the licensee uses this form to document the agreed modification. All changes must be agreed to by both buyer and seller, and both parties must sign the completed amendment. Failing to use the correct form or executing unauthorized amendments can expose the licensee to disciplinary action.

Problems discovered by the title company, the surveyor, the home inspector, or the lender may all generate the need for a contract amendment. The Amendment to Contract references the standard residential contract by paragraph number, so the licensee and client must understand which paragraph of the original contract is being changed.

The first blank on the form is for the property address, taken from the original contract. The ten permissible changes are:

Sales Price Changes (Paragraph 1)

Paragraph 1 is used when the agreed sales price, down payment, or loan amount needs to change after execution. Three sub-entries address each component: Paragraph 1.A adjusts the down payment, Paragraph 1.B adjusts the total loan amount, and Paragraph 1.C adjusts the total sales price. These three numbers must always balance: the down payment plus the total financing must equal the sales price. Dollar amounts are always used in these blanks; percentages are never entered here.

Repairs (Paragraph 2)

Paragraph 2 is used to require the seller to complete specific repairs. This paragraph is most commonly used after the home inspection report is received. Any repair request that cannot be accommodated within the original closing timeline may also require a closing date extension in Paragraph 3.

Closing Date Extension (Paragraph 3)

Paragraph 3 changes the closing date set in Paragraph 9 of the original contract. The blank requires an exact calendar date. A licensee who enters language such as at lender's discretion instead of a specific date violates TREC rules and could be found to be practicing law. The closing date may be extended more than once; each extension should be documented with a new amendment.

Seller's Contribution to Brokerage Fees (Paragraph 4)

Paragraph 4 modifies the amount the seller agreed to contribute toward brokerage fees payable by the buyer in Paragraph 12A(1)(b) of the residential contract. In Form 39-11 this entry must be stated as a specific dollar amount. The percentage option that this entry previously offered has moved to Paragraph 5.

Seller's and Buyer's Contributions Under Paragraph 12B (Paragraph 5)

Paragraph 5 modifies the amounts in Paragraph 12B of the residential contract. It provides separate entries for the seller and for the buyer, and each amount may be entered either as a specific dollar amount or as a percentage of the sales price. Paragraph 5 is the one entry in the amendment form where a percentage is permissible.

Lender-Required Repairs (Paragraph 6)

Paragraph 6 modifies Paragraph 7.E of the residential contract, which governs lender-required repairs and who will pay for them. This paragraph is used most often in VA and FHA transactions, where the lender's appraiser may generate a required repair list as a condition of loan approval. After the lender's appraiser has inspected the property and issued a repair list, the buyer and seller negotiate which items each party will address and what dollar amounts each will contribute. Once agreed, those amounts are documented in Paragraph 6 and an itemized list of repairs is attached.

Termination Option Extension (Paragraph 7)

Paragraph 7 extends the Termination Option period established in Paragraph 5.B of the residential contract. An extension may be needed when the home inspector identifies an issue requiring a follow-up inspection by a specialist and the time to complete that review extends beyond the original option period.

The seller does not have to agree to an extension. When the Termination Option period is extended under Paragraph 7, a corresponding extension of the closing date under Paragraph 3 may also be necessary if the new option expiration date falls near or beyond the original closing date.

Waiver of Termination Option (Paragraph 8)

Paragraph 8 is used when the buyer chooses to waive the remaining unrestricted right to terminate under the Termination Option before the option period has expired. By completing this paragraph, the buyer effectively declares that the contract is final before the option period ends.

Extension of Financing Notification Deadline (Paragraph 9)

Paragraph 9 modifies the buyer's obligation in the Third Party Financing Addendum (Form 40-11) to notify the seller within a stated number of days if financing cannot be obtained. An extension under this paragraph may be needed when the buyer has moved the loan to a different lender to obtain better terms or to qualify for a loan the first lender declined. A specific calendar date is required; vague language violates TREC rules.

Other Modifications (Paragraph 10)

Paragraph 10 provides a catch-all for any other agreed modification to the ratified contract that is not addressed by Paragraphs 1 through 9. The form includes a reminder that real estate brokers and sales agents are prohibited from practicing law. License holders should use Paragraph 10 only for factual business details and should advise clients to consult an attorney when any proposed modification involves legal rights or remedies not covered by the other nine paragraphs.

Third Party Financing Addendum (Form 40-11)

The Third Party Financing Addendum (Form 40-11, effective January 3, 2025) is used whenever the buyer is obtaining financing from a third-party lender, meaning any institutional or private lender that is not a named party in Paragraph 1 of the contract. It is required for conventional, Texas Veterans, FHA, VA, USDA, reverse mortgage, and other financing types. It is not used when the seller is providing all of the financing or when the parties are exchanging properties with no financing required.

The addendum requires the property address and contains a numbered section identifying each financing type the buyer may elect. The total loan amount entered in this addendum must match the amount entered in Paragraph 3.B of the residential contract.

Conventional Financing (Paragraph 1.A)

When the buyer is obtaining a conventional loan, Paragraph 1.A is checked. The form provides entries for a first mortgage loan and a second mortgage loan. For each loan, the buyer enters the principal amount excluding any financed PMI premium, the loan term in years, the maximum interest rate for the first year, the number of years that rate applies, and the maximum origination charges as shown on the Loan Estimate. For a fixed-rate loan, the same term is entered in both the loan term and rate-adjustment period blanks. For an adjustable-rate mortgage, the initial fixed-rate period is entered in the adjustment period blank.

Some transactions require multiple loans. For example, an 80-10-10 loan program has the buyer contribute 10 percent as a down payment, borrow 80 percent from a primary lender, and borrow the remaining 10 percent from a second lender. If the second 10 percent is provided by the seller, Paragraph 1.A is checked for the primary loan and the Seller Financing Addendum is attached for the seller's portion.

Texas Veterans Loan (Paragraph 1.B)

When the buyer is applying for a Texas Veterans Land Board loan, Paragraph 1.B is checked and the loan amount and term are entered. Licensees should verify the current maximum loan amount directly with the Texas Veterans Land Board, as it is updated periodically.

FHA Insured Financing (Paragraph 1.C)

When the buyer is obtaining an FHA-insured loan, Paragraph 1.C is checked. The FHA loan section number is entered in the first blank; the FHA 203(b) loan is most commonly used because it allows a lower down payment than conventional financing. The FHA 203(k) loan combines home purchase financing with rehabilitation financing in a single loan. The loan amount excludes any financed mortgage insurance premium. The last blank in the FHA section identifies the contract sales price, informing all parties of the amount at which the property must appraise.

VA Guaranteed Financing (Paragraph 1.D)

When the buyer is obtaining a VA-guaranteed loan, Paragraph 1.D is checked. The loan amount entered should exclude any financed VA Funding Fee. The VA Funding Fee is the charge the VA imposes to protect the lender from default; it is similar in purpose to mortgage insurance premiums on FHA loans and PMI on conventional loans. The loan term, interest rate, and origination fee limitations are entered in the applicable blanks.

USDA Guaranteed Financing (Paragraph 1.E)

When the buyer is obtaining a USDA-guaranteed loan, Paragraph 1.E is checked. The loan amount entered excludes any financed funding fee. The loan term, interest rate for the first year, and origination charge limit are entered as with the other loan types. USDA-guaranteed loans are available for eligible rural and suburban properties and are administered through the U.S. Department of Agriculture's Rural Development program.

Reverse Mortgage Financing (Paragraph 1.F)

When the buyer is obtaining a reverse mortgage, also known as a Home Equity Conversion Mortgage loan, Paragraph 1.F is checked. The original principal amount is entered, excluding any financed PMI premium or other costs, along with the maximum interest rate and origination charges. The form includes a checkbox for whether the reverse mortgage will be FHA insured.

Other Financing (Paragraph 1.G)

Paragraph 1.G is available for any loan type not described in Paragraphs 1.A through 1.F. The lender's name, principal amount, term, interest rate, and origination charge limit are entered. This paragraph also contains a checkbox allowing the buyer to optionally waive all rights to terminate the contract under the Property Approval provision of Paragraph 2.B for the loan described in this paragraph.

Approval of Financing (Paragraph 2)

Paragraph 2 establishes that financing approval is deemed obtained when both Buyer Approval and Property Approval are obtained. Time is of the essence for this paragraph.

Paragraph 2.A addresses Buyer Approval. Two checkboxes are available: the parties may make the contract subject to the buyer obtaining Buyer Approval, or they may elect that the contract is not subject to Buyer Approval. If subject to Buyer Approval, the buyer must notify the seller of an inability to obtain approval within the stated number of days after the effective date. The notice must include both a termination notice and a written statement from the lender setting forth the reason for the lender's determination. If the buyer does not terminate by the deadline, the financing contingency for Buyer Approval is deemed waived and the buyer must close or be in default.

Paragraph 2.B addresses Property Approval. If the buyer's lender determines that the property does not satisfy the lender's underwriting requirements, including appraisal, insurability, and lender-required repairs, the buyer may terminate the contract on or before the third day before the closing date by delivering notice of termination and a copy of the lender's written statement to the seller. If the buyer does not terminate under this paragraph, Property Approval is deemed to have been obtained. The FHA and VA required provision in Paragraph 4 of the addendum provides additional protections for buyers using those loan programs and is not subject to the three-day notice requirement.

Authorization to Release Information (Paragraph 5)

Paragraph 5.A authorizes the buyer's lender to furnish the seller, the buyer, or their representatives with information relating to the status of financing approval. Paragraph 5.B authorizes the buyer's lender, the title company, and the escrow agent to disclose and furnish copies of closing disclosures and settlement statements to the parties' respective brokers and sales agents identified in the Broker Information section of the contract. Licensees should be aware of this authorization because it establishes a clear basis for the flow of financial information among the transaction's service providers.

Loan Assumption Addendum (Form 41-3)

The Loan Assumption Addendum (Form 41-3, effective February 1, 2023) is used when the buyer agrees to take over the seller's existing mortgage loan rather than obtaining new financing. Loan assumptions require the lender's approval in virtually all cases because most modern loan documents include a due-on-sale clause that requires the full loan balance to be paid when the property is transferred. Loan assumptions are uncommon today but do still occur, particularly when the interest rate on the existing loan is significantly below current market rates.

Creditworthiness and Approval (Paragraphs A and B)

Paragraph A addresses the documentation the buyer must provide to the seller to demonstrate creditworthiness. The seller and buyer agree on the type of documentation required, and the buyer must deliver it within the number of days entered in the blank.

Paragraph B establishes that if the credit documentation is not delivered within the specified time, the seller may terminate the contract and the earnest money will be paid to the seller. If the documentation is delivered but the seller determines the buyer's credit is unacceptable, the seller may terminate the contract within seven days after the delivery deadline or actual delivery, whichever is later, and the earnest money will be refunded to the buyer. If the seller does not terminate within the time specified, the seller is deemed to have approved the buyer's creditworthiness.

Loan Details (Paragraph C)

Paragraph C identifies the existing loan or loans being assumed. The lender's name, the current unpaid balance, and the monthly payment amount are entered for each loan. Because the seller may make additional payments between the contract date and the closing date, the actual payoff balance at closing may differ from the amount entered. The addendum provides two options for handling the variance at closing: the buyer pays the seller cash at closing for any difference between the stated balance and the actual lower balance, or the sales price is reduced to reflect the actual lower balance.

If the variance between the stated balance and the actual closing balance exceeds the dollar amount agreed to by the parties in the blank provided, either party has the right to terminate the contract, with the earnest money returned to the buyer. Alternatively, either party may choose to pay the other the difference and allow the transaction to proceed. Within seven days after the effective date, the seller must deliver to the buyer copies of the note or notes to be assumed, the deed or deeds of trust, and the most recent loan statements from the lender.

Assumption Terms and Lender Consent (Paragraphs D and E)

Paragraph D specifies the conditions under which the buyer may terminate the contract if the lender's assumption requirements are unacceptable. These include an assumption fee that exceeds the stated maximum dollar amount, an increase in the interest rate above a stated maximum, or any other unacceptable modification the lender imposes as a condition of the assumption. Paragraph E confirms that if the noteholder fails to consent to the assumption, either party may terminate the contract and the earnest money will be refunded to the buyer.

An assumption may be attractive for two reasons: the interest rate on the existing loan is significantly below current market rates, or the existing loan has been substantially paid down, giving the buyer a lower balance and a more favorable principal-to-interest payment ratio.

Seller's Liens (Paragraph F)

Unless the seller is formally released from liability on the assumed note by the lender, the seller remains personally liable on the loan even after the buyer assumes it. Paragraph F requires that a vendor's lien and deed of trust to secure assumption be used whenever the seller is not released. The vendor's lien is automatically released on delivery of an executed release by the noteholder.

Tax and Insurance Escrow (Paragraph G)

Many sellers maintain an escrow account with the lender that holds funds for property taxes, insurance premiums, and mortgage insurance. Paragraph G provides that if the assumption proceeds, this escrow account is transferred to the buyer, who reimburses the seller for the account balance at closing. Buyers are advised to review all existing loan documents before signing the addendum, particularly if the loan has an adjustable-rate feature. Sellers are advised to request release of liability through the TREC

Addendum for Release of Liability on Assumed Loan (Form 12-3) if they want to eliminate their ongoing exposure.

Authorization to Release Information (Paragraph H)

Paragraph H.1 authorizes the lenders of notes being assumed to furnish the seller, the buyer, or their representatives with information relating to the status of the consent to the assumption. Paragraph H.2 authorizes the lenders, the title company, and the escrow agent to disclose and furnish copies of closing disclosures and settlement statements to the parties' respective brokers and sales agents identified in the Broker Information section of the contract.

Seller Financing Addendum (Form 26-8)

The Seller Financing Addendum (Form 26-8, effective February 1, 2023) is used when the seller agrees to carry all or part of the purchase price as a loan to the buyer. The seller acts as the lender, the property serves as collateral, and the buyer makes payments to the seller under the terms set out in the addendum. The loan documents used are a promissory note and a deed of trust, the same instruments a conventional lender would use.

The form carries a prominent notice that seller financing agreements can be complicated and may be subject to laws regulating loans, and that the seller may have accounting or reporting obligations in connection with the arrangement. Both parties are advised to consult an attorney and a financial professional before signing. License holders may not give legal or financial advice on these matters.

Creditworthiness and Approval (Paragraphs A and B)

Paragraph A requires the buyer to provide the seller with detailed financial information so the seller can assess whether the buyer is a suitable credit risk. Paragraph B sets a deadline for the buyer to deliver the required financial documentation to the seller. If the buyer fails to deliver it within that period, the seller may terminate the contract and the earnest money will be paid to the seller. If the documentation is delivered in a timely manner, the seller then has seven days to decide whether to approve the buyer's credit. If the seller declines, the contract terminates and the earnest money is returned to the buyer. If the seller does not respond within seven days of receiving the documentation, approval is deemed to have occurred.

Interest Rate and Payment Terms (Paragraph C)

Paragraph C establishes the interest rate, which is agreed between the buyer and seller. The note will contain a late fee of five percent of any installment not paid within ten days of the due date. Matured unpaid amounts bear interest at 18 percent per annum or the highest lawful rate, whichever is less. The buyer may prepay the note in whole or in part at any time without penalty; any prepayments are applied to the installments of principal last maturing and interest immediately ceases on the prepaid principal.

Three payment structures are available. Paragraph C.1 is used for a lump sum payment at a specified future date. Paragraph C.2 is used for monthly installment payments including both principal and interest, which is the most commonly used format. Paragraph C.3 is used for interest-only payments for an initial period followed by installment payments thereafter.

Deed of Trust Provisions (Paragraph D)

Paragraph D addresses the deed of trust that secures the seller's promissory note and contains four sub-paragraphs.

Paragraph D.1 governs whether the buyer may transfer the property without the seller's consent while the seller's note remains outstanding. If Paragraph D.1.a is selected, the property may be sold, conveyed, or leased without the seller's consent, provided any subsequent buyer assumes the note. If Paragraph D.1.b is selected, the seller's consent is required before any transfer; if the buyer transfers without consent, the seller may call the note due and payable in full immediately. Exceptions include subordinate liens, condemnation conveyances, deeds solely between buyers, and passage of title by death or operation of law. In either case, the buyer remains personally liable on the note until formally released by the seller.

Paragraph D.2 addresses casualty insurance. The parties elect whether the deed of trust will require the buyer to obtain casualty insurance naming the seller as a mortgagee loss payee effective on the date of closing. This election protects the seller's security interest in the event the property is damaged or destroyed during the loan period.

Paragraph D.3 determines how property taxes and hazard insurance are handled during the loan period. If Paragraph D.3.a is selected, no escrow is required; the buyer pays taxes and insurance directly and provides proof of payment to the seller. If Paragraph D.3.b is selected, the buyer makes escrow deposits with each installment payment and the seller pays the tax and insurance bills from the collected escrow funds, maintains a separate escrow account, and provides an annual accounting. The parties elect whether a third-party servicer will manage the escrow and who bears the cost of that service.

Paragraph D.4 addresses prior liens. Any default under any lien superior to the lien securing the seller's note constitutes a default under the deed of trust securing that note. This provision protects the seller when there is an existing first mortgage on the property by allowing the seller to act if the buyer fails to make payments on a superior lien.

Addendum for Release of Liability on Assumed Loan (Form 12-3)

The Addendum for Release of Liability on Assumed Loan and/or Restoration of Seller's VA Entitlement (Form 12-3, effective December 5, 2011) is used to protect a seller who allows a buyer to assume an existing loan. Without this addendum, the seller may remain personally liable on the assumed loan for as long as the loan remains outstanding, even though the buyer has taken over the payments and the property has been transferred. This addendum is attached to the contract when the parties need the lender to formally release the seller from that ongoing obligation.

Release of Liability (Paragraph A)

Paragraph A requires the buyer to initiate the lender's release of the seller's liability within a stated number of days after the contract's effective date. If the release has not been approved by the stated closing date, the parties must choose one of two options: Paragraph A.1 terminates the contract and returns the earnest money to the buyer, or Paragraph A.2 allows the parties to proceed to closing with the seller remaining liable on the assumed loan.

Restoration of VA Entitlement (Paragraph B)

If the existing loan is a VA-guaranteed loan, Paragraph B addresses restoration of the seller's VA entitlement. When a VA-eligible seller's loan is assumed by another party, the seller's VA entitlement that backed the original loan remains tied to that loan until the loan is paid off or the entitlement is formally restored. Without restoration, the seller cannot use full VA entitlement on a future purchase. To restore entitlement, the buyer assuming the loan must be a veteran with sufficient unused VA entitlement to substitute for the seller's and must otherwise qualify under VA requirements.

If the VA entitlement is not restored by the closing date, the seller must choose between Paragraph B.1, which terminates the contract, or Paragraph B.2, which allows the seller to proceed even though entitlement may not be restored. The seller bears the cost of securing both the release of liability and the restoration of entitlement, since those outcomes benefit the seller directly.

Chapter 7 Snapshot Review

The following review summarizes the key rules and concepts from Chapter 7.

Contingencies

- A contingency must be satisfied or waived before the contract becomes fully binding; a missed deadline typically waives the contingency and obligates the buyer to proceed
- Contingency release dates must be specific calendar dates; vague language like within a reasonable time can lead to disputes and TREC disciplinary action
- Appraisal contingency: property must appraise at or above stated value; Form 49-1 is the promulgated vehicle
- Financing contingency: buyer must obtain loan approval within stated days; managed through Form 40-11; waived if buyer fails to give timely written notice
- House sale contingency: buyer must sell existing home within stated days; two structures: settlement contingency and sale-and-settlement (kick-out) contingency
- Kick-out clause: seller continues marketing; if a better offer arrives, original buyer has 24-72 hours to remove the contingency or have the contract terminate
- Inspection contingency: buyer has the right to inspect and terminate; in Texas, managed primarily through the Termination Option in Paragraph 5.B of Form 20-19
- Title contingency: buyer may object to title defects; governed by Paragraph 6 of Form 20-19
- Insurance contingency: purchase contingent on buyer obtaining adequate homeowner's insurance
- HOA documents contingency: purchase contingent on receipt and approval of association documents; Form 36-11
- Home business contingency: purchase contingent on written zoning approval for specified business use; verbal approvals are not sufficient

Amendments vs. Addenda

- An addendum is executed simultaneously with the original contract and is part of it from the beginning
- An amendment modifies an already-ratified contract and requires signatures from all parties after execution
- The TREC Amendment to Contract (Form 39-11) provides ten defined categories of permissible change; closing date extensions and financing deadline extensions require specific calendar dates; vague language violates TREC rules
- Paragraph 5 of Form 39-11 is the one entry where a percentage is permissible: the amounts in Paragraph 12B may be set for both the seller and the buyer, each as a dollar amount or a percentage of the sales price; Paragraph 4 and all other dollar-amount blanks require dollar figures only

Amendment to Contract (Form 39-11) -- Ten Uses

- Paragraph 1: sales price, down payment, or loan amount change
- Paragraph 2: seller-required repairs after inspection
- Paragraph 3: closing date extension
- Paragraph 4: change in seller's contribution to buyer's brokerage fees (Paragraph 12A(1)(b)); dollar amount only

- Paragraph 5: change in the seller's and buyer's contributions under Paragraph 12B; dollar amount or percentage of sales price
- Paragraph 6: reallocation of lender-required repair costs between buyer and seller
- Paragraph 7: extension of Termination Option period
- Paragraph 8: waiver of remaining Termination Option right
- Paragraph 9: extension of financing notification deadline
- Paragraph 10: other modifications not covered by Paragraphs 1 through 9; licensees may not add language creating legal rights or remedies

Third Party Financing Addendum (Form 40-11)

- Required for all conventional, Texas Veterans, FHA, VA, USDA, reverse mortgage, and other financed transactions; loan amount must match Paragraph 3.B of the residential contract
- Financing types: Paragraph 1.A conventional, Paragraph 1.B Texas Veterans, Paragraph 1.C FHA, Paragraph 1.D VA, Paragraph 1.E USDA, Paragraph 1.F reverse mortgage, Paragraph 1.G other financing
- VA Funding Fee and FHA mortgage insurance premium are excluded from the loan amounts entered in the addendum
- Paragraph 2.A Buyer Approval: the contract may or may not be made subject to Buyer Approval; if subject to it, the buyer must give written notice and a lender statement if financing is denied within the deadline or the contingency is waived
- Paragraph 2.B Property Approval: if the property fails to satisfy lender underwriting requirements, the buyer may terminate by the third day before closing with written notice and a lender statement
- Paragraph 5 authorizes the lender to share financing status with the parties and their agents, and authorizes the lender, title company, and escrow agent to share closing disclosures and settlement statements with the parties' brokers

Loan Assumption, Seller Financing, and Release of Liability

- Loan Assumption Addendum (Form 41-3): required when buyer assumes seller's existing loan; lender approval required; seller may remain personally liable without Form 12-3
- Form 41-3 Paragraph B: buyer delivers credit documentation within agreed days; seller has 7 days to approve or reject after delivery; non-response is deemed approval
- Form 41-3 Paragraph C: the variance threshold between the stated loan balance and the actual closing balance is agreed to by the parties in a blank; if the variance exceeds that threshold, either party may terminate
- Form 41-3 Paragraph H: authorizes lenders, title company, and escrow agent to share assumption status and closing disclosures with brokers and agents
- Seller Financing Addendum (Form 26-8): required when seller carries the note; buyer has 7 days to deliver financials; seller has 7 days to approve; note and deed of trust are the loan instruments
- Form 26-8 Paragraph D: contains four sub-paragraphs -- D.1 (property transfer consent), D.2 (casualty insurance election naming seller as mortgagee loss payee), D.3 (tax and insurance escrow options), D.4 (default under prior liens is also a default under the seller's deed of trust)
- Form 26-8: no prepayment penalty; late fee of 5 percent after 10 days; overdue amounts bear interest at 18 percent per annum or the highest lawful rate, whichever is less
- Addendum for Release of Liability on Assumed Loan (Form 12-3): releases seller from ongoing liability; both Paragraph A and Paragraph B required for VA loans; seller pays the cost

- Contracts for deed have no TREC promulgated form; buyer and seller must retain an attorney
- All addenda must include the names of all parties and the legal address of the subject property

CHAPTER 7 QUIZ:
CONTINGENCIES, ADDENDA, AND AMENDMENTS

1. A contingency clause is included in a sales contract. If the specified condition is not met, what right does the contingency give the buyer?
   a. The right to sue the seller for specific performance
   b. The right to request TREC mediation before making any further decisions
   c. The right to apply to a court for an extension of the contract term
   d. The right to exit the contract without default and to recover the earnest money

2. What typically happens if a buyer misses a contingency release deadline without providing the seller with written notice?
   a. The contingency is deemed waived and the buyer becomes obligated to proceed with the purchase
   b. The contract automatically terminates and the earnest money is returned to the buyer
   c. The contingency period is extended by an additional 14 days as a matter of law
   d. The seller must give the buyer a 72-hour cure period before the waiver takes effect

3. Which TREC form is the promulgated vehicle for addressing appraisal contingency rights in a Texas residential transaction?
   a. Third Party Financing Addendum (Form 40-11)
   b. Addendum for Property Subject to Mandatory Membership in a Property Owners Association (Form 36-11)
   c. Addendum Concerning Right to Terminate Due to Lender's Appraisal (Form 49-1)
   d. Environmental Assessment, Threatened or Endangered Species, and Wetlands Addendum (Form 28-2)

4. Which of the following correctly describes how a financing contingency protects a buyer in a Texas residential transaction?
   a. It guarantees that the lender will approve the loan at the interest rate stated in the contract
   b. It gives the buyer a specified number of days to obtain loan approval; if financing cannot be secured in time, the buyer may cancel and recover the earnest money
   c. It requires the seller to reduce the price if the property appraises below the contract amount
   d. It obligates the seller to provide seller financing if the buyer's lender declines the application

5. Under the Third Party Financing Addendum (Form 40-11), what is the consequence if a buyer fails to provide the seller with written notice of an inability to obtain financing by the stated deadline?
   a. The financing contingency is waived and the buyer must close the transaction or be in default
   b. The contract terminates automatically and the seller must return the earnest money within three business days
   c. The financing deadline is extended by ten days as provided by TREC rule
   d. The buyer may continue seeking financing indefinitely without risk of default

6. In a sale-and-settlement contingency with a kick-out clause, how much time does the original buyer typically have to remove the house sale contingency after the seller receives another acceptable offer?
   a. Immediately upon notification, with no grace period allowed
   b. Five to seven business days from the date the seller notifies the original buyer
   c. Up to ten calendar days as required by TREC guidelines
   d. 24 to 72 hours from the time the seller notifies the original buyer

7. In a Texas residential transaction, the inspection contingency is most commonly managed through which provision of the standard sales contract?
   a. The title objection procedure in Paragraph 6 of Form 20-19
   b. The Termination Option in Paragraph 23 of Form 20-19, which gives the buyer an unrestricted right to terminate during the option period
   c. The seller's disclosure notice provision in Paragraph 7 of Form 20-19
   d. The financing contingency in the Third Party Financing Addendum (Form 40-11)

8. Which of the following correctly describes the key difference between a settlement contingency and a sale-and-settlement contingency with a kick-out clause?
   a. In a settlement contingency, the seller retains the right to continue marketing; in a sale-and-settlement contingency, the seller must stop showing the property
   b. A settlement contingency applies only when the buyer's existing home has not yet been listed; a kick-out clause applies only when that home is already under contract
   c. In a settlement contingency, the seller is typically prohibited from accepting other offers; in a sale-and-settlement contingency, the seller retains the right to continue marketing
   d. A settlement contingency requires the buyer to waive the earnest money; a kick-out clause does not

9. A buyer plans to operate a tax preparation business from a residential property. To be properly protected by a home business contingency, which of the following must the buyer obtain before closing?
   a. A written letter from the appropriate zoning authority confirming that the specified business may legally operate from the property address
   b. A verbal approval from the local zoning officer, documented in a note by the buyer's agent
   c. A statement from the homeowners association confirming that home businesses are generally permitted
   d. A signed affidavit from the seller acknowledging that the property has been used for business purposes before

10. Which TREC form is used to manage the HOA documents contingency in a Texas residential transaction where the property is subject to a mandatory property owners association?
   a. Addendum for Back-Up Contract (Form 11-9)
   b. Addendum for Sale of Other Property by Buyer (Form 10-6)
   c. Short Sale Addendum (Form 45-2)
   d. Addendum for Property Subject to Mandatory Membership in a Property Owners Association (Form 36-11)

11. Which of the following best distinguishes an addendum from an amendment in Texas real estate practice?
    a. An addendum is used only for financing changes; an amendment is used for all other contract modifications
    b. An addendum is executed at the same time as the original contract and is part of it from the start; an amendment modifies a contract that has already been fully ratified by all parties
    c. An addendum is signed only by the buyer; an amendment must be signed by all parties including the brokers
    d. An addendum is used after closing to confirm the transfer of possession; an amendment is used only before closing

12. The TREC Amendment to Contract (Form 39-11) allows a licensee to modify a ratified residential contract for how many defined categories of permissible changes?
    a. Five
    b. Seven
    c. Ten
    d. Twelve

13. When a licensee uses the TREC Amendment to Contract (Form 39-11) to extend the closing date, what must be entered in the date blank?
    a. The number of additional days requested, expressed as a whole number
    b. The language at lender's discretion if the delay is caused by the lender
    c. An estimated date followed by a note indicating that the exact date is subject to lender confirmation
    d. A specific calendar date. Entering vague language such as at lender's discretion violates TREC rules

14. Paragraph 6 of the TREC Amendment to Contract (Form 39-11) governs lender-required repairs. In which type of transaction does this paragraph most commonly arise?
    a. VA and FHA transactions, where the lender's appraiser may generate a required repair list as a condition of loan approval
    b. Conventional transactions, where private lenders routinely require buyers to replace all major appliances before closing
    c. Cash transactions, because cash buyers have no lender to impose repair requirements
    d. Seller-financed transactions, where the seller acts as the lender and sets repair conditions

15. Which TREC addendum is required whenever a buyer obtains financing from a conventional lender, the Texas Veterans Land Board, an FHA-insured lender, a VA-guaranteed lender, a USDA-guaranteed lender, or through a reverse mortgage?
    a. Seller Financing Addendum (Form 26-8)
    b. Loan Assumption Addendum (Form 41-3)
    c. Third Party Financing Addendum (Form 40-11)
    d. Addendum for Release of Liability on Assumed Loan (Form 12-3)

16. When a buyer is obtaining a VA-guaranteed loan and completing the Third Party Financing Addendum (Form 40-11), which amount should be excluded from the loan amount entered in the addendum?
    a. The VA Funding Fee
    b. The buyer's down payment
    c. The title insurance premium
    d. The earnest money deposit already paid to the escrow agent
17. Under the Loan Assumption Addendum (Form 41-3), if a seller does not respond to the buyer's submitted credit documentation within how many days is the seller considered to have approved the buyer's creditworthiness?
    a. Three days
    b. Five days
    c. Ten days
    d. Seven days
18. Under the Loan Assumption Addendum (Form 41-3), if the variance between the loan balance stated in the addendum and the actual balance at closing exceeds what amount does either party have the right to terminate the contract?
    a. One hundred dollars
    b. Two hundred fifty dollars
    c. Five hundred dollars
    d. One thousand dollars
19. Under the Seller Financing Addendum (Form 26-8), if the buyer fails to deliver required financial documentation to the seller within seven days, what may the seller do?
    a. Extend the deadline by an additional seven days and then terminate if still not received
    b. Terminate the contract and retain the earnest money
    c. File a complaint with TREC requesting mandatory arbitration of the dispute
    d. Proceed to closing and demand the documentation at the closing table
20. Under the Seller Financing Addendum (Form 26-8), what prepayment penalty applies if the buyer pays off the seller-financed loan early?
    a. A penalty equal to six months of accrued interest on the outstanding balance
    b. A penalty of two percent of the remaining principal balance at the time of payoff
    c. A penalty calculated using the schedule specified in the promissory note
    d. No prepayment penalty; the buyer may prepay all or any portion of the loan at any time without penalty
21. What is the primary purpose of the Addendum for Release of Liability on Assumed Loan (Form 12-3)?
    a. To formally release the seller from ongoing personal liability on a mortgage loan that the buyer has assumed
    b. To require the buyer to obtain a new loan at closing rather than assuming the seller's existing loan
    c. To waive the due-on-sale clause in the seller's existing loan so that the assumption may proceed
    d. To transfer the seller's escrow account balance to the buyer at the time of closing

22. When the Addendum for Release of Liability on Assumed Loan (Form 12-3) is used, who bears the cost of securing both the release of liability and the restoration of VA entitlement?
   a. The buyer, because the buyer is the party benefiting from the loan assumption arrangement
   b. The seller, because those outcomes directly benefit the seller
   c. The costs are split equally between buyer and seller as a matter of TREC rule
   d. The title company, which deducts the costs from the closing proceeds before disbursing to either party

23. For a VA loan assumption to qualify for restoration of the seller's VA entitlement under Form 12-3, which of the following conditions must the buyer who is assuming the loan satisfy?
   a. The buyer must be a first-time homebuyer and must not have used VA entitlement on a prior purchase
   b. The buyer must pay the VA Funding Fee in cash at closing rather than financing it into the loan
   c. The buyer must be a veteran with sufficient unused VA entitlement to substitute for the seller's entitlement
   d. The buyer must have a credit score of at least 680 as required by current VA underwriting guidelines

24. A buyer and seller wish to structure their transaction as a contract for deed. Which of the following correctly states what the parties must do because no TREC promulgated form exists for that purpose?
   a. Retain an attorney to prepare the appropriate documents
   b. Use the standard One to Four Family Residential Contract (Form 20-19) with the Seller Financing Addendum attached
   c. Request a special-purpose form from TREC through the Broker-Lawyer Committee
   d. Use the Loan Assumption Addendum (Form 41-3) and modify the blank spaces to reflect installment sale terms

25. In a seller financing arrangement governed by the Seller Financing Addendum (Form 26-8), which instruments does the seller use to secure the loan?
   a. A title commitment and a certificate of title issued by the title company
   b. A warranty deed and a release of lien filed with the county clerk
   c. A commitment for title insurance and a general warranty deed
   d. A promissory note and a deed of trust

Chapter 7 Case Study:

Contingencies, Addenda, and Amendments

The Situation

Greg and Ann Mettling are purchasing a home in Fort Worth through Performance Programs Realty. Their agent, Rob Vance, negotiated a ten-day option period and a 21-day financing deadline in the Third Party Financing Addendum (Form 40-11). The contract also included a sale-and-settlement contingency with a kick-out clause, giving Greg and Ann 48 hours to remove the contingency if the seller received another acceptable offer while the Mettlings waited for their current home to sell.

On day eight of the option period, the home inspector issued a report identifying a significant foundation crack that the inspector recommended be evaluated by a structural engineer. Rob called Greg and told him the finding was probably minor and not to worry about it. He did not extend the option period or schedule the follow-up inspection. The option period expired on day ten without a termination notice from the Mettlings and without the structural engineer's report.

On day nineteen, the Mettlings' lender notified Rob that the loan had been declined because Greg had recently co-signed a car loan for his adult son, which pushed his debt-to-income ratio above the qualifying threshold. Rob had been aware of the co-signed loan since the application stage but assumed it would not be a problem. He did not notify the seller's agent in writing. Day 21 passed without written notice from the Mettlings.

On day 22, a competing buyer submitted a full-price offer on the same property. The seller invoked the kick-out clause and gave the Mettlings 48 hours to remove their sale contingency or have the contract terminate. Greg called Rob and asked him to prepare an amendment extending the financing notification deadline so they could switch lenders and try again. Rob prepared the amendment using the TREC Amendment to Contract (Form 39-11) and entered the language financing deadline extended at lender's discretion in the date blank.

Discussion Questions

Question 1

The home inspector recommended a structural engineering evaluation but the option period expired before the follow-up inspection could be completed. Analyze Rob Vance's handling of this situation, identify the tool available to extend the option period, and explain what the Mettlings lost when the option period expired without a termination notice being sent.

____

____

____

____

____

Question 2

Greg Mettling's lender declined the loan on day 19 but Rob did not provide the seller with written notice of the financing failure before day 21. Explain the consequence of missing that written notice deadline under the Third Party Financing Addendum (Form 40-11), and describe what the Mettlings' correct course of action should have been once the loan was declined.

____

____

____

____

____

Question 3

Rob prepared an amendment to extend the financing notification deadline but entered the language financing deadline extended at lender's discretion in the date blank rather than a specific calendar date. Identify the TREC rule Rob violated, explain why vague date language is prohibited, and describe what he should have written instead.

____

____

____

____

____

CHAPTER 8:

FINANCING REAL ESTATE

Chapter Overview

Learning Objectives

Upon completing Chapter 8, the student will be able to:

1. Describe the legal theories of mortgage ownership, explain the roles of the mortgagor and mortgagee, and identify the three basic financing instruments used in Texas.
2. Define a promissory note, distinguish between a straight note and an installment note, and identify the key provisions found in most notes.
3. Describe the standard provisions of a mortgage document and explain how a mortgage is created, enforced, and released.
4. Explain how a deed of trust differs from a mortgage, identify the three parties involved, describe the covenants contained in a deed of trust, and explain why lenders prefer it in Texas.
5. Define and explain the key clauses found in mortgage and deed of trust documents, including late payment, prepayment, lock-in, due-on-sale, subject to, subordination, release, and exculpatory clauses.
6. Describe land contracts, explain the benefits and disadvantages for buyers and sellers, and identify the Texas Property Code requirements that apply to executory contracts.
7. Explain the three types of mortgage foreclosure, describe the non-judicial foreclosure process used in Texas, and identify the tax consequences a borrower may face after a foreclosure sale.
8. Define a short sale, describe the TREC Short Sale Addendum (Form 45-2), and explain how a short sale benefits lenders, borrowers, buyers, and licensees.
9. Define a lien, describe its legal features, classify liens by type and priority, and illustrate how lien priority affects the distribution of foreclosure proceeds.
10. Identify the primary and secondary mortgage market participants and explain the role of Fannie Mae, Freddie Mac, and Ginnie Mae.
11. Describe the most common loan repayment plans, explain the features of conventional loans, adjustable rate mortgages, and private mortgage insurance, and identify the specialty loan options available to borrowers.
12. Explain the major federal lending laws affecting real estate transactions, including RESPA and TRID, Regulation Z and the Truth in Lending Act, ECOA, the Community Reinvestment Act, the Fair Credit Reporting Act, and the Home Mortgage Disclosure Act.

Contents

- Special Mortgage Clauses
- Land Contracts
- Foreclosure
- Non-Judicial Foreclosure in Texas
- Tax Consequences of Foreclosure
- Short Sales
- Liens
- Sources of Real Estate Loans
- The Secondary Mortgage Market
- Loan Repayment Plans
- Conventional Loans and Private Mortgage Insurance
- Specialty Loan Options
- Federal Lending Legislation

Mortgage Law and Financing Instruments

A mortgage involves the transfer of an interest in land as security for a loan or other obligation. It is the most common method of financing real estate transactions. The mortgagor is the borrower who transfers the security interest. The mortgagee is the lender, usually a financial institution, who provides the loan in exchange for the security interest.

Title Theories

Three legal theories govern who holds legal title to a mortgaged property. Under the title theory, the legal title to the security interest rests with the mortgagee throughout the loan period. Most states, however, follow the lien theory, under which the legal title remains with the mortgagor unless there is a foreclosure. Texas follows the lien theory, meaning the borrower retains legal title and the lender holds only a security interest. Finally, the intermediate theory applies the lien theory until a default occurs, at which point the title theory applies.

The Garn-St Germain Depository Institutions Act of 1982 made due-on-sale and due-on-encumbrance clauses enforceable nationwide, allowing lenders to accelerate loans when a property is transferred. Most lenders today sell the loans they originate on the secondary mortgage market. Revenue earned from selling a loan is called the Service Release Premium.

Three Basic Financing Instruments in Texas

There are three basic legal documents used to finance real estate in Texas:

- Note and mortgage
- Note and deed of trust
- Land contract

The concept of leverage drives most real estate financing. Leverage means using other parties' money to make a purchase, such as making a modest down payment and borrowing the balance. When a buyer pledges property as collateral for a loan, the loan is secured. Real estate loans are always secured loans.

The loan document must be in writing, describe the collateral accurately, detail all repayment terms, be signed by all parties, and be properly witnessed.

The Promissory Note

A promissory note, commonly called simply the note, is the legal evidence of the debt incurred. When a buyer borrows money to purchase a home, the note describes the amount borrowed, the repayment terms, and the consequences of default. A note is itself a complete and legally enforceable contract once signed. It does not require a mortgage or deed of trust to be valid. When a note has no related collateral, it is unsecured. Real estate notes, however, are always paired with either a mortgage or a deed of trust as security instruments, making them secured loans.

Types of Notes

Straight note An interest-only note in which the borrower pays only interest periodically and repays the entire principal in a single payment when the note matures.

Installment note A note requiring periodic payment of both principal and interest; the most common type used in residential real estate.

Key Note Provisions

Most notes include the following provisions:

- Identity of borrower and lender
- Promise to pay, creating the legal obligation
- Amount borrowed (the face amount of the note)
- Interest rate, either fixed or adjustable; if adjustable, the note specifies how it will change
- Due dates and frequency of payments
- Amount of each payment, determined by loan amount, term, and interest rate
- Maturity date when the debt is fully due
- Reference to the real estate as security, identifying the mortgage or deed of trust
- Signatures; only one original is signed and it remains with the lender until the debt is satisfied

Additional provisions typically address how payments are applied (usually first to late charges, then to interest, then to principal), penalties for late payment and any grace period, notification of default and the lender's right to accelerate, prepayment rights and any penalty, the conditions under which the loan may be assumed, the lender's assignment rights, and the process for lien release when the loan is satisfied.

Mortgage Provisions

A mortgage pledges real property as security for the repayment of a debt. Standard mortgage documents include the following provisions:

Identification of participants The names of the mortgagor (borrower) and mortgagee (lender).

Granting clause The statement pledging the mortgagor's property rights, using words such as grant, bargain, sell, and convey to create a lien on the property.

Property description A legal description of the property, including a statement pledging everything permanently attached to the land as collateral.

Covenant of seisin The mortgagor's warranty that it actually holds title to the property and has the authority to pledge it.

Attachment of note A reference to the note or, in some forms, an actual copy of the note attached to the mortgage document.

Property taxes A requirement that the mortgagor pay all taxes, assessments, and charges; failure to do so constitutes default. Many lenders require the borrower to make monthly escrow deposits toward future tax bills.

Insurance A requirement that the mortgagor maintain hazard insurance in an amount that adequately covers the lender's interest; the lender must be named as a co-insured. Insurance premiums are often escrowed with the monthly payment.

Preservation of property A requirement that the borrower maintain the physical condition of the property.

Defeasance clause States that if the borrower repays the debt when due, the mortgage is canceled and title is returned to the borrower free of the lien.

Acceleration clause States that if the borrower fails to pay or breaches any covenant of the mortgage, the lender may declare the entire remaining balance immediately due and payable.

Signatures and acknowledgment The borrowers' signed acceptance of all conditions, dated and notarized so the document may be recorded.

Once the mortgagor has paid off the mortgage in full, the lender executes and records a mortgage release, also called a satisfaction of mortgage, to remove the lien from the public record.

Deed of Trust

A deed of trust, also called a trust deed, is a legal document that transfers title to a property to a neutral third-party trustee as security for the loan. Three parties are involved: the trustor (borrower), the beneficiary (lender), and the trustee. Texas almost exclusively uses the deed of trust when financing residential mortgages.

At closing, the borrower signs both the promissory note and the deed of trust. The deed of trust conveys title to the trustee, who holds it on behalf of the lender until the loan is repaid. When the borrower fully repays the note, the trustee reconveys title to the borrower using a deed of reconveyance, also called a release deed. If the borrower defaults, the lender contacts the trustee, who exercises the power of sale granted in the deed of trust. The property is sold and the proceeds go to the lender without requiring a court proceeding.

Why Lenders Prefer the Deed of Trust

Lenders prefer the deed of trust for several reasons:

- The trustee may sell the property after default without the time-consuming judicial foreclosure process
- The statute of limitations does not bar action on the power of sale in a deed of trust, as it might on a mortgage note
- A deed of trust can secure more than one note
- The lender may remain anonymous by not being named directly in the deed of trust

- There is generally no statutory right of redemption after a power-of-sale foreclosure in Texas

Deed of Trust Covenants

Like a mortgage, a deed of trust identifies the parties, describes the collateral, repeats the note terms, and provides for signatures and notarization. Unlike a mortgage, it conveys title to the trustee. The deed of trust also includes the following covenants:

- Property maintenance: the borrower must maintain the property in good condition
- Fire insurance: the borrower must carry fire insurance naming the lender as beneficiary
- Legal action: the borrower will defend against claims affecting the property and pay costs arising from foreclosure
- Payment of taxes: the borrower will pay all taxes, assessments, and trust costs when due
- Expenditures: the borrower will reimburse the lender for money spent on the borrower's behalf
- Injury to property: condemnation awards or damage payments are applied to reduce the loan balance
- Late payment: acceptance of a late payment does not waive the lender's right to timely future payments
- Trustee actions: the trustee may reconvey the property, consent to plats, grant easements, and execute extension agreements at the lender's request
- Reconveyance: the trustee must reconvey the property to the borrower when the loan is fully paid
- Assignment of rents: the borrower may collect rents during the loan period, but upon default the lender may collect all property income
- Acceleration: breach of any covenant permits the lender to call the entire loan balance due and the trustee to sell the property after proper notice

Mortgage vs. Deed of Trust

Although mortgages and deeds of trust both secure real estate loans, they differ in important ways. The table below summarizes the key distinctions.

Parties A mortgage involves two parties: borrower and lender. A deed of trust involves three: borrower (trustor), lender (beneficiary), and trustee.

Title In a mortgage (lien theory), legal title remains with the borrower. In a deed of trust, the borrower conveys title to the trustee, who holds it until the loan is satisfied.

Foreclosure type A mortgage default requires judicial foreclosure through the courts. A deed of trust default allows non-judicial foreclosure through the trustee's power of sale.

Discharge A mortgage is discharged by recording a satisfaction of mortgage. A deed of trust is discharged by recording a reconveyance of title.

Recording of assignments Mortgage assignments may need to be recorded under state law. Deed of trust assignments typically do not need to be recorded.

Special Mortgage Clauses

Late Payment Penalty

A late payment clause requires the borrower to pay a penalty for payments received after the due date. Many lenders allow a grace period of 10 to 15 days before assessing a late fee. Texas has no statutory restrictions on late fees; the customary standard follows the Fannie Mae guideline of five percent of the payment amount after 15 days.

Prepayment Privilege

If a note has no prepayment clause, the borrower may repay the loan at any time without penalty. Some loans limit prepayment to a specific percentage of the principal or a fixed amount above regular payments in any single year.

Prepayment Penalty

A lender who wants to protect a high-interest loan from early payoff may include a prepayment penalty clause allowing an additional charge if the loan is paid early. The penalty is typically a percentage of the original loan amount or the outstanding balance. Texas Finance Code Section 302.102 prohibits prepayment penalties on residential mortgage loans secured by a borrower's homestead if the interest rate on the loan exceeds 12 percent, unless the charge is required by a federally-created agency.

Lock-In Clause

A lock-in clause prohibits the borrower from paying off the entire mortgage before a specified date. Lenders use this clause in limited circumstances to protect a very favorable interest rate for as long as possible. Lenders sometimes combine the prepayment privilege, prepayment penalty, and lock-in clause: for example, no prepayment for the first four years, followed by limited prepayment with a penalty for a further period before full prepayment is permitted.

Due-on-Sale Clause

Also called an alienation clause, nonassumption clause, call clause, or right-to-sell clause, the due-on-sale clause requires the borrower to pay off the entire loan balance when the property is sold. This clause effectively prevents assumption of the loan without lender approval. If a new buyer wishes to assume an existing loan, the lender typically conditions approval on increased interest rates, assumption fees, a larger down payment, or some combination of those requirements. The Garn-St Germain Act of 1982 made due-on-sale clauses in loans from federally-chartered institutions enforceable nationwide.

Subject To Provision

When a loan has no due-on-sale clause, the new buyer of the property has two options for handling the existing loan. The buyer may assume the loan, taking personal responsibility for it. Alternatively, the buyer may purchase the property subject to the existing mortgage. With a subject-to purchase, the new buyer makes loan payments as long as it benefits them to do so but cannot be held personally liable for the debt if they default. The original seller, however, remains personally and legally responsible to the lender throughout.

For the seller to be fully released from liability, the lender must agree to a novation, replacing the original borrower with the new buyer on the loan instrument. The new buyer qualifies with the lender, and upon approval the lender executes and records an amendment to the loan agreement.

Subordination Clause

A subordination clause is an agreement to reduce the priority of one lien to a lien that will be recorded in the future. For example, a developer who purchases land carries the purchase loan as the first lien. When construction financing is arranged, the construction lender wants first lien priority. The subordination clause allows the original land purchase loan to be moved to second position behind the construction mortgage.

Release Clause

A release clause, also called a partial release clause, is used when two or more parcels are pledged as collateral for a single loan. As a developer sells individual lots from the mortgaged tract, a portion of each sale's proceeds pays down the mortgage, and the lender executes and records a partial release of the sold lot, giving the buyer clear title to that lot while the mortgage continues on the remaining lots.

Exculpatory Clause

An exculpatory clause is a lender's agreement to waive the right to a deficiency judgment in the event of default. If this clause is present, the lender may foreclose and take the property but may not pursue the borrower's other assets for any remaining balance.

Land Contracts

A land contract, also called a contract for deed, installment sales contract, agreement for deed, or agreement to convey, is a complete financing contract executed directly between a seller (vendor) and a buyer (vendee), without a separate promissory note or institutional lender. Under a land contract, the seller retains legal title and the buyer receives equitable title and immediate possession. The seller continues to be primarily liable for any existing mortgage on the property. The deed transfers to the buyer only when the buyer completes all obligations stated in the contract.

Land contracts are classified as executory contracts under Texas law and are subject to extensive requirements under Texas Property Code Chapter 5, Subchapter D (sections 5.061 and following). These requirements include mandatory pre-execution disclosures: a survey or plat, copies of all liens and encumbrances, a Seller's Disclosure Notice, and, if not in a recorded subdivision, written notice that utilities may not be available. The seller must also provide tax certificates and evidence of insurance.

Benefits of Land Contracts

In an appreciating market, a land contract allows buyers who cannot qualify for conventional financing to take possession and benefit from appreciation before the final payment comes due. Sellers benefit from access to a larger pool of buyers, a potentially faster transaction, and the ability to defer capital gains recognition until installment payments are received. Land contracts are particularly suited to buyers whose incomes are expected to increase during the contract period, enabling them to eventually refinance and pay off the land contract balance.

Disadvantages for Buyers

- The buyer makes payments before receiving a deed and must continue paying even if questions arise about the seller's ability to deliver clear title at the end of the term

- If the seller has placed additional mortgages or liens on the property during the contract period, those encumbrances can cloud the eventual title transfer
- If the seller dies or becomes missing at the time of final payment, the property may become tied up in probate, delaying the title transfer
- A covenant against assignment in the contract may prevent the buyer from transferring the interest to another party
- The seller may fail to apply the buyer's payments to the existing mortgage, potentially triggering foreclosure

Disadvantages for Sellers

- If the buyer defaults, clearing the title can be time-consuming and expensive, especially if the buyer is in bankruptcy or is a nonresident
- Because a land contract is a contract, it is subject to varying interpretations that can lead to disputes and litigation

Foreclosure

Foreclosure is the legal process through which a lender or other lienholder forces the sale of mortgaged property to satisfy an unpaid debt when the borrower has defaulted. Foreclosure brings the rights of all parties to an end and passes the property's title either to the holder of the mortgage or to a third-party purchaser at the foreclosure sale. All liens can be enforced through court action, operation of law, or powers granted in the original loan agreement.

Three types of foreclosure enforce mortgage liens: judicial foreclosure, non-judicial foreclosure, and strict foreclosure.

Judicial Foreclosure

Judicial foreclosure occurs when a lender files suit and obtains a court order to sell the foreclosed property. It is used when the mortgage document does not contain a power-of-sale clause. The lender first accelerates the loan and, if the borrower fails to pay off the balance, files a foreclosure suit naming the borrower as defendant. The suit asks the court to terminate the defendant's interest in the property, order a public sale, and apply the proceeds to the debt.

A lis pendens gives public notice that litigation affecting the property has been filed. Other lienholders may join the suit to protect their interests. If the defendant does not meet the demands of the suit within the prescribed period, the court issues a writ of execution authorizing the sheriff to seize and sell the property. After public notice, the property is auctioned. The proceeds are distributed to lienholders in order of priority. If proceeds are insufficient, the lender may seek a deficiency judgment against the borrower's other assets. A deficiency judgment is the outstanding debt remaining after the foreclosure sale.

The borrower has the right of redemption, also called equity of redemption, which is the right to reclaim the foreclosed property by paying all amounts owed before the foreclosure sale takes place. Some states provide a statutory redemption period allowing reclamation for up to one year after the sale.

Judicial foreclosure can be used with conventional mortgages, FHA-insured mortgages, VA-guaranteed mortgages, and junior mortgages. Most lenders prefer judicial foreclosure when they want to obtain a deficiency judgment.

Non-Judicial Foreclosure

When the mortgage or deed of trust contains a power-of-sale clause, the lienholder may force the sale of the property without going to court. The lender or trustee records and delivers notice to the borrower and other lienholders, publishes a notice of sale after the required period, conducts the auction, and extinguishes all junior liens. The highest bidder receives unencumbered title. In a non-judicial proceeding, the lender cannot obtain a deficiency judgment through the foreclosure itself; the lender must instead file a separate deficiency suit.

The primary method of foreclosure in Texas is non-judicial foreclosure through the deed of trust's power-of-sale clause. This method eliminates the statutory redemption period available in judicial foreclosure, making it faster and less expensive for the lender.

Strict Foreclosure

Strict foreclosure is a court proceeding that gives the lender title directly, by court order, rather than through a public sale. The court establishes a period within which the defaulting borrower must repay amounts owed. If the borrower fails to repay, the court transfers full legal title to the lender. Strict foreclosure is rarely used because there is no public auction to establish market value, making it difficult to calculate a deficiency judgment. Many states prohibit deficiency judgments in strict foreclosure proceedings.

Deed in Lieu of Foreclosure

A defaulting borrower who faces foreclosure may voluntarily deed the property to the mortgagee to avoid court proceedings. This deed in lieu of foreclosure transfers legal title to the lienholder. However, it does not extinguish any other existing liens on the property; the lender receives title subject to those encumbrances.

Redemption Rights in Texas

In Texas, the right of redemption after a foreclosure sale is limited. For property that is the defaulted taxpayer's homestead or that is designated for agricultural use, the owner may redeem the property within two years after the sheriff's deed is recorded following a tax lien foreclosure. For other properties, the redemption period for tax lien foreclosures is six months. There is no right of redemption when foreclosure is accomplished through a non-judicial deed-of-trust power-of-sale proceeding or through the judicial enforcement of a vendor's lien.

Non-Judicial Foreclosure in Texas

Because Texas uses the deed of trust almost exclusively for residential mortgage financing, non-judicial foreclosure is the standard process. The requirements are strict, and the deed of trust must contain the power-of-sale language for this method to be used.

Notice Requirements

Before a non-judicial foreclosure sale may occur in Texas, the following notice requirements must be satisfied:

- The lender must send the borrower a demand letter giving 20 days to cure the default before foreclosure proceedings begin

- After the 20-day notice and at least 21 days before the foreclosure sale, the lender must file notice with the county clerk of the county where the property is located, mail notice to the defaulting borrower and other creditors whose liens affect the property, and post notice at the county courthouse
- Foreclosure sales must occur on the first Tuesday of each month, even if that date falls on a legal holiday, between 10 a.m. and 4 p.m. at the courthouse

The Foreclosure Sale

The trustee auctions the property to the highest bidder. The lender is entitled to credit bid up to the amount of the outstanding indebtedness. The trustee may reject bids deemed inadequate and may postpone the sale up to three times by announcement at the time and location of the sale. More than three postponements require recording, publishing, mailing, and posting a new notice of sale

The successful bidder receives a trustee's deed to the property, but there is no guarantee that the title is entirely clear. Outstanding senior liens including federal tax liens, real property taxes, assessments, and valid mechanic's liens may survive the sale. Recording the trustee's deed extinguishes all junior liens, any encumbrances subordinate to the foreclosing deed of trust, and the defaulted borrower's right of reinstatement. The new purchaser is entitled to immediate possession but may need to pursue eviction of the prior occupant.

Proceeds are distributed in this order: first to the trustee for sale expenses, then to the first lienholder, then to junior lienholders in order of priority, and any remaining amount to the defaulted borrower.

Tax Consequences of Foreclosure

Many borrowers assume that losing a property through foreclosure creates no tax liability. That assumption is incorrect. The IRS treats a foreclosure as a sale. If the amount of the forgiven debt exceeds the borrower's tax basis in the property, the IRS considers that a taxable gain has occurred.

Examples of how this works: if a borrower owes $600,000 on a property purchased for $550,000 and the property is now worth $480,000, the borrower is taxed as if the property sold for $600,000, producing a $50,000 gain subject to applicable exemptions. If a borrower owes $600,000 on a property purchased for $720,000 that is now worth $480,000, the borrower is treated as selling for $600,000, producing an apparent loss of $120,000. This loss may be deductible if the property was a rental or investment property but is generally not deductible if it was the borrower's personal residence.

Because the tax consequences of a foreclosure can be significant and complex, every borrower facing foreclosure should consult a qualified tax advisor before proceeding.

Short Sales

A short sale occurs when a lender allows a borrower who is in default to sell the mortgaged property for less than the outstanding loan balance. The lender releases the lien so the property can be conveyed free and clear to a new purchaser, and typically forgives the remaining balance. Lenders agree to short sales to avoid the delay and expense of foreclosure and to avoid carrying a Real Estate Owned (REO) property on their books.

The TREC Short Sale Addendum (Form 45-2, effective April 1, 2021) is attached to contracts involving a short sale. The addendum states that the contract is contingent on the lienholder's consent to the sale, the lienholder's agreement to accept the seller's net proceeds as full satisfaction of the loan, and the lienholder's delivery of an executed release of lien in recordable form.

Short Sale Candidates

A short sale candidate is a homeowner who is late or will soon be late on mortgage payments and can document the inability to make payments. A short sale can proceed even while a foreclosure is in process, as long as the foreclosure sale has not yet occurred or the owner has filed for bankruptcy protection.

Why Short Sales Benefit All Parties

- The lender recovers as much of the non-performing loan as possible without the time and expense of foreclosure and property management
- The borrower has a portion of the debt forgiven and experiences a less severe impact on credit; a foreclosure can reduce a credit score by 300 points or more, while a short sale's impact is typically in the range of 80 to 100 points
- The buyer acquires a property priced at or near current market value
- The licensee gains a listing opportunity, commission income, and the chance to provide significant added value to clients in distress

From a broader perspective, keeping properties out of foreclosure helps stabilize neighborhood values and the overall real estate market. A single foreclosure can reduce surrounding property values by a significant amount, compounding losses in an already weak market.

Liens

A lien is a creditor's claim against personal or real property as security for a debt owed by the property owner. If the owner defaults, the lien gives the creditor the right to force a sale of the property to satisfy the debt. This right to force a sale is what distinguishes a lien from other types of encumbrances. Liens are subject to Texas Homestead laws.

A recorded lien reduces the owner's effective equity in the property to the extent of the lien amount. The creditor placing a lien is the lienor; the debtor whose property is liened is the lienee.

Legal Features of Liens

A lien does not convey ownership The lienor holds only an equitable interest in the property. The exception is in a title-theory state where a mortgage conveys legal title to the lender. Texas is a lien-theory state, so lenders hold only a security interest and borrowers retain title.

A lien attaches to the property When the property is transferred, the new owner acquires it subject to the lien, and the creditor may pursue foreclosure against the new owner to satisfy the debt.

A property may be subject to multiple liens Multiple lienholders may have claims against the same property simultaneously. The more liens recorded, the less secure the collateral becomes.

A lien terminates on payment and recording Full payment of the debt and recording of a satisfaction or release document extinguishes the lien. Default triggers a judicial or foreclosure action to enforce the lien.

Types of Liens

Liens may be classified along three dimensions:

Voluntary vs. involuntary A voluntary lien is created by the property owner, such as a mortgage. An involuntary lien is imposed by legal process regardless of the owner's wishes. If imposed by statute, it is a statutory lien; if by court action, it is an equitable lien.

General vs. specific A general lien attaches to all real and personal property owned by the debtor, such as an inheritance tax lien. A specific lien attaches only to a single identified property, such as a mortgage lien.

Superior vs. inferior Superior (senior) liens outrank inferior (junior) liens in priority. Real estate tax liens, special assessments, and inheritance tax liens are typically superior. Other liens, including most income tax liens, are inferior.

Lien Priority

Priority determines the order in which lienholders receive payment from foreclosure proceeds. Two factors establish priority: whether the lien is superior or junior, and the date of recordation. All superior liens take precedence over all junior liens regardless of recording date, because they are matters of public record not requiring additional notice. Among junior liens, earlier recording dates establish higher priority.

The mechanic's lien is an exception to the recording rule: its priority dates from the point when work commenced or ended, as determined by state law, rather than from its recording date.

Example of lien priority distribution: A homeowner is foreclosed on a second mortgage of $75,000 taken in 2021. The first mortgage from 2018 has a balance of $350,000. Unpaid real estate taxes for the current year are $6,500. There is a mechanic's lien of $15,000 for work performed in 2019. The home sells for $450,000. Proceeds are distributed as follows: $6,500 real estate taxes, $350,000 first mortgage, $15,000 mechanic's lien, $75,000 second mortgage, and $3,500 balance to the homeowner. The second mortgage holder needed the property to sell for at least $446,500 to recover the full loan amount.

Judgment Liens

A judgment lien attaches to real and personal property as a result of a money judgment entered by a court in favor of a creditor. In Texas, an example is a court-ordered lien against all property of a parent who defaults on child support. The creditor may obtain a writ of execution to force the sale of attached property. After paying the debt from proceeds, the debtor may obtain a satisfaction of judgment to clear the title records on other property.

During litigation, a creditor may also secure a writ of attachment to prevent the debtor from selling or concealing property. Certain properties are exempt from judgment liens in Texas, including homestead property. If a judgment lien has been applied to homestead property and no exemptions apply, the owner may file an affidavit with the county clerk to release the lien, subject to certain notice requirements.

Other Texas Lien Types

Mortgage and trust deed lien In Texas (a lien-theory state), the lender records a lien against the property as security for the loan.

Vendor's lien Secures a purchase money mortgage; arises by statute in Texas even if not recorded in the deed. A vendee's lien arises when a buyer files a claim after a seller fails to deliver title despite full performance by the buyer.

Municipal utility lien Placed against a property for failure to pay municipal utility bills.

Surety bail bond lien Recorded in Texas when a property owner pledges real estate instead of cash to secure bail; homestead property is exempt.

TWC wage lien Filed against an employer's real and personal property when the employer owes back wages to an employee.

Sources of Real Estate Loans

The primary mortgage market consists of lenders who originate loans directly to borrowers. The major types of primary market lenders are:

Savings Associations

Savings and loan associations, also called savings banks or thrifts, promote thrift and homeownership by accepting deposits and investing in residential mortgage loans. State-chartered Texas savings institutions are regulated by the Department of Savings and Mortgage Lending (SML). Federally-chartered institutions are regulated by the Office of the Comptroller of the Currency, with accounts insured by the FDIC.

Commercial Banks

Commercial banks primarily make short-term loans including construction loans, home improvement loans, and manufactured housing loans. They operate under state or federal charters; the Texas Department of Banking licenses state-chartered banks and the Comptroller of the Currency licenses nationally-chartered banks.

Credit Unions

Credit unions are nonprofit financial cooperatives that pay no income tax, allowing them to offer higher deposit rates and lower loan rates than commercial competitors. Under the Federal Credit Union Act, credit unions may make 30-year loans to finance members' principal residences and may offer FHA and VA loans at competitive rates.

Insurance Companies

Life insurance companies are a major source of credit for large commercial projects, including shopping centers, office buildings, hotels, industrial buildings, and apartment complexes. Texas ranks second only to California in total dollar volume of insurance company real estate loans.

Real Estate Investment Trusts

A REIT is an investment vehicle created by federal tax law in 1960. REITs receive favorable tax treatment if they invest at least 75 percent of assets in real estate and distribute at least 95 percent of annual real estate income to investors. They focus on income-producing properties and major development projects.

Mortgage Bankers

Mortgage bankers originate and service loans on behalf of other lenders such as insurance companies and investment trusts. They earn an origination fee plus a servicing percentage.

Mortgage Brokers

A mortgage broker arranges financing for a borrower but does not invest its own capital in the loan and does not service the loan after closing. The broker earns a commission paid by the borrower. Under the Texas Secure and Fair Enforcement for Mortgage Licensing Act of 2009 (Texas SAFE Act), any individual acting as a residential mortgage loan originator must hold a valid mortgage loan originator license.

The Secondary Mortgage Market

The secondary mortgage market consists of entities that purchase loans originated in the primary market, assemble them into packages, and resell them to investors. Primary lenders sell their loans to generate capital for new originations. Investors purchase fractional interests in mortgage pools through securities brokers. The secondary market shifts capital from surplus areas to shortage areas and stabilizes the flow of mortgage credit nationwide.

The three major government-sponsored enterprises (GSEs) that dominate the secondary market are:

Ginnie Mae (GNMA) Government National Mortgage Association; a government agency that guarantees mortgage-backed securities backed by FHA and VA loans.

Fannie Mae (FNMA) Federal National Mortgage Association; became a private corporation in 1968 but retained a government-sponsored enterprise status; purchases and securitizes conventional conforming loans.

Freddie Mac (FHLMC) Federal Home Loan Mortgage Corporation; a quasi-government agency that purchases conventional conforming loans and issues mortgage-backed securities; provides the Loan Product Advisor automated underwriting system.

When lenders follow Fannie Mae and Freddie Mac underwriting standards, they can sell their loans in the secondary market rather than holding them in their own portfolios, freeing up capital for new lending. Loans meeting these standards are called conforming loans; loans exceeding the conforming loan limits set annually by the Federal Housing Finance Agency are called jumbo loans and are not purchased by the GSEs.

Loan Repayment Plans

When obtaining a loan, both borrower and lender must agree on a repayment plan that suits the borrower's financial circumstances while providing the lender an acceptable return. The most common repayment structures are:

Straight (Interest-Only) Loan

Monthly payments cover only interest; no principal is repaid during the loan term. At maturity, the borrower must pay the entire principal balance or refinance. Interest-only loans can be appropriate for buyers who plan a short holding period and expect the property to appreciate, but they carry the risk that the appreciation may not materialize and the borrower may owe more than the property is worth.

Amortized Loan

With a fully amortized loan, the borrower makes a fixed monthly payment of principal and interest. Each payment is applied first to interest and then to principal. In the early years, most of the payment goes to interest and little to principal; as the loan matures, the proportion reverses and equity builds more rapidly. A 30-year fixed rate loan of $550,000 at 7.0 percent has a monthly principal and interest payment of approximately $3,660. During the first payment, only a small fraction reduces the principal balance; by year 25, the majority of each payment reduces the balance.

With a straight amortized loan (as distinguished from a fully amortized loan), the principal reduction per payment is fixed, while the interest payment decreases as the balance declines, producing a declining monthly payment over the life of the loan.

Balloon Payment Loan

A balloon mortgage is partially amortized: the monthly payments are calculated as if the loan were a longer term (such as 30 years), but the loan matures at a shorter date (such as 5, 7, or 10 years), at which time the remaining unpaid balance (the balloon) becomes due in full. Balloon loans are often used by borrowers who expect to sell or refinance before the balloon comes due. If the borrower cannot pay or refinance at maturity, the lender is not obligated to extend the loan.

Adjustable-Rate Mortgage (ARM)

With an ARM, the interest rate is fixed for an initial period and then adjusts periodically based on a designated index plus a margin set by the lender at origination. ARMs carry an initially lower rate, called a teaser rate, which can make them more accessible to borrowers who might not qualify for a fixed-rate loan. Key ARM components include:

> **Index** A measure of economic conditions used as the basis for rate adjustments; common indexes include the one-year Treasury Bill, the five-year Treasury note, the Cost of Funds Index, and the Secured Overnight Financing Rate (SOFR).
>
> **Margin** The lender's fixed markup, typically two to three percentage points, added to the index to produce the note rate.
>
> **Adjustment period** The interval at which the rate may change; one, three, and five years are most common.
>
> **Periodic (rate) cap** Limits the amount the interest rate may increase or decrease in any single adjustment period.
>
> **Lifetime cap** The maximum interest rate increase permitted over the life of the loan.
>
> **Payment cap** Limits the change in the monthly payment amount; can cause negative amortization when the payment cap prevents full interest coverage.
>
> **Negative amortization** Occurs when the monthly payment is insufficient to cover the full interest charge; the unpaid interest is added to the principal balance, causing the balance to grow rather than decline.
>
> **Negative amortization cap** Limits the total amount of unpaid interest that may be added to the principal, typically capped at 125 percent of the original loan amount.

Conventional Loans and Private Mortgage Insurance

Conventional loans are not insured or guaranteed by a government agency; they are the most common type of residential mortgage and are generally considered the most secure. Standard down payment requirements for conventional loans are established by lending guidelines:

- 65 percent loan-to-value (LTV) for land acquisition
- 75 percent LTV for land development
- 80 percent LTV for multi-family and commercial property
- 85 percent LTV for one-to-four family residences

Fixed-Rate Conventional Loans

Most conventional loans are fixed-rate loans with level monthly payments for the life of the loan. The interest rate does not change regardless of market conditions. Fixed-rate loans are offered in a variety of terms, with 30-year and 15-year mortgages being the most common. Biweekly mortgages, in which half the monthly payment is made every two weeks, effectively make 13 monthly payments per year, shortening the loan term and reducing total interest significantly.

Private Mortgage Insurance (PMI)

A borrower who makes a down payment of less than 20 percent on a conventional loan must purchase private mortgage insurance (PMI) to protect the lender against the increased risk. PMI typically insures the top 20 to 30 percent of the loan amount. The lender purchases the policy from a private mortgage insurer and passes the cost to the borrower as an upfront fee at closing plus a monthly premium.

Under the Homeowners Protection Act, PMI on loans originated after July 1999 must be terminated automatically when the borrower's equity reaches 22 percent of the original purchase price or appraised value (an LTV of 78 percent) and the borrower is current on payments. Borrowers may request cancellation when equity reaches 20 percent. Lenders must send borrowers an annual written notice of PMI cancellation rights.

An alternative to PMI is lender-paid mortgage insurance, in which the lender purchases the policy but charges the borrower a slightly higher interest rate (typically about one-half percentage point above market) instead of a separate premium. Because the higher rate is built into the loan, all interest remains tax-deductible, and the rate persists for the life of the loan.

Another common PMI avoidance strategy is 80-10-10 financing: an 80 percent first mortgage, a 10 percent second mortgage, and a 10 percent cash down payment. Because neither loan exceeds 80 percent LTV, PMI is not required. The second mortgage typically carries a higher rate than the first but the combined monthly payment is often less than a single first mortgage with PMI.

Conventional loans have several advantages over government-backed loans: faster processing, fewer forms, no dollar limits on loan amounts, access to multiple lenders if rejected, and greater flexibility in loan structuring. Conventional loans may have higher down payment requirements and may carry prepayment penalties, which government-backed loans generally do not.

Specialty Loan Options

A variety of specialty loan structures are available to borrowers who need alternatives to standard fixed-rate financing:

Graduated payment mortgage (GPM) Monthly payments start low and increase by a fixed percentage each year for a specified number of years before leveling off. Designed for buyers who expect income growth; may produce negative amortization in early years.

Pledged account mortgage (PAM) A type of GPM in which the borrower deposits a lump sum into a pledged account that supplements monthly payments during the first three to five years, reducing the borrower's out-of-pocket payment during that period.

Buydown The seller, builder, or a family member makes a lump sum payment to the lender at closing to temporarily reduce the interest rate on the borrower's loan for the first few years.

Open-end loan An expandable loan up to a stated maximum; each advance is secured by the original mortgage; useful for seasonal operating needs.

Blanket mortgage A single loan covering more than one parcel of property; commonly used by land developers; typically includes a partial release clause allowing individual parcels to be released from the lien as they are sold.

Wraparound mortgage A second lender issues a new larger loan that wraps around the existing first loan; the borrower pays the second lender, who then pays the first lender; requires that the original loan documents permit assumption.

Bridge loan A short-term loan bridging the gap between two financing transactions, such as between the end of a construction loan and the permanent loan, or between a buyer's need for funds and the closing of the sale of a current property.

Purchase money mortgage A seller provides financing to the buyer as part of the purchase transaction; the seller takes back a second mortgage for a portion of the price when the buyer cannot fully qualify for institutional financing.

Construction loan Finances the construction of improvements; disbursements are made in stages as construction progresses; short-term with higher rates than permanent loans; replaced or converted to a permanent loan at completion.

Home equity loan Allows a homeowner to borrow against accumulated equity; may be a fixed amount or a revolving line of credit; commonly used for improvements, debt consolidation, or major expenses.

Package mortgage Includes personal property and appliances installed on the property as part of the collateral; used extensively in furnished condominium sales.

Reverse annuity mortgage (RAM) The lender makes monthly payments to the borrower, allowing older homeowners to access the equity in a paid-off property without selling; the loan and accumulated interest are repaid when the home sells or from the borrower's estate.

Shared equity mortgage The lender shares in the appreciation of the mortgaged property upon sale; the borrower accepts lender participation in future gains in exchange for more favorable loan terms.

Sale-leaseback The property owner sells the property and simultaneously enters into a lease as tenant; frees tied-up capital for business use; should be undertaken only with qualified legal and tax counsel.

Federal Lending Legislation

RESPA and TRID

The Real Estate Settlement Procedures Act (RESPA) requires that parties to covered residential transactions receive accurate information about their closing costs. RESPA is administered by the Consumer Financial Protection Bureau (CFPB). It applies to purchases of residential property (one-to-four family homes, cooperatives, and condominiums) financed by federally-related loans, including FHA and VA loans and loans that will be sold to Fannie Mae, Freddie Mac, or Ginnie Mae. RESPA does not apply to seller-financed loans or to most loan assumptions.

In October 2015, the TILA-RESPA Integrated Disclosure (TRID) Rule replaced the prior HUD-1 settlement statement and Good Faith Estimate with two new forms:

- Loan Estimate: must be provided to the borrower at the time of loan application or within three business days of application; discloses estimated loan terms, projected monthly payments, and closing cost estimates
- Closing Disclosure: must be delivered to the borrower at least three business days before closing; details all financial particulars of the transaction for both buyer and seller

RESPA prohibits kickbacks and unearned referral fees for settlement services including title search, inspection, survey, appraisal, loan origination, credit reporting, and attorney services. Business relationships among real estate firms, mortgage brokers, and title companies are permitted when disclosed in writing, when the consumer is free to use other providers, and when no fees are exchanged solely for referrals.

Truth in Lending Act and Regulation Z

The Truth in Lending Act (TILA), Title I of the Consumer Credit Protection Act, is implemented through Regulation Z. TILA requires lenders to disclose the true cost of credit so borrowers can compare loan offers on an equal basis. Regulation Z applies to all loans secured by a residence. It does not apply to commercial loans or agricultural loans without a principal dwelling.

Key Regulation Z requirements include:

- Disclosure of all finance charges and the annual percentage rate (APR) on the Loan Estimate form
- The right to rescind a transaction within three business days (applies to refinancing and home equity loans, not residential first mortgages)
- Advertising standards: if any financing term is mentioned in an advertisement, all relevant terms including APR must be disclosed

Violations of Regulation Z advertising requirements carry penalties of twice the finance charge or a minimum of $100 to a maximum of $1,000, plus court costs, attorney fees, and actual damages. Willful violation is a criminal misdemeanor punishable by a fine of up to $5,000, one year in prison, or both.

Equal Credit Opportunity Act

The Equal Credit Opportunity Act (ECOA), enforced by the Consumer Financial Protection Bureau and the Federal Trade Commission, prohibits lenders from discriminating against credit applicants on the basis of race, color, religion, national origin, sex, marital status, age, or dependency on public assistance. The law applies to all organizations that regularly extend credit, including banks, credit card companies, and real estate brokers who arrange financing.

When evaluating a credit application, a lender must base the decision on income, net worth, job stability, and credit history. A lender may not discount income because of the applicant's sex or marital status, refuse to consider part-time income, Social Security, pensions, or annuities, or assume that a woman of childbearing age will leave the workforce. If an application is denied, the lender must provide a written explanation within 30 days.

Community Reinvestment Act

The Community Reinvestment Act (CRA), passed in 1977, was designed to prevent redlining and to encourage banks and thrifts to meet the credit needs of all segments of their communities, including low- and moderate-income neighborhoods. Federal financial institution regulators assess each bank's and thrift's CRA performance and consider that record when evaluating applications for charters, mergers, acquisitions, and branch openings. CRA ratings range from outstanding to substantial noncompliance.

Fair Credit Reporting Act

The Fair Credit Reporting Act (FCRA), Title VI of the Consumer Credit Protection Act of 1968, requires lenders to keep credit information confidential, to obtain the consumer's authorization before obtaining a credit report, and to disclose the sources of credit information so consumers can identify and correct errors. The three nationwide credit reporting agencies, Equifax, Experian, and TransUnion, are each required to provide consumers a free copy of their credit report once every 12 months upon request.

Lenders today typically order a tri-merge credit report combining data from all three bureaus. Each bureau may produce a different FICO score. The FICO score, developed by Fair Isaac and Company, ranges from 300 to 900 and is based on payment history (35 percent), amounts owed (30 percent), length of credit history (15 percent), new credit inquiries (10 percent), and credit mix (10 percent). Most lenders use the middle of the three scores, not an average. Many mortgage lenders decline to consider scores below 620.

Home Mortgage Disclosure Act

The Home Mortgage Disclosure Act (HMDA) of 1975 requires qualifying financial institutions to maintain and annually disclose data about home purchase loans, pre-approvals, home improvement loans, and refinance applications for one-to-four unit and multifamily dwellings. The data enables public officials to distribute public-sector investments, evaluate whether financial institutions are serving community housing needs, and identify discriminatory lending patterns. HMDA applies to depository institutions meeting asset and activity thresholds and to for-profit mortgage lending institutions meeting origination volume thresholds.

Computerized Loan Origination

Under RESPA, a real estate firm may offer a computerized loan origination (CLO) system that provides mortgage product information to prospective borrowers, prequalifies borrowers, and initiates loan applications for a fee. Only the borrower may pay the fee. The broker must disclose that competing mortgage products exist that are not part of the CLO system.

Automated underwriting systems, such as Fannie Mae's Desktop Underwriter (DU) and Freddie Mac's Loan Product Advisor (LPA), evaluate borrower and property information electronically and can produce loan approval decisions in a fraction of the time previously required. Loan servicers must provide borrowers with an annual escrow statement summarizing all account activity over the prior 12 months, disclosing any shortfalls or overages and how they will be resolved.

Chapter 8 Snapshot Review

The following review summarizes the key rules and concepts from Chapter 8.

Financing Instruments and Documents

- Texas is a lien-theory state; the borrower retains legal title and the lender holds only a security interest through a deed of trust or mortgage
- Three basic financing instruments in Texas: note and mortgage, note and deed of trust, and land contract
- Promissory note: the foundational document; straight (interest-only) or installment (principal plus interest); straight note is unsecured; real estate notes are always secured
- Mortgage: two-party lien instrument; discharged by satisfaction of mortgage; requires judicial foreclosure
- Deed of trust: three parties (trustor, beneficiary, trustee); trustee holds title; non-judicial power-of-sale foreclosure; discharged by reconveyance; preferred in Texas
- Land contract: seller retains legal title; buyer gets equitable title and possession; subject to Texas Property Code Chapter 5 requirements; attorney and title company strongly recommended

Special Mortgage Clauses

- Late payment penalty: Texas has no statutory restrictions; customary standard is 5 percent after 15 days
- Prepayment penalty: prohibited on Texas homestead loans with interest rates above 12 percent (Texas Finance Code Section 302.102) unless required by a federally-created agency
- Lock-in clause: prohibits early payoff before a specified date; rarely used
- Due-on-sale clause: requires full repayment when property is transferred; also called alienation clause; enforceable nationwide since the Garn-St Germain Act of 1982
- Subject to: buyer takes ownership without personal liability for the existing loan; seller remains primarily responsible; novation is required to fully release the seller
- Subordination clause: reduces an existing lien's priority to accommodate a new higher-priority lien
- Release clause: allows individual parcels to be released from a blanket mortgage upon partial payment
- Exculpatory clause: lender waives the right to a deficiency judgment; limits recourse to the property only

Foreclosure in Texas

- Non-judicial foreclosure is the primary method in Texas; requires a 20-day demand letter, then at least 21 days' further notice filed with the county clerk, mailed to the borrower and other lienholders, and posted at the courthouse
- Foreclosure sales occur on the first Tuesday of each month between 10 a.m. and 4 p.m. at the courthouse
- There is no right of redemption after a non-judicial deed-of-trust foreclosure in Texas
- Two-year redemption right exists for homestead and agricultural property after a tax lien foreclosure; six months for other properties

- Judicial foreclosure: court proceeding; enables deficiency judgment; requires lis pendens, writ of execution, and public sale
- Strict foreclosure: court awards title directly to lender without public sale; rarely used
- Deed in lieu of foreclosure: voluntary transfer to lender; does not extinguish junior liens
- Foreclosure is treated as a sale by the IRS; if the forgiven debt exceeds the borrower's tax basis, a taxable gain may result

Liens

- Four legal features: does not convey ownership (except in title-theory states); attaches to and transfers with the property; multiple liens possible; terminates on payment and recording of a release
- Voluntary vs. involuntary; general vs. specific; superior vs. inferior
- Lien priority: superior liens (real estate taxes, special assessments) always outrank junior liens regardless of recording date; among junior liens, earlier recording date wins
- Mechanic's lien priority dates from when work commenced or ended (as state law determines), not from when it was recorded
- Judgment liens do not attach to Texas homestead property

Loan Programs and PMI

- PMI must be automatically terminated when a borrower's LTV reaches 78 percent (22 percent equity) on loans originated after July 1999; borrowers may request cancellation at 20 percent equity
- Conforming loans meet Fannie Mae and Freddie Mac standards; jumbo loans exceed the FHFA conforming loan limits and are not eligible for GSE purchase
- Secondary mortgage market: Fannie Mae (FNMA), Freddie Mac (FHLMC), and Ginnie Mae (GNMA) purchase, package, and resell loans from the primary market
- ARM components: index (SOFR and Treasury rates are common), margin, periodic rate cap, lifetime cap, payment cap, negative amortization cap

Federal Lending Laws

- TRID requires a Loan Estimate within three business days of application and a Closing Disclosure at least three business days before closing
- RESPA prohibits kickbacks and unearned referral fees for settlement services; affiliated business arrangements permitted with disclosure, consumer freedom, and no fees for mere referrals
- Regulation Z (TILA): disclose APR and all finance charges; right to rescind refinancing and home equity loans within three business days; strict advertising requirements apply to all media
- Regulation Z advertising violations: penalties of twice the finance charge ($100 minimum, $1,000 maximum); willful violation is a criminal misdemeanor
- ECOA: prohibits credit discrimination based on race, color, religion, national origin, sex, marital status, age, or public assistance dependency; written denial reasons required within 30 days
- Community Reinvestment Act: prevents redlining; requires lenders to serve all community credit needs
- Fair Credit Reporting Act: consumer authorization required for credit pulls; consumers entitled to one free annual report from each of Equifax, TransUnion, and Experian; errors must be investigated within 30 days
- HMDA: annual disclosure of mortgage lending data; identifies discriminatory patterns; enables public officials to target public-sector investments

CHAPTER 8 QUIZ:

FINANCING REAL ESTATE

1. Texas follows which legal theory governing who holds title to mortgaged property?
   a. Title theory, meaning the lender holds legal title until the loan is repaid
   b. Lien theory, meaning the borrower retains legal title and the lender holds only a security interest
   c. Intermediate theory, meaning title passes to the lender at origination and returns to the borrower upon full payment
   d. Trust theory, meaning a court-appointed third party holds title until the transaction is fully executed

2. Which federal act passed in 1982 made due-on-sale clauses in loans from federally-chartered institutions enforceable nationwide?
   a. The Equal Credit Opportunity Act
   b. The Community Reinvestment Act
   c. The Real Estate Settlement Procedures Act
   d. The Garn-St Germain Depository Institutions Act

3. In a straight promissory note, how does the borrower repay the principal?
   a. In a single lump sum payment at the maturity date, after making periodic interest-only payments throughout the loan term
   b. In equal monthly installments that include both principal and interest throughout the loan term
   c. In progressively larger installments that increase annually until the loan is fully amortized
   d. In a series of balloon payments due at the end of each calendar year during the loan term

4. A deed of trust involves three parties. Which of the following correctly identifies all three?
   a. Mortgagor, mortgagee, and title company
   b. Vendor, vendee, and escrow agent
   c. Trustor, beneficiary, and trustee
   d. Borrower, lender, and closing attorney

5. A due-on-sale clause in a mortgage document requires the borrower to do which of the following when the property is sold?
   a. Transfer the existing loan to the new buyer without the lender's approval
   b. Obtain the lender's written consent to transfer the property at least 90 days before the scheduled closing
   c. Purchase new title insurance coverage that names the lender as the primary insured on the replacement policy
   d. Pay off the entire remaining loan balance so the property can be conveyed free of the lender's lien

6. Under Texas non-judicial foreclosure procedures, how many days must elapse between the lender's demand letter to the borrower and the start of the formal foreclosure process?
   a. 20 days
   b. 30 days
   c. 45 days
   d. 60 days

7. Under the Homeowners Protection Act, PMI on a conventional loan originated after July 1999 must be automatically terminated when the borrower's equity in the property reaches which threshold?
   a. 15 percent equity, corresponding to an 85 percent loan-to-value ratio
   b. 20 percent equity, corresponding to an 80 percent loan-to-value ratio
   c. 22 percent equity, corresponding to a 78 percent loan-to-value ratio
   d. 25 percent equity, corresponding to a 75 percent loan-to-value ratio

8. Under a seller financing arrangement, which two documents does the seller use to secure the loan made to the buyer?
   a. A general warranty deed and a title insurance policy
   b. A promissory note and a deed of trust
   c. A vendor's lien and a satisfaction of mortgage
   d. A certificate of title and a commitment for title insurance

9. Under the TRID Rule, within how many business days of a borrower's loan application must the lender provide the Loan Estimate?
   a. Three business days
   b. Five business days
   c. Seven business days
   d. Ten business days

10. Which secondary mortgage market entity guarantees mortgage-backed securities that are backed by FHA and VA loans?
   a. Fannie Mae
   b. Freddie Mac
   c. The Federal Housing Finance Agency
   d. Ginnie Mae

11. In an adjustable-rate mortgage, the margin is best described as which of the following?
   a. The maximum interest rate increase permitted over the entire life of the loan
   b. The initial below-market rate offered to attract borrowers at the start of the loan term
   c. The lender's fixed markup, added to the index rate to produce the note rate on the loan
   d. The limit on how much the monthly payment amount may change in any single adjustment period

12. When is the TREC Short Sale Addendum (Form 45-2) attached to a Texas residential sales contract?
   a. Whenever the buyer is purchasing a property through a court-ordered foreclosure proceeding
   b. When the seller's net proceeds at closing will be insufficient to pay off the existing mortgage balance and the seller requires the lienholder's consent to sell
   c. When the buyer intends to assume the seller's existing mortgage loan rather than obtaining new financing
   d. Whenever the property is being sold at a price below the county appraisal district's assessed value

13. Under a land contract, which party retains legal title during the contract period?
   a. The buyer, who holds both legal and equitable title from the moment of possession
   b. A neutral trustee appointed by both the buyer and seller at the time of closing
   c. The buyer's title insurance company, which holds title in escrow until all payments are complete
   d. The seller, while the buyer holds only equitable title and possesses the property

14. The Equal Credit Opportunity Act (ECOA) prohibits a lender from denying credit to an applicant on the basis of which of the following?
   a. Race, color, religion, national origin, sex, marital status, age, or dependency on public assistance
   b. Insufficient income, unstable employment history, or an outstanding judgment lien on a prior property
   c. A prior foreclosure, short sale, or bankruptcy within the past seven years
   d. A credit score below the lender's minimum threshold as established by its underwriting guidelines

15. Which of the following is a feature that distinguishes judicial foreclosure from non-judicial foreclosure?
   a. Judicial foreclosure is faster than non-judicial foreclosure and is therefore preferred by most Texas lenders
   b. Judicial foreclosure is used only when the borrower has already vacated the property before the foreclosure sale
   c. Judicial foreclosure allows the lender to obtain a deficiency judgment against the borrower for any balance remaining after the sale
   d. Judicial foreclosure extinguishes all existing liens on the property, including those that are senior to the foreclosing lender's lien

16. Under the Truth in Lending Act and Regulation Z, a borrower has the right to rescind a transaction within three business days of closing. To which type of transaction does this rescission right apply?
   a. The original purchase of a primary residence financed with a conventional first mortgage
   b. The refinancing of an existing mortgage or the taking out of a home equity loan on a primary residence
   c. Any VA-guaranteed loan used to purchase a primary residence
   d. Any purchase money mortgage that requires the buyer to pay private mortgage insurance

17. On which day of the week and at which location do non-judicial foreclosure sales in Texas take place?
   a. On the third Monday of each month at the county tax office
   b. On any business day chosen by the trustee, provided at least 21 days' notice has been given
   c. On the last Friday of each month at the address of the foreclosing lender
   d. On the first Tuesday of each month at the courthouse, between 10 a.m. and 4 p.m.

18. RESPA specifically prohibits paying or receiving fees in connection with which of the following settlement services?
   a. Title search, inspection, survey, appraisal, loan origination, credit reporting, and attorney services, when no service has actually been rendered
   b. Only title insurance services, because the Texas Department of Insurance regulates rates and prohibits unearned premiums
   c. Only broker compensation, because TREC rules forbid any form of referral fee between cooperating brokers
   d. Any service where the fee exceeds the amount customarily charged in the local market for that type of service

19. How is the priority of a mechanic's lien determined, compared with other junior liens recorded against the same property?
   a. The mechanic's lien always ranks last among all junior liens regardless of the date work commenced
   b. The mechanic's lien priority is determined by the date the lien was recorded with the county clerk
   c. The mechanic's lien priority dates from when work commenced or ended under state law, not from the date it was recorded
   d. The mechanic's lien always outranks all other liens, including a recorded first mortgage, regardless of the order of recording

20. In a judicial foreclosure, which legal instrument authorizes the sheriff to seize and sell the foreclosed property after the borrower fails to meet court demands?
   a. A lis pendens
   b. A writ of execution
   c. A trustee's deed
   d. A deed in lieu of foreclosure

21. A subordination clause in a real estate loan document is used to accomplish which of the following?
   a. Reduce the priority of an existing lien to a position behind a new lien that will be recorded in the future
   b. Release individual parcels from a blanket mortgage as they are sold by the developer
   c. Prevent the borrower from paying off the entire mortgage balance before a specified date
   d. Waive the lender's right to pursue a deficiency judgment against the borrower after foreclosure

22. When the IRS treats a foreclosure as a sale, which of the following may result in a taxable gain for the borrower?
   a. When the property sells at the foreclosure auction for less than its current fair market value
   b. When the lender forgives the remaining balance but files a deficiency judgment the following year
   c. When the borrower surrenders the property through a deed in lieu of foreclosure rather than a public auction
   d. When the amount of the forgiven debt exceeds the borrower's tax basis in the property

23. Conventional loans that meet the underwriting standards and loan limits set by Fannie Mae and Freddie Mac are called conforming loans. What are loans that exceed those limits called?
    a. Non-qualifying loans
    b. Jumbo loans
    c. Portfolio loans
    d. Super conforming loans

24. The FHA 203(k) loan differs from the more common FHA 203(b) loan in which of the following ways?
    a. The FHA 203(k) loan requires a higher down payment because it is used for investment properties rather than owner-occupied homes
    b. The FHA 203(k) loan is only available to first-time homebuyers who have never previously used FHA financing
    c. The FHA 203(k) loan combines home purchase financing with rehabilitation financing in a single loan, while the FHA 203(b) is a standard purchase loan
    d. The FHA 203(k) loan is insured by a private mortgage insurer rather than the Federal Housing Administration

25. The Community Reinvestment Act was enacted to address which practice in mortgage lending?
    a. Steering minority borrowers toward higher-rate loan products to maximize lender profit
    b. Charging excessive origination fees on government-backed loans in low-income markets
    c. Requiring excessive documentation from applicants whose income is derived from Social Security or disability payments
    d. Redlining, in which lenders refused to make loans in certain neighborhoods based on the racial or economic composition of those areas

26. A borrower chooses a biweekly mortgage instead of a standard monthly mortgage. What is the primary benefit of the biweekly payment structure?
    a. The monthly payment amount is reduced by approximately one-half because payments are made more frequently
    b. The borrower effectively makes 13 monthly payments per year, which shortens the loan term and reduces total interest paid
    c. The interest rate is locked at a fixed level and cannot adjust regardless of market conditions during the loan term
    d. The borrower is protected from prepayment penalties because the accelerated payment schedule satisfies the note ahead of schedule

27. A land developer uses a blanket mortgage to finance the acquisition of a tract that will be subdivided into individual lots for sale. Which clause in the blanket mortgage allows the lender to release each lot from the lien as the developer sells it?
    a. The subordination clause
    b. The exculpatory clause
    c. The release clause, also called the partial release clause
    d. The lock-in clause

28. The FICO credit score model gives the greatest weight to which factor when calculating a borrower's score?
    a. Payment history, which accounts for 35 percent of the score
    b. Length of credit history, which accounts for 30 percent of the score
    c. New credit inquiries, which account for 25 percent of the score
    d. Credit mix, which accounts for 20 percent of the score

29. In an 80-10-10 financing arrangement, how does a buyer avoid paying private mortgage insurance?
    a. The buyer qualifies for a government-backed loan that is exempt from PMI requirements by statute
    b. The seller agrees to carry a note for the full 20 percent second mortgage, satisfying the lender's equity requirement
    c. The lender waives the PMI requirement in exchange for a higher origination fee paid at closing
    d. Neither the first mortgage nor the second mortgage exceeds an 80 percent loan-to-value ratio, so PMI is not triggered on either loan

Chapter 8 Case Study:

Financing Real Estate

The Situation

Dan and Carol Mettling are purchasing a home in Austin for $620,000. They are putting 10 percent down and financing the remaining $558,000 through Performance Lending Programs, a conventional mortgage lender. Because their down payment is less than 20 percent, their lender requires private mortgage insurance. Their loan officer, Rita Voss, quoted them an interest rate and explained that the rate would be fixed for the first five years and then adjust annually based on a market index plus the lender's margin. Rita told the Mettlings the initial rate was low enough that they would easily qualify and that they should not worry about future adjustments.

Six months before the Mettlings close on their new home, they learn that the seller of the property, Warren Oakes, is a foreign national who has been living outside the United States for the past three years. Warren has not filed U.S. income tax returns during that period. The Mettlings' agent, Cheryl Webb, tells them not to worry about it because the title company will handle any tax issues at closing.

During the loan application process, Rita pulls a tri-merge credit report on Dan Mettling and finds that one of the three bureaus shows a collection account for $1,400 that Dan does not recognize. Dan disputes the account as an error but Rita tells him the lender will simply use the middle score of the three, which is acceptable, and that he does not need to bother with a formal dispute. The closing occurs without the error being corrected. Two years later Dan applies for a home equity loan and the same erroneous collection account, now listed as unresolved, causes his application to be denied.

Discussion Questions

Question 1

Rita Voss told the Mettlings their adjustable-rate mortgage was nothing to worry about. Identify the key ARM components the Mettlings should have been told about before accepting the loan, and explain the specific risk that neither Rita nor the Mettlings addressed by focusing only on the initial rate.

____

____

____

____

____

Question 2

The seller, Warren Oakes, is a foreign national with no recent U.S. tax filings. Cheryl Webb told the Mettlings the title company would handle any tax issues at closing. Evaluate whether Cheryl's response was adequate, identify the federal law that applies to this situation, and explain what the Mettlings were actually required to do as the buyers.

____

____

____

____

____

Question 3

Dan Mettling discovered an erroneous collection account on one of his three credit bureau reports. Rita Voss told him not to bother with a formal dispute because the lender uses the middle score. Evaluate Rita's advice, identify the federal law that governs credit report errors, explain what steps Dan was entitled to take, and describe the consequences of leaving the error unresolved.

CHAPTER 9:

CONVEYANCE OF TITLE

Chapter Overview

Learning Objectives

Upon completing Chapter 9, the student will be able to:

1. Explain voluntary alienation, describe the essential elements of a valid deed in Texas, and distinguish among the major deed types and their levels of protection for the grantee.
2. Identify the primary methods of involuntary alienation, including adverse possession, estoppel, and escheat, and explain how property owners can protect themselves from each.
3. Distinguish between legal and equitable title, describe the transfer of a decedent's property by will, and explain both testate and intestate proceedings including the probate process.
4. Explain the purpose of public recording in Texas, describe constructive and actual notice, and distinguish the Torrens system from standard recording systems.
5. Define marketable title, explain the chain of title, and describe the two primary forms of title evidence including title search, abstract and opinion, and title insurance.

Contents

Title and Voluntary Alienation

When a buyer purchases real property, the buyer acquires an interest in that property along with all of the rights attached to it. When an owner sells property, the owner transfers those ownership rights, collectively called title, to the new owner. This transfer of title is called alienation. When the transfer is accomplished through a written instrument, it is called a conveyance.

Voluntary alienation is an unforced transfer of title by sale or gift from an owner to another party. When a government entity transfers property to a private party, the conveyance is a public grant. When a private party transfers property to another private party, the conveyance is a private grant. A living owner makes a private grant by executing a deed. A private grant that takes effect at the owner's death is a transfer by will.

Deeds

A deed is the legal instrument used by an owner to voluntarily transfer title to real property to another party. The person transferring title is the grantor. The person receiving title is the grantee. To be effective, a deed must satisfy specific legal requirements, but recording is not required to make a deed valid between the parties. Recording is, however, essential to protect the grantee's interest against future claims by third parties, because it gives the public constructive notice of the grantee's ownership.

Essential Elements of a Valid Deed in Texas

In Texas, the minimum requirements for a valid deed are:

- Properly identifies the grantor and grantee
- Includes consideration (something of value exchanged)
- Contains a sufficient and identifiable legal description of the property
- Contains words of conveyance (granting language)
- Is signed by a competent grantor or an authorized representative
- Is delivered to a legitimate grantee and accepted

More complete deeds include additional elements such as the habendum clause (defining the extent of the estate conveyed), designation of limitations, exemptions and reservations affecting the title, acknowledgment before a notary, and recording in the county clerk's office.

Types of Deeds

General Warranty Deed

A general warranty deed, also called a full covenant and warranty deed, is the most widely used deed in real estate transfers and offers the greatest protection of any deed type. The grantor warrants the title against all claims, whether they arose before or during the grantor's period of ownership. The overall covenant is: I own and I will defend.

A general warranty deed typically carries five covenants:

> **Covenant of seisin** Assures that the grantor actually owns the estate being conveyed and has the legal right to convey it.

Covenant against encumbrances Assures that no encumbrances exist on the property other than those specifically named in the deed.

Covenant of quiet enjoyment Assures that the grantee will not be disturbed by third-party title disputes.

Covenant of further assurance Assures that the grantor will take whatever additional steps are needed to correct any title problems discovered after the transfer.

Covenant of warranty forever Assures that the grantee will receive good title and that the grantor will defend any future claims to the contrary.

In Texas, warranty covenants are largely implied by statute through the use of the granting language grant, bargain, and sell. The two warranties actually recognized in Texas are the covenant of seisin and the covenant against encumbrances.

Special Warranty Deed

A special warranty deed warrants the title only against defects or encumbrances that arose during the grantor's period of ownership or trusteeship. It does not protect the grantee against claims that predate the grantor's ownership. The overall covenant is: I own and will defend against my acts only. Special warranty deeds are commonly used by trustees, corporate grantors, and parties who acquired the property through a tax sale.

Bargain and Sale Deed

A bargain and sale deed without covenants implies that the grantor holds title but makes no warranty against encumbrances and offers no promise to defend against third-party claims. The overall covenant is: I own, but will not defend. This form is frequently used in foreclosure and tax sales.

Quitclaim Deed

A quitclaim deed conveys whatever interest, if any, the grantor may hold in the property, without any warranty of ownership. The grantor makes no claim to any interest and offers no protection to the grantee. The overall covenant is: I may or may not own, and I will not defend.

Quitclaim deeds are commonly used to clear title rather than convey it. Where prior recording errors or other instruments have clouded the title, the relevant parties execute a quitclaim deed conveying any and all interest to the grantee. They are also used for transfers within families and in divorce settlements. If a party responsible for an encumbrance refuses to execute a quitclaim, the property owner may file a quiet title suit, requiring the encumbering party to prove the validity of the interest. If the party cannot, the court removes the cloud by decree.

A subdivision developer who conveys subdivision roads or common areas to a local government does so through dedication by deed, which typically uses a quitclaim deed form.

Special Purpose Deeds

Special purpose deeds are tailored to particular parties, properties, or circumstances. The most common types are:

Personal representative's deed (executor's deed) Used by an executor or executrix to convey property from a decedent's estate.

Referee's deed Used in bankruptcies and foreclosures to convey property under court supervision.

Guardian's deed Used by a court-appointed guardian to transfer property owned by a minor or mentally incompetent person.

Sheriff's deed Used to convey foreclosed property that has been sold at a public auction.

Deed of trust Used to convey property to a third-party trustee as collateral for a loan; when the loan is satisfied, the trustee uses a reconveyance deed to return title to the borrower.

Deed in trust Used to convey property to the trustee of a land trust; not to be confused with a deed of trust.

Master deed Used by a condominium developer to convey land and establish the condominium; recorded together with the condominium declaration.

Partition deed Used to convey co-owned property in compliance with a court order when co-owners cannot agree to dissolve their co-ownership relationship voluntarily.

Land patent deed Used to transfer government property to a private party in what is called a public grant.

Tax deed Used to convey property sold at a tax sale.

Involuntary Alienation

Involuntary alienation is a transfer of title to real property without the owner's consent. It occurs through several legal mechanisms:

- Laws of descent and distribution: when a title holder dies without a valid will, the state's laws of descent identify heirs and their respective shares
- Escheat: when a property owner dies without heirs, or property is abandoned for a statutory period, title transfers to the state
- Foreclosure: when a property owner fails to meet loan obligations or pay taxes, the estate may be lost through a foreclosure proceeding
- Eminent domain: government entities may take private property for public use, with compensation paid to the owner; the transfer is involuntary even though the owner receives payment
- Adverse possession: state law may allow a person who has occupied and used another's property openly and continuously for a statutory period to claim legal title
- Estoppel: a prior conveyance or prior conduct may prevent an owner from reclaiming a property

Adverse Possession

Adverse possession is the process by which a person who enters, occupies, and uses another's property without the owner's consent, or with the knowledge of an owner who fails to act over a statutory period, may obtain legal title to the property. To succeed in a claim of adverse possession, the possessor must meet all of the following criteria:

- Claim of right or color of title: the possessor must occupy and maintain the property as if the legal owner, or must hold a colorable but defective instrument of ownership
- Notorious possession: the possession must be open and unconcealed so that the public, including the legal owner, has constructive notice of it

- Hostile possession: the possessor must consistently assert ownership without the owner's permission
- Continuous occupation for the full statutory period
- In some states, payment of taxes over the required period

Satisfying these criteria does not automatically transfer title. The adverse possessor must bring a legal action to quiet title in order to receive a court judgment establishing ownership. If the possessor has paid rent of any kind to the owner during the period, the claim of adverse possession may be defeated because rent payments are inconsistent with a claim of ownership.

A property owner can prevent the risk of adverse possession by periodically inspecting the property within the statutory deadlines and evicting any trespassers found, or by filing a suit to quiet title to extinguish any adverse claim that may be developing.

Estoppel

Estoppel prevents a party from asserting a right or interest that is inconsistent with the party's prior statements or actions. In real estate, estoppel can operate as a basis for involuntary alienation by preventing an owner from reclaiming property that was transferred under false pretenses.

A classic example: a grantor conveys property while fully aware of a title defect but discloses nothing to the grantee. The grantor later cures the defect at personal expense and then claims to be the rightful owner on the basis of having cleared the title. Estoppel bars the grantor's new claim because of the prior act of conveyance. The grantee remains the legal owner and benefits from the cleared title as well.

Estoppel can also arise in landlord-tenant relationships. If a landlord informs a tenant that rent is reduced because of a construction disruption or a utility outage, and the tenant reasonably relies on that statement in deciding to remain on the premises, the landlord may be estopped from collecting the original full rent for that period.

Escheat

Escheat is an involuntary alienation doctrine that transfers the property of a person who dies intestate and without heirs to the state. It ensures that property is not left without a recognized owner. The term applies specifically when a person dies without a will and is not survived by any heir recognized under the applicable intestacy statute. When those circumstances are present, the entire estate escheats to the state after all claims and debts are settled.

In some jurisdictions, escheat also applies to dormant financial accounts held by banks or other institutions. If an account shows no activity for a statutory period and the owner cannot be located, the funds may escheat to the state. Similarly, property that has been physically abandoned for a statutory period may escheat.

Legal and Equitable Title

Legal title refers to the complete bundle of ownership rights in a property, including the right of possession. A party who holds all ownership interests holds legal title. Equitable title is a different, more limited interest: it is the right or enforceable expectation to obtain legal title in accordance with a contract between the legal owner and a buyer or creditor.

During the contractual period before a sale is completed, the buyer holds equitable title while the seller retains legal title. This distinction is most clearly illustrated in a contract for deed transaction. The seller lends the buyer most of the purchase price and retains legal title until the final payment is made. The buyer takes possession of the property and makes payments throughout the contract term. During that entire period, the seller holds legal title and the buyer holds equitable title. When the buyer fulfills all contract obligations, the buyer has an enforceable right to receive the deed conveying legal title.

A similar principle applies in mortgage lending. The lender's contractual right to execute a strict foreclosure and thereby obtain legal title in the event of default gives the lender equitable title to the property during the loan term. In everyday practice, the terms title and legal title are often used interchangeably.

Transfer of a Decedent's Property

A will, more formally a last will and testament, is the legal instrument through which a property owner voluntarily directs the transfer of real and personal property after death. The person who creates the will is the testator or testatrix. The people or entities receiving property under the will are beneficiaries, also called heirs or devisees. The property transferred by will is called the devise.

A will takes effect only at the testator's death and may be amended at any time during the testator's lifetime. A common amendment is called a codicil. The testator typically names an executor or executrix to administer the estate and carry out the will's instructions. If the estate involves minor heirs, the testator may also designate a guardian to handle legal affairs on the minor's behalf.

Forms of Wills

Witnessed will A written will signed in the presence of at least two competent witnesses who also sign to attest to the signature and the testator's capacity.

Holographic will A will written entirely in the testator's own handwriting, dated, and signed; recognized in Texas without witnesses.

Approved will A will prepared on a pre-printed form that meets the requirements of state law.

Nuncupative will An oral will dictated to a witness; generally not valid for the transfer of real property.

Validity of a Will and Probate

Texas law establishes the requirements for a valid will. Generally, the testator must be of legal age, be mentally competent, and must expressly state that the document is the last will and testament. The will must be signed in the presence of two witnesses who are at least 14 years of age and who are willing to be named as witnesses. The witnesses must sign the will, and the entire process must be completed voluntarily without duress or undue influence.

After the testator's death, a court proceeding called probate settles the decedent's estate whether the person died with or without a valid will. Real property is exempt from probate if it is held in a land trust. Probate of real property is conducted by courts in the state where the property is physically located, regardless of where the deceased resided. The probate court validates the will if one exists, identifies and settles all claims and outstanding debts of the estate, and distributes the remaining assets to the rightful heirs. If the will does not name an executor, the court appoints an administrator to fulfill that role.

Testate and Intestate Proceedings

Testate Proceeding

When a person dies with a valid will, the person is said to have died testate. The probate court hears and evaluates claims from lienors and creditors. Superior liens are satisfied first: these include real estate taxes, assessment taxes, federal estate taxes, and state inheritance taxes. If the liquid assets of the estate are insufficient to cover all obligations, the court may order the sale of personal or real property to generate the needed funds.

The court must also recognize and satisfy legal life estate claims, including those for homestead, dower, curtesy, and elective share. These statutory interests may prevail even if the will does not provide for them. Once all obligations are satisfied, the balance of the estate passes to the named heirs free and clear.

Intestate Proceeding

When a person dies without a valid will, the person is said to have died intestate. The estate passes to the lawful heirs according to the state's laws of descent and distribution, also called succession. These laws stipulate who inherits and in what proportions, without regard to the wishes of the heirs or the presumed intentions of the deceased. The typical order of descent is the surviving spouse first, followed by children, then parents, then siblings, and then more distant relatives.

Texas distinguishes between separate property and community property in its laws of descent and distribution, applying different rules to each. Separate property generally descends first to the surviving spouse and then to children. Community property passes according to different statutory formulas depending on whether there are children from outside the marriage.

If an intestate decedent has no recognized heirs, the estate escheats to the state or county after all claims and debts have been validated and paid.

Public Records and Recording

Texas law requires public officials to maintain land records in county clerk offices, land offices, offices of county surveyors, assessors, and other courts of record. These records include deeds, mortgages, most leases, and other documents that affect title to or interests in real property. The Statute of Frauds requires that such documents be in writing to be enforceable, and recording statutes require that they be filed in the public record.

The act of recording provides legal, public, and constructive knowledge to everyone about the ownership of a property. Texas law provides that unless the documents relating to a property have been recorded, a deed or mortgage is not fully effective against subsequent purchasers or creditors who lack actual knowledge of the prior transaction. A prospective buyer who searches the public record should be able to rely on what that search discloses about the property's title condition.

Recording Acts in Texas

All documents relating to any interest in land in Texas must be recorded in the office of the county clerk in the county where the property is located. To be eligible for recording, a document must be prepared and executed in accordance with the state's recording statutes.

Under Texas Property Code Section 12.001(b), an instrument conveying real property may not be recorded unless it is signed and acknowledged before two or more credible subscribing witnesses or acknowledged before an authorized notarial officer. The law further provides that a paper document concerning real or personal property may not be recorded unless it contains an original signature that is acknowledged, sworn to with a proper jurat, or proved according to law, or unless it is attached as an exhibit to a paper affidavit that meets those requirements. Original signatures are not required for documents electronically submitted for recording.

Constructive and Actual Notice

Recording a deed gives the grantee protection against any future title claims that are not yet recorded in the public record. This protection is provided through the mechanism of constructive notice.

Constructive notice, also called legal notice, is knowledge of a fact that a person could have or should have obtained through the exercise of reasonable diligence. The primary method of imparting constructive notice in real estate is recording ownership documents in the public title records. Because public records are open to everyone, the law presumes that when evidence of ownership is properly recorded, the public at large has received constructive notice of that ownership. The law also presumes that the owner of record is the legal owner.

Actual notice is direct, personal knowledge of something learned through direct experience or communication. A party receives actual notice of ownership by reviewing the deed directly, reading title records in person, or visiting the property to observe who is in physical possession of it. Actual possession of a property gives others in the chain constructive notice even if no deed has been recorded, because inspection of the property would reveal the occupant.

The Torrens System

A small number of states and jurisdictions use the Torrens System of title registration as an alternative to the standard recording system. The Torrens system differs fundamentally from the standard system in that the title certificate itself is the title. Title passes only when the conveyance has been registered directly on the Torrens certificate, and encumbrances have no legal effect until they appear on the certificate. There is no need to search the broader public record to determine the state of the title; the certificate shows everything.

To bring a property into the Torrens system, the owner must initiate a court action that gives notice to all potential interest holders, requiring them to assert any claims they may have. At the conclusion of the proceeding, the court decrees that the title is accepted into Torrens registration. Subsequent transactions must follow specific Torrens recording procedures.

Approximately ten states have adopted the Torrens system, including Minnesota, Massachusetts, Colorado, Georgia, Hawaii, New York, North Carolina, Ohio, and Washington. Torrens-registered property is not subject to general judgment liens and cannot be lost through adverse possession.

Proof of Ownership and Marketable Title

A seller is required to deliver marketable title at closing. A marketable title is one so free of defects that the buyer can be confident the title will not need to be defended against valid claims by third parties. To deliver marketable title, the seller must have and provide evidence of ownership of the property.

Chain of title refers to the succession of property owners of record from the original grant of title from the state to a private party through every subsequent transfer to the present day. If there is a break in the chronology of owners, a defective conveyance, or an undisclosed encumbrance, the chain is said to be broken or the title clouded. An owner whose title is clouded may need to file a quiet title suit, a legal proceeding that clears the title records of unrecorded or questionable claims so that the owner can demonstrate clear title to future purchasers and lenders.

Title Search

Before a lender agrees to finance a purchase, the lender orders a title search on the subject property. The title search examines public records to reveal three things: the legal description of the property, the current owners of record, and any outstanding liens or encumbrances on the property.

A lien is an indication of debt secured by the property. Common examples include outstanding property tax bills, mortgage loans, and court-ordered money judgments. An encumbrance indicates that some other party has a right, claim, or interest in the property short of ownership. Examples include utility rights-of-way, fence or structure encroachments from neighboring properties, and driveway easements crossing the property.

A title search alone does not reveal all possible defects. Items such as encroachments, forgeries, undisclosed heirs, or errors that never made it into the public record will not appear in a standard search. This is one reason title insurance exists: to protect against defects that a reasonable search would not disclose.

Abstract and Opinion

An abstract of title is a chronological summary of all recorded documents that affect the title to a specific property, beginning with the original grant of title and continuing through every subsequent deed, mortgage, court judgment, lien, easement, and other instrument. The person who prepares the abstract is called an abstractor. The abstractor searches documents registered with the county recorder, county registrar, circuit court, and other official sources, summarizes the findings, and arranges them in chronological order.

Historically, sellers passed the abstract to buyers before closing, adding entries for any transactions that occurred during the seller's period of ownership. The buyer would have an attorney review the abstract and provide an opinion. That opinion could be informal or a formal written opinion of title, in which the attorney accepted personal liability for any loss arising from a matter overlooked in the abstract.

In today's transactions, an abstract prepared by a private abstractor is not considered an official document. The abstractor is responsible only for accurately summarizing what appears in the public record and cannot be held liable for defects that do not appear there. Even an attorney who issues a formal opinion on an abstract does not insure the title or guarantee against defects outside the record. Because of these limitations, title insurance has largely replaced the abstract and opinion as the preferred form of title evidence in Texas and most of the country.

Title Insurance

A title insurance policy is the most widely accepted evidence of marketable title. It combines the abstracting process with an insurance program, guaranteeing the validity and accuracy of the title search and protecting the insured against financial loss arising from defects in the title, undiscovered liens, or encumbrances on the property. The title company also agrees to defend the insured's title in court against any lawsuits arising from defects covered by the policy.

Title insurance protects against hidden defects that a reasonable public record search would not reveal, including:

- Forged documents such as deeds or mortgages
- Undisclosed heirs with claims to the property
- Incorrect interpretation of a prior will
- Misfiled or improperly indexed documents
- Confusion arising from similarity of names
- Incorrectly stated marital status in prior documents
- Conveyances made by mentally incompetent grantors

The title company's underwriting process includes examining all records pertaining to the property's recorded history, reviewing risks that may not appear in the public record, interpreting the legality of the records, assisting the property owner in correcting any defects found, and insuring the property against economic loss from covered claims.

If the title search does not disclose any uninsurable defects, the company issues a title commitment, also called a binder, which recapitulates the property description, the interest to be insured, the names of the insured parties, and any exceptions to coverage. Unlike most insurance, title insurance is a one-time premium paid at closing. The policy remains in effect until the property is transferred again.

Title Insurance in Texas

In Texas, both the buyer and the lender should carry title insurance. The buyer's policy protects the investment against claims that challenge ownership. The lender's policy protects the lender's security interest in the property. The Texas Department of Insurance regulates title insurance rates in Texas; rates are set by the state and are the same regardless of which title company issues the policy.

Loan Policies

Most lending institutions require the buyer to purchase a loan policy as a condition of financing. This policy protects the lender up to the outstanding principal balance of the loan if a title claim voids the lender's security interest. A loan policy remains in effect until the loan is repaid. If the owner refinances the property, most lenders require a new loan policy because the old policy expires when the loan it protected is paid off by the new loan.

Owner Policies

An owner policy protects the property owner against covered title claims for as long as the owner or the owner's heirs own the property or remain liable under any title warranties made when the property is sold. Coverage is for the value of the property at the time the policy is purchased. It does not automatically cover increases in value after the purchase unless the owner separately purchases an increased-value endorsement.

In Texas, when a buyer purchases a property and the lender requires a loan policy, the title company will automatically issue an owner policy as well unless the owner specifically rejects it in writing. A property owner should retain the owner policy permanently, even after selling the property, because it protects against claims related to the period of ownership.

What Title Insurance Covers

If a third party asserts a claim against an insured owner's title, the title company will defend the title in court and pay any actual loss up to the policy limits for covered claims. Circumstances triggering coverage include:

- A prior owner's failure to pay a mortgage, a court judgment, property taxes, special assessments, or homeowners association fees
- A lien for contractor labor and materials provided to a previous owner without the current owner's consent
- Other liens or title claims not listed as exceptions in the policy
- Undisclosed leases, contracts, or options on the property that were not recorded and not disclosed to the current owner
- Undisclosed restrictions on the use of the property
- Easements not appearing in the public record
- Missing or defective signatures in the chain of title
- Documents in the chain of title that are invalid because of forgery, fraud, or other legally recognized causes

Chapter 9 Snapshot Review

The following review summarizes the key rules and concepts from Chapter 9.

Voluntary Alienation and Deeds

- Voluntary alienation is the unforced transfer of title by sale or gift; when accomplished through a written instrument it is a conveyance
- A deed is the primary instrument of voluntary alienation during the grantor's lifetime; a will is used at death
- Texas minimum requirements for a valid deed: identifies the parties, states consideration, contains a sufficient legal description, contains words of conveyance, is signed by a competent grantor, and is delivered to and accepted by the grantee
- Recording is not required for validity between the parties but is essential to protect the grantee against subsequent third-party claims
- General warranty deed: grantor warrants title against all claims past and present; greatest grantee protection; Texas covenants are implied by the granting language grant, bargain, and sell
- Texas recognizes two warranty covenants: covenant of seisin and covenant against encumbrances
- Special warranty deed: grantor warrants only against claims arising during the grantor's period of ownership; used by trustees and parties acquiring through tax sales
- Bargain and sale deed without covenants: implies ownership but makes no warranty; common in foreclosure and tax sales
- Quitclaim deed: conveys whatever interest the grantor may hold with no warranty; used to clear title, for family transfers, and in divorce settlements
- If a party refuses to execute a quitclaim, the owner may file a quiet title suit requiring the encumbering party to prove the validity of the interest

Involuntary Alienation

- Involuntary alienation transfers title without the owner's consent through six primary mechanisms: laws of descent and distribution, escheat, foreclosure, eminent domain, adverse possession, and estoppel
- Adverse possession requirements: open and notorious possession, hostile claim of ownership, continuous occupation for the statutory period, and a claim of right or color of title; some states also require payment of taxes
- Meeting adverse possession requirements does not automatically transfer title; the possessor must file a quiet title action to obtain a court judgment
- Payment of rent to the owner during the possession period defeats an adverse possession claim
- Owner prevention: periodically inspect the property within statutory deadlines, promptly evict trespassers, or file a quiet title suit
- Estoppel prevents a party from asserting rights inconsistent with prior conduct; protects a grantee when a grantor conveyed with a defective title, later cured the defect, and then tried to reclaim the property
- Escheat transfers property to the state when an owner dies intestate with no heirs, or when property is abandoned for a statutory period

Legal and Equitable Title

- Legal title is the complete bundle of ownership rights including the right of possession
- Equitable title is the enforceable right to obtain legal title under a contract
- In a contract for deed: seller holds legal title, buyer holds equitable title during the contract period; legal title transfers at final payment
- In a mortgage transaction: the lender's contractual right to foreclose gives the lender equitable title during the loan period

Wills and Probate

- A will is a legal instrument for the voluntary transfer of property after death; it takes effect only at the testator's death and may be amended at any time during the maker's lifetime
- Texas requires the testator to be of legal age, mentally competent, and to sign in the presence of two witnesses who are at least 14 years of age
- A holographic will in Texas does not require witnesses if it is entirely in the testator's own handwriting, dated, and signed
- A nuncupative (oral) will is generally not valid for the transfer of real property
- Probate validates the will, settles all claims and debts, and distributes the remaining estate to the heirs
- Real property held in a land trust is exempt from probate; probate is administered in the state where the property is located
- Superior liens paid first in probate: real estate taxes, assessment taxes, federal estate taxes, and state inheritance taxes; homestead and other legal life estate claims may prevail even if not addressed in the will
- Intestate with heirs: estate passes under laws of descent and distribution; Texas applies different rules to separate property and community property
- Intestate without heirs: estate escheats to the state after all claims and debts are settled

Public Records, Recording, and Notice

- All documents affecting real property interests in Texas must be recorded in the county clerk's office in the county where the property is located
- To be eligible for recording: document must be signed and acknowledged before a notary or two credible subscribing witnesses; original signatures are not required for electronically submitted documents
- Recording gives constructive (legal) notice to the world; the law presumes the recorded owner is the legal owner
- Actual notice is direct personal knowledge gained through direct experience or communication such as reviewing the deed, reading title records, or visiting the property
- Actual physical possession of a property provides constructive notice to others even without a recorded deed
- The Torrens system treats the title certificate itself as the title; title passes only when the conveyance is registered on the certificate; Texas does not use the Torrens system
- Torrens-registered property is not subject to general judgment liens and cannot be lost through adverse possession

Marketable Title and Title Evidence

- Marketable title is one so free of defects that the buyer is certain of not having to defend it against valid third-party claims; sellers must deliver marketable title at closing
- Chain of title is the chronological succession of recorded owners from the original government grant to the present day; a break in the chain or defective conveyance produces a clouded title
- A quiet title suit clears the title records of unrecorded or questionable claims
- A title search reveals the legal description, the owners of record, and all outstanding liens and encumbrances; it does not reveal defects outside the public record such as forgeries, undisclosed heirs, or encroachments
- An abstract of title is a chronological summary of all recorded documents affecting the property; an attorney's opinion evaluates the abstract but does not insure against undiscovered defects
- Title insurance is the most widely accepted form of title evidence; the title company issues a commitment listing the property, insured parties, and policy exceptions before issuing the policy
- Loan policy: protects the lender up to the outstanding loan balance; expires when the loan is repaid; a new policy is required on refinance
- Owner policy: protects the buyer at the purchase price at the time of issuance; remains in force as long as the owner or heirs hold the property or are liable under title warranties; does not cover increases in value unless an endorsement is purchased
- In Texas, title insurance rates are set by the Texas Department of Insurance and are the same from all title companies; when a lender requires a loan policy, the title company automatically issues an owner policy as well unless the owner rejects it in writing

CHAPTER 9 QUIZ:
CONVEYANCE OF TITLE

1. A general warranty deed is considered the most protective deed type. Which of the following best describes the overall covenant made by the grantor in a general warranty deed?
    a. The grantor warrants title only against claims that arose during the grantor's own period of ownership
    b. The grantor conveys whatever interest the grantor holds but makes no warranty of any kind
    c. The grantor warrants the title against all claims whether they arose before or during the grantor's period of ownership
    d. The grantor warrants that no encumbrances exist but offers no promise to defend the title in court

2. Under Texas law, which two warranty covenants are actually recognized when a deed uses the statutory granting language grant, bargain, and sell?
    a. The covenant of seisin and the covenant against encumbrances
    b. The covenant of quiet enjoyment and the covenant of warranty forever
    c. The covenant of further assurance and the covenant of seisin
    d. The covenant against encumbrances and the covenant of quiet enjoyment

3. A quitclaim deed is most commonly used for which purpose?
    a. To convey a fee simple interest from a seller to a buyer in a standard residential resale
    b. To transfer property out of a decedent's estate by the executor named in the will
    c. To convey property to a trustee of a land trust for privacy purposes
    d. To clear a clouded title by conveying any and all interest a party may hold in the property

4. If a party responsible for a title encumbrance refuses to sign a quitclaim deed to release the claim, what legal action may the property owner take?
    a. The owner may record an affidavit of ownership stating that the encumbrance is invalid
    b. The owner may file a quiet title suit requiring the encumbering party to prove the validity of the interest in court
    c. The owner may ask TREC to arbitrate the dispute under the standard residential contract mediation provision
    d. The owner may apply to the county clerk to have the encumbrance removed from the public record

5. Which of the following correctly describes the hostile possession requirement for a successful adverse possession claim?
    a. The possessor must physically prevent the legal owner from entering the property at all times during the statutory period
    b. The possessor must file a formal notice of claim with the county clerk before occupying the property
    c. The possessor must consistently assert ownership of the property without the legal owner's permission
    d. The possessor must demonstrate that the legal owner abandoned the property intentionally

6. Satisfying all the requirements for adverse possession does not automatically transfer legal title. What additional step must the adverse possessor take to obtain a court judgment establishing ownership?
   a. The possessor must pay all outstanding property taxes owed by the legal owner for the period of occupation
   b. The possessor must record an affidavit of adverse possession signed by two witnesses
   c. The possessor must obtain a written release from the legal owner acknowledging the possessor's right to the property
   d. The possessor must bring a legal action to quiet title and obtain a court judgment establishing ownership

7. Escheat transfers ownership of real property to the state under which of the following circumstances?
   a. A property owner dies intestate with no recognized heirs, or property is abandoned for a statutory period
   b. A property owner fails to pay property taxes for three or more consecutive years
   c. A property owner is declared mentally incompetent and no guardian has been appointed
   d. A lender forecloses on a property and no qualified buyer purchases it at the public auction

8. During a contract for deed transaction, which party holds legal title and which party holds equitable title while installment payments are being made?
   a. The buyer holds legal title and the seller holds equitable title during the contract period
   b. The seller holds legal title and the buyer holds equitable title during the contract period
   c. Both parties hold an undivided equal interest in legal title until all payments are completed
   d. Neither party holds title during the contract period because title is held in escrow by the title company

9. A holographic will in Texas has a distinctive feature that sets it apart from a standard witnessed will. Which of the following correctly describes a holographic will?
   a. It is prepared by an attorney on a standard pre-printed form and signed by the testator and three witnesses
   b. It is dictated orally by the testator to a notary public who records and certifies the testator's wishes
   c. It is a witnessed will that has been notarized and then recorded in the county deed records
   d. It is written entirely in the testator's own handwriting, dated, and signed, and does not require any witnesses

10. When a probate court processes a testate estate, which category of obligations must be satisfied first before the remaining estate is distributed to the named heirs?
   a. Bequests to charitable organizations named in the decedent's will
   b. Claims from general unsecured creditors who had business relationships with the decedent
   c. Superior liens including real estate taxes, assessment taxes, federal estate taxes, and state inheritance taxes
   d. Homestead claims from surviving family members who occupied the property

11. When a Texas property owner dies intestate, in what order does the estate generally pass to surviving relatives under the state's laws of descent and distribution?
   a. The surviving spouse first, then children, then parents, then siblings, then more distant relatives
   b. Children first, then the surviving spouse, then parents, then siblings
   c. Parents first, then the surviving spouse, then children, then more distant relatives
   d. Siblings first, then children, then parents, then the surviving spouse

12. When a deed is recorded in the county clerk's office, what type of notice does the recording provide to the general public?
    a. Actual notice, because every person in the county receives direct personal communication of the ownership change
    b. Constructive notice, because the law presumes that recorded information is available to and known by the public
    c. Provisional notice, which becomes permanent only after the deed has been on record for 30 days
    d. Equitable notice, which protects only the grantee and does not affect third-party purchasers

13. How does the Torrens system of title registration differ fundamentally from the standard recording system used in most states?
    a. In the Torrens system, a court must approve every title transfer before the new owner may take possession
    b. In the Torrens system, deeds must be recorded within 30 days of execution or they become void
    c. In the Torrens system, the title certificate itself is the title; title passes only when the conveyance is registered directly on the certificate
    d. In the Torrens system, all title disputes are resolved by a state title registrar rather than by a court

14. A title search of a property's public records reveals three items of information. Which of the following correctly lists those three items?
    a. The property's current market value, the outstanding loan balance, and the identity of the current occupant
    b. The property's zoning classification, any pending permit applications, and the identity of the original grantor
    c. The property's square footage, the names of all prior owners, and the amount of any existing HOA dues
    d. The legal description of the property, the current owners of record, and any outstanding liens or encumbrances

15. An abstract of title is a chronological summary of recorded documents affecting a property. Which person is responsible for preparing an abstract of title?
    a. An abstractor, who searches documents registered with the county recorder and other official sources and arranges them in chronological order
    b. The county clerk, who prepares the abstract automatically when any document affecting the property is recorded
    c. The buyer's real estate agent, who compiles a history of ownership based on MLS records
    d. The title insurance underwriter, who prepares the abstract as part of the commitment process

16. Title insurance protects the insured against certain hidden defects that a standard public record search would not reveal. Which of the following is an example of a defect that a title insurance policy typically covers?
    a. Damage to the property caused by a flood that occurs after the policy date
    b. A forged deed appearing in the chain of title
    c. A boundary dispute caused by a neighbor who builds a fence after the closing date
    d. An easement that is created and recorded by a utility company after the title policy is issued

17. Before issuing a title insurance policy in Texas, a title company issues a title commitment. Which of the following correctly describes the contents of a title commitment?
    a. It is a final title insurance policy that takes immediate effect upon execution and delivery
    b. It is a written guarantee from the title company that the buyer will receive marketable title with no exceptions
    c. It is a formal opinion from the county attorney confirming that no liens exist against the property
    d. It recapitulates the property description, the interest to be insured, the names of the insured parties, and any exceptions to coverage

18. In Texas, how are title insurance rates determined, and does the rate vary from one title company to another?
    a. Title insurance rates in Texas are set by the Texas Department of Insurance; the rate is the same regardless of which title company issues the policy
    b. Title insurance rates in Texas are set by each individual company and may vary significantly based on the company's underwriting standards
    c. Title insurance rates in Texas are negotiated between the buyer and the title company before closing
    d. Title insurance rates in Texas are established by the Texas Real Estate Commission and apply only to residential transactions

19. An owner's title policy in Texas protects the property owner against covered title claims for how long?
    a. For ten years after the date the policy is issued, with an option to renew at the then-current rate
    b. Until the outstanding mortgage loan on the property is repaid in full
    c. For as long as the owner or the owner's heirs hold the property or remain liable under any title warranties
    d. Until the property is transferred to a new owner, at which point the new owner must assume the policy

20. In Texas, when a lender requires the buyer to purchase a loan title policy, what does the title company automatically do unless the owner rejects it in writing?
    a. The title company provides a full survey of the property at no additional cost to the buyer
    b. The title company also issues an owner's title policy to the buyer
    c. The title company records the deed on behalf of the buyer within three business days of closing
    d. The title company sends a title commitment to all parties naming the listing broker as an additional insured

Chapter 9 Case Study:
Conveyance of Title

The Situation

Diane and Paul Mettling are purchasing a home in San Antonio that has been in the Ochoa family for three generations. The current seller, Rosa Ochoa, inherited the property from her mother, whose name on the deed was listed as Maria Elena Ochoa-Garza. Rosa has always gone by her married name and her mother's estate was never formally probated. Rosa signed the listing agreement in her married name without mentioning the title discrepancy to her agent, Frank Voss of Performance Programs Realty.

During the title search, the title company discovered two problems. First, because Maria Elena Ochoa-Garza's estate was never probated, there is no recorded instrument transferring title from the deceased mother to Rosa. The chain of title has a gap. Second, a review of older records revealed that thirty years ago a neighboring property owner named Gil Trevino had obtained a court judgment against Rosa's grandfather for an unpaid debt. The judgment was recorded in the county records at that time but was never satisfied or released. Gil Trevino passed away fifteen years ago and his estate has been closed.

Frank Voss told the Mettlings that both issues were minor and that they should proceed to closing on schedule. He suggested that the Mettlings simply waive their title objection rights so the seller would not feel pressured. The Mettlings' own agent, Carol Webb, did not object to Frank's suggestion and did not advise the Mettlings to consult an attorney.

Discussion Questions

Question 1

The title search revealed a gap in the chain of title because Rosa's mother's estate was never probated, and an old recorded judgment lien that was never released. Classify each of these as a type of title problem, explain why each one creates a cloud on title, and describe what would typically need to happen to resolve each before the Mettlings could receive marketable title.

Question 2

Frank Voss advised the Mettlings to waive their title objection rights so the seller would not feel pressured, and Carol Webb did not intervene. Evaluate the conduct of both agents, explain what fiduciary duties were implicated, and describe what each agent should have done instead.

CHAPTER 10:

TRANSACTION PROCESS AND CLOSING

Chapter Overview

Learning Objectives

Upon completing Chapter 10, the student will be able to:

1. Describe the complete real estate transaction process from accepted offer through post-closing, including the roles of the listing broker and cooperating broker under 2024 NAR settlement rules.
2. Explain the purpose and structure of transaction checklists and describe a standard residential closing checklist used to track all pre-closing and closing requirements.
3. Identify the forms required for a residential loan application, describe the TRID Loan Estimate and Closing Disclosure requirements, and explain what information lenders need to process and underwrite a loan.
4. Explain how credit reports are obtained and evaluated, identify the factors that raise or lower credit scores, and describe the steps a borrower can take to correct credit report errors.
5. Describe the types of property inspections used in a residential transaction, explain how inspection reports and repair negotiations are handled, and identify the parties responsible for each step.
6. Explain the title work process including the title search, chain of title, quiet title actions, and the title commitment delivered under the One to Four Family Residential Contract (Form 20-19).
7. Describe the escrow process, the preliminary title report, the survey, and the pre-closing activities that must be completed before the closing date.
8. Calculate prorated items using both the 12-month/360-day method and the 365-day method, explain how debits and credits appear on the settlement statement, and describe the closing, disbursement of funds, and IRS reporting obligations.

Contents

- The Real Estate Transaction Process
- Roles of the Brokers
- The Role of the Listing Broker
- Cooperating Broker Responsibilities
- Relevance of Checklists
- Residential Closing Checklist
- Loan Application
- Loan Estimate and Verifications
- Required Loan Information
- Processing and Underwriting the Loan
- Credit Reports and Scores
- RESPA and TRID
- Property Inspections

- Types of Inspections
- Inspection Reports and Repairs
- Title Work
- Chain of Title and Title Commitment
- Closing a Transaction
- Preliminary Title Report and Survey
- The Escrow Process
- Pre-Closing Procedures
- Prorations
- Proration Methods and Examples
- Conducting the Closing
- Disbursement of Funds and IRS Reporting

The Real Estate Transaction Process

The real estate transaction process is the sequence of tasks that agents and other parties complete between the time an offer is accepted and the transaction closes. Managing this process well is one of the most important services a licensee provides. The key phases are offer and contract management, due diligence and inspections, title work, loan processing, closing preparation, and post-closing activities.

Offer and Contract Management

From the moment an offer is received through the final signed contract, the listing agent coordinates a series of tasks that protect the seller's interests and keep the transaction on track:

- Receive and review all purchase offers submitted by buyers or buyer's agents
- Prepare a net sheet for each offer so the seller can compare proceeds
- Counsel the seller on the merits and weaknesses of each offer component
- Contact buyer's agents to discuss buyer qualifications and the terms of the offer
- Deliver the Seller's Disclosure Notice (Form 55-1) to the buyer's agent or buyer as required
- Confirm that the buyer is pre-qualified and obtain a pre-qualification letter from the lender
- Negotiate all offers on the seller's behalf, establish a time limit for loan approval, and set a closing date
- Prepare and deliver any counteroffers, acceptances, or amendments to the buyer's agent
- Distribute copies of the executed contract and all addenda to the title company
- Promptly deposit the buyer's earnest money into the escrow account
- Disseminate showing restrictions per the seller's instructions after the contract is executed
- Deliver copies of the fully signed contract to the seller, the buyer's agent, and the lender
- Change the MLS status to Pending and update transaction management systems
- Review the buyer's credit report results and advise the seller of the range of possible outcomes
- Order any required inspections, including septic system, well flow, termite, and mold inspections, and deliver reports to the lender and buyer

Closing Preparations

As the closing date approaches, the listing agent monitors and coordinates the following:

- Confirm the contract is signed by all parties
- Coordinate the closing process with the buyer's agent and the lender
- Update all closing forms and transaction files
- Confirm the closing date, time, and location, and notify all parties
- Assist in resolving title problems such as boundary disputes and unrecorded easements
- Ensure that all parties have the documents and information needed to close

Roles of the Brokers

Every residential transaction involves at least one, and typically two, brokers. Their roles and responsibilities differ but are complementary.

The Role of the Listing Broker

The listing broker represents the seller and bears responsibility for using reasonable efforts to complete the sale. This responsibility continues from the time the contract is signed through closing and into post-closing activities. The listing broker is responsible for the accuracy of all settlement statements and must ensure that all parties receive signed copies.

The listing broker's core closing duties include:

- Ensuring that all information and documents called for by the contract are produced accurately and on time
- Overseeing financial arrangements for both buyer and seller, including working with the lender to obtain the loan package and with the seller's lender to obtain payoff figures
- Working with the title company to ensure that all documents needed to clear title are produced
- Ensuring that all liens and taxes are paid by closing
- Following up on utility charges and verifying that prorations are calculated correctly
- Notifying the buyer about insurance requirements
- Preparing and documenting closing worksheet information
- Advising the buyer and seller of the closing date and time
- Informing the buyer of the exact amount of cash needed at closing
- Complying with all IRS and state reporting and withholding requirements
- Properly disbursing funds and ensuring the availability of good funds
- Ensuring that all documents are properly recorded

Cooperating Broker Responsibilities

Under the 2024 NAR settlement rules adopted in Texas, all buyer's agents must have a signed written buyer agreement before showing a buyer any property. Cooperating brokers are those who earn a commission split by representing the buyer. The Commission requires the listing broker to obtain the seller's consent before offering any commission split to a cooperating broker. If the listing broker plans to offer different commission levels to different types of cooperating brokers, that tiered structure must be disclosed to the seller in advance, along with the possibility that it may limit the property's market exposure.

Under the post-settlement model, the buyer's agent's compensation is established in the written buyer representation agreement between the buyer and the cooperating broker. Compensation to the cooperating broker may be offered by the seller or paid directly by the buyer, depending on the terms negotiated.

Cooperative commission terms must be agreed upon in advance and cannot be communicated through MLS in a way that violates NAR rules.

The cooperating broker's primary duties during the transaction include:

- Attending all property inspections with the buyer and service providers
- Handling all discussions and negotiations on behalf of the buyer
- Participating in all transaction-related meetings with brokers and sellers
- Maintaining open and timely communication with the listing broker and other service providers
- Actively participating in finalizing all business, financial, and contract terms
- Coordinating the timely transfer, execution, and delivery of all transaction-related documents
- Completing all commission-related documents in a timely manner
- Keeping all transaction and client information confidential unless directed otherwise

Relevance of Checklists

The business of real estate is fundamentally checklist-driven. In Texas, the standard TREC residential purchase contract is itself largely a checklist structure: it contains blanks to fill in and provisions that direct the parties to address questions that might otherwise be overlooked. Who pays the HOA transfer fee? Does the buyer get occupancy on the day of closing or a few days after? How many days does the buyer have to obtain loan approval? The contract does not always determine the answers, but it ensures the questions are asked.

When a property goes under contract, that event should generate additional checklists covering inspections to be ordered, disclosures to be made, the title report to be reviewed, financing deadlines to be tracked, and a host of other tasks. In a standard residential transaction, it makes sense to use at least three checklists reviewed at predetermined dates after contract execution and before closing.

A checklist is not a step-by-step instruction manual. It is a quick, simple tool that helps skilled professionals avoid overlooking items that, while routine, are critical to a successful closing. Checklists free up the judgment and attention needed to respond to unexpected complications that arise in every transaction. Reviewing a transaction checklist only after closing to release a commission check is far too late; a disclosure that was not made at the proper time cannot be retroactively corrected in any risk-management sense.

Residential Closing Checklist

Residential closing companies use a detailed checklist to confirm that every element of the closing has been assembled before the parties meet to sign. The checklist provides a column for initialing each completed item and for noting the responsible party. Items covered in a standard residential closing checklist include:

- Executed copy of the contract and all addenda received
- Closing date and possession date confirmed
- Exact legal names of all sellers and buyers verified
- Broker names and commission splits confirmed, including the amount and to whom each portion is payable
- Contact information for seller's and buyer's attorneys
- Escrow amount and holder identified (usually the title company)
- Property type confirmed (single family, rental, condo, commercial, etc.)

- Copies of all existing leases obtained for rental properties
- Deadline and status for abstract or title commitment ordered and delivered
- Existing mortgage identified: lender name, assumption or payoff status, estoppel letter requested and received
- Buyer's new mortgage status: lender, loan type (conventional, FHA, VA), commitment deadline, and terms
- Whether seller is carrying back financing and the specific terms
- Building inspection status and any required repairs
- Termite and roof inspection status
- Buyer's insurance arrangements confirmed
- Inventory of personal property included in the sale
- HOA status: dues, maintenance receipts, association approval, and any pending assessments
- Municipal improvement lien status checked with city and county
- All seller utility bills and real estate taxes verified as paid
- Corporate seller's Certificate of Good Standing obtained
- Title defects identified, cure deadline set, and defects resolved
- Deed prepared and sent for recording
- Non-lien affidavit, disbursement sheet, closing statement, and bill of sale prepared
- Title policies prepared and delivered
- Transaction file reviewed and date of closing recorded

Loan Application

A residential loan application requires the borrower and the loan officer to complete several forms at the initial interview. The standard application forms are Fannie Mae Form 1003 and Freddie Mac Form 65, also called the Uniform Residential Loan Application. The loan officer assists the borrower in completing the application, and a clean typed copy is provided for signature prior to settlement. The application covers eleven sections: type of mortgage and loan terms; property information and purpose of loan; borrower information; employment information; monthly income and combined housing expense information; assets and liabilities; details of transaction; declarations; acknowledgment and agreement; information for government monitoring purposes; and addendum for additional information.

Additional forms completed during the application process include:

- Permission to request a credit report, signed by the borrower authorizing the lender to obtain credit information
- Loan Estimate, delivered by the lender within three business days of receiving the application
- Verification of Employment (VOE), or alternatively copies of at least 30 days of pay stubs and two years of W-2 forms
- Verification of Deposit (VOD), or alternatively three months of bank statements

Loan Estimate and Verifications

Under the TRID Rule that took effect in October 2015, the Loan Estimate replaced the prior Good Faith Estimate and Truth in Lending Statement. The Loan Estimate is a standardized three-page form that discloses the loan terms, projected monthly payments, and an itemized estimate of all closing costs. Lenders must provide the Loan Estimate within three business days of receiving the borrower's application. The form must contain a good faith estimate of all credit costs and transaction terms including the annual percentage rate, must be in writing in the form prescribed by the CFPB, must be delivered in a manner satisfying TRID timing requirements, and may be revised only under specific circumstances.

Employment verification today is commonly accomplished by reviewing current pay stubs and two years of W-2 forms rather than waiting for a formal written VOE. Lenders may also request proof of pension, retirement, Social Security, or disability income; documentation of rental or investment income; and documentation of any child support or alimony paid or received. Bank deposit verification is commonly accomplished by reviewing three months of bank statements.

Required Loan Information

The following documents and information speed the application process when brought to the initial interview:

- Social Security card and driver's license or government-issued photo identification
- Residential addresses for the past two years
- Employment history for the past two years
- Gross monthly income from all sources including Social Security, alimony, child support, pension, and disability
- Account numbers, minimum monthly payments, and current balances for all installment loans, credit cards, student loans, auto loans, and other mortgage loans, including any co-signed obligations
- Account numbers and current balances for all checking accounts, savings accounts, stocks, and bonds
- Pay stubs for the most recent 30 days
- W-2 forms for the most recent two years

Special circumstances require additional documentation:

- Child support or alimony counted as income or debt: copy of the court order and evidence of regular receipt or payment
- VA loans: Certificate of Eligibility or a statement from a commanding officer confirming continued service
- Self-employed borrowers: federal tax returns for the most recent two years, a current year profit and loss statement, and possibly a current balance sheet

Processing and Underwriting the Loan

After the application is complete, it is forwarded to a loan processor who packages the file for the underwriter. The underwriter must validate three things: the borrower, the property, and the title to the property. Validating the borrower involves verifying employment and income, confirming the availability of funds to close, reviewing credit information, preparing the case file, and obtaining any required explanations for irregularities.

Employment verification focuses on the length of time on the current job, the probability of continued employment, any job changes in the prior two years, and unexplained gaps in employment. Hourly income is calculated as the hourly rate multiplied by 40 hours multiplied by 52 weeks, divided by 12 for gross monthly income. Overtime, part-time income, and bonuses must show a two-year history plus evidence of expected continuation. Anticipated salary increases require written documentation before they can be counted.

Funds to close are verified through bank statements from the prior two to three months, written bank verification, or a copy of the contract for a property being sold to generate the down payment funds. If sale proceeds are the source of the down payment, the lender will require a copy of the Closing Disclosure from that sale to confirm actual receipt of the funds.

Credit Reports and Scores

Lenders request a tri-merge credit report that pulls information from all three major credit repositories: Experian, Equifax, and TransUnion. Each bureau may report different information and produce a different credit score. The lender typically uses the middle of the three scores rather than an average. Credit scores are statistical measures of the likelihood that a borrower will repay a loan. They are calculated using the FICO model developed by Fair Isaac and Company and range from a low of approximately 300 to a high of 850 or above.

A rough interpretation of score ranges is:

- Below 580: high risk of default; many lenders will not consider applicants in this range
- 580 to 619: elevated risk of default; limited loan products available
- 620 to 679: moderate risk; most conventional loan programs become accessible at this threshold
- 680 to 749: low risk; favorable rates and terms typically available
- 750 and above: very low risk; best available rates and terms

The credit report contains the following information:

- Types and amounts of credit in use
- Length of credit history
- Payment history showing how promptly bills have been paid
- Amount of available credit and current utilization
- Number of open accounts
- Number of recent credit inquiries
- Public record entries including any bankruptcy, foreclosure, judgment, or lien

Factors Affecting Credit Scores

Actions that lower a credit score include not paying bills on time, carrying too many open credit accounts, maintaining excessively high credit limits relative to income, and carrying balances near the credit limit on existing accounts. The debt-to-credit-limit ratio, also called credit utilization, is particularly significant; accounts that are at or near their maximum limits substantially reduce a borrower's score.

Steps that can improve a credit score over time include paying all bills on or before the due date, avoiding opening unnecessary new credit accounts, keeping the total number of credit cards to a manageable amount, and maintaining balances well below credit limits.

Obtaining and Correcting Credit Reports

Under the Fair Credit Reporting Act, each of the three major credit reporting agencies must provide every consumer one free copy of their credit report per year upon request. Reports can be obtained through AnnualCreditReport.com, by telephone, or through each bureau directly. The three agencies are Equifax (equifax.com), TransUnion (transunion.com), and Experian (experian.com).

Consumers who discover errors in their credit reports may correct them by writing to all three agencies disputing the inaccurate item. Each agency must investigate and respond within 30 days. A borrower in the loan application process who is waiting for an error to be corrected should provide the lender with a written explanation of the discrepancy so that the underwriter can evaluate the full picture.

RESPA and TRID

The Real Estate Settlement Procedures Act (RESPA), administered by the Consumer Financial Protection Bureau (CFPB), requires that parties to covered residential transactions receive accurate figures related to their closing costs. RESPA applies to purchases of residential property (one-to-four family homes, cooperatives, and condominiums) that involve first or second mortgages financed by federally-related loans, including FHA and VA loans and loans that will be sold to Fannie Mae, Freddie Mac, or Ginnie Mae. RESPA does not apply to seller-financed loans or to loan assumptions unless the lender changes the assumed loan's terms or charges more than $50 for the assumption.

Under the TRID Rule effective October 2015:

- Lenders must give every loan applicant a copy of the CFPB booklet Your Home Loan Toolkit at the time of application
- Lenders must provide a Loan Estimate of settlement costs at application or within three business days of application
- A Closing Disclosure detailing all financial particulars of the transaction must be delivered to the buyer at least three business days before closing; the settlement agent must also provide the seller with the Closing Disclosure, which may be done at consummation

RESPA specifically prohibits the payment or receipt of fees or kickbacks for any settlement service that has not actually been rendered. Referral fees are strictly forbidden for title search, inspection, survey, appraisal, loan origination, credit reporting, and attorney services. RESPA permits commission sharing among cooperating brokers and MLS services. Affiliated business arrangements among real estate firms, mortgage brokers, and title companies are permitted if the relationship is disclosed in writing to the consumer, the consumer is free to use other providers, and no fees are exchanged merely for referrals.

A real estate firm may offer a computerized loan origination (CLO) system that provides mortgage product information, prequalifies borrowers, and initiates loan applications, but only the borrower may pay the CLO fee and the broker must disclose that competing products exist outside the system. Loan servicers must provide borrowers with an annual escrow statement summarizing all account activity in the prior 12 months and disclosing any escrow shortfall or overage and how it will be resolved.

Property Inspections

Most buyers make the purchase contingent on one or more professional inspections, and many lenders condition loan approval on the completion of at least one inspection. Inspections must be ordered as early as possible in the transaction so that reports can be reviewed, repairs negotiated and completed, and re-inspections scheduled without jeopardizing the closing date. For every inspection ordered, the reports must be approved or rejected by the buyer or lender, required repairs must be completed and re-inspected, and all parties must receive notification of the final results.

A home inspection is a limited, non-invasive examination of the condition of a home conducted by a licensed inspector. The inspector prepares a written report describing the condition of the home at the time of inspection. The inspector does not guarantee the future performance or life expectancy of any system or component.

Types of Inspections

Standard home inspection Covers the home's major mechanical systems (electrical, plumbing, heating, and cooling) and its construction from roof to foundation, exterior to interior.

Pest inspection A check for damage caused by wood-destroying insects such as termites, carpenter ants, and beetles.

Soil inspection An examination of soil conditions to identify settling or drainage problems that could affect the structure.

Structural inspection A visual inspection of the foundation, bearing walls, beams, columns, floor slabs, framing, crawlspace areas, and drainage to assess structural integrity.

Environmental inspection An assessment of environmental conditions such as radon, asbestos, lead-based paint, underground storage tanks, and contaminated water.

If buyers do not have a preferred inspector, the licensee should provide at least three names to choose from rather than directing the buyer to a single recommended inspector, to avoid the appearance of a conflict of interest and to comply with RESPA's restrictions on kickbacks and referral fees.

Inspection Reports and Repairs

Once an inspection is complete, the inspector prepares a written report identifying areas of concern, recommending repairs, noting poor workmanship or deterioration, and flagging conditions that could become problematic if the property is later remodeled. For example, a report might note that a septic system adequate for the current three-bedroom home would need to be upgraded before a fourth bedroom could be added.

Depending on the contingency terms, the buyer may disapprove the report and terminate the contract, or may identify specific unsatisfactory items and request that the seller make the repairs before closing. If the lender required the inspection, the lender's list of required repairs becomes a condition of loan approval that the seller must satisfy and document. In most cases, all required repairs must be completed and the property re-inspected before the sale can close.

Title Work

The seller is required to deliver marketable title at closing. Marketable title is one so free of defects that the buyer can be confident of not having to defend it. To deliver marketable title, the seller must have and provide evidence of title, which is the documented proof of ownership. Before lending on a property, the lender orders a title search to confirm that no undisclosed liens or encumbrances exist. The buyer is typically responsible for the title search fee.

A title search is the process of retrieving and examining recorded documents in the history of a property to determine the interests and encumbrances affecting it. The search answers three core questions: does the seller have a saleable interest in the property; what restrictions or encumbrances pertain to the use of the land; and do any liens exist that must be satisfied at closing.

Chain of Title and Quiet Title

Chain of title is the chronological succession of owners of record from the original government grant through every subsequent transfer to the present day. If there is a break in the chain, a defective conveyance, or an undisclosed encumbrance, the title is said to be clouded. A cloud on title includes a mechanic's lien, income or property tax lien, encroachment, zoning violation, or a deed defect such as a missing signature or an incorrectly stated name. The seller is typically given a period of time to cure any discovered defect before closing.

To remove a cloud on title, the owner may file a suit to quiet title. This is a legal action asking a court to establish ownership of the property and prevent the respondent from making any further claims. The court's order clears the title record of the defect so the transaction can proceed. The two most commonly used forms of title evidence following a title search are the abstract of title with attorney's opinion and the title insurance policy.

Title Commitment Under Form 20-19

Paragraph 6 of the One to Four Family Residential Contract (Form 20-19, effective July 1st, 2026) governs the title commitment. Under this paragraph, the title company has 20 days after receiving the executed contract to furnish a title commitment to the buyer. The title commitment is in the same format as a title insurance policy but is not a policy. It is a document setting out the terms and conditions under which the company will issue a policy. Title examiners search all public records related to the property looking for encumbrances that might affect the title.

Three items must be delivered to the buyer under Paragraph 6.B:

- The title commitment
- Copies of any restrictive covenants (deed restrictions) affecting the property
- Copies of all documents showing exceptions to the title insurance coverage

All documents are to be delivered as provided in Paragraph 21 of the contract, which identifies the parties' addresses, fax numbers, and email addresses. If the title company cannot deliver the documents within 20 days, an automatic extension of 15 additional days or until the closing date (whichever comes first) applies.

Closing a Transaction

Once the buyer and seller have an executed contract, the closing process begins in earnest. The buyer must secure financing, complete inspections, and review the preliminary title report. The seller must clear any liens against the property, make required repairs, execute the deed, and arrange to vacate. This entire pre-closing sequence is what practitioners refer to as the closing process.

Preliminary Title Report

The person preparing the closing documents orders a preliminary title report as early as possible to start the title search. This report shows the condition of the title before the sale and loan are consummated. It includes the owner's name and property description, a list of outstanding assessments such as taxes or bonds, any covenants, conditions, or restrictions on the property, and all recorded liens or encumbrances that must be removed before the loan can proceed. If the report reveals a judgment lien against the property, the seller must either clear the lien or prove it was placed in error.

A preliminary title report is not an insurance policy. It reflects items the title company would exclude from coverage if a policy were issued at that time. Its purpose is to identify problems early enough for them to be addressed before the closing date.

Survey

In addition to the preliminary title report, a land survey is typically ordered to show the physical footprint of the improvements on the property, including the house, any deck, patio, garage, carport, fence, swimming pool, or other structure. The survey identifies whether any neighbor's structure encroaches on the subject property and whether the subject property's structures are within the property boundaries. It also confirms whether any fencing is properly located on the lot lines. Any physical encroachment identified on the survey is a cloud on title that must be resolved before the loan can close.

The Escrow Process

Escrow is the process in which a neutral third party holds all money and documents relating to the transaction until all terms and conditions of the escrow instructions have been satisfied. The person coordinating this process is the escrow agent or escrow holder. In Texas, the escrow agent may be an attorney, a title company, a trust company, an escrow company, or the escrow department of a lending institution.

The buyer and seller select the escrow company through negotiation in the purchase agreement. When a TREC-promulgated sales contract is used, the escrow agreement is incorporated into the contract itself. The escrow holder opens the escrow in the names of the parties and needs information about the length of the escrow period, loan terms, commission arrangements, inspection instructions, personal property included in the sale, the legal description of the property, and the earnest money deposit.

Pre-Closing Procedures

During the escrow period, numerous activities occur simultaneously:

- Appraisal: the appraisal report is sent to the lender; if buyers or sellers want to see the results their agents must contact the lender; if the appraisal comes in below the contract price, the parties must negotiate a resolution
- Inspections: pest control, structural, and other reports are sent to the buyer through the buyer's agent, who may provide copies to the lender; if lender-required repairs are identified, the seller must complete and document them
- Financing: when the loan is approved, the lender issues a commitment outlining exact loan terms and an expiration date; the lender sends all documents to the escrow agent who schedules a signing appointment with the buyer
- Title work: the escrow agent orders the complete title search and coordinates title insurance; the preliminary report is sent to both the lender and the buyer for review
- Property insurance: the escrow agent verifies that the buyer has obtained homeowner's insurance at the required replacement value and that a copy has been delivered to the lender
- Final settlement statements: the escrow agent prepares the final Closing Disclosure for the closing meeting

Prorations

Some expenses associated with owning real estate must be prorated at closing, meaning they are divided proportionately between the seller and the buyer based on each party's period of ownership during the year. The most common prorated items are property taxes, hazard insurance, mortgage interest, utilities, and rent on income properties.

On the settlement statement, every prorated item appears as a debit to one party and a credit to the other party for the same amount.

Prepaid and Accrued Expenses

Expenses that were paid in advance by the seller for a period extending beyond closing are prepaid expenses. The buyer owes the seller a credit for the unused portion. For example, if the seller prepaid property insurance for the full calendar year and the closing is September 18, the buyer receives a debit and the seller receives a credit for the coverage from September 19 through December 31.

Expenses that were incurred by the seller but not yet paid at the time of closing are accrued expenses or expenses paid in arrears. The buyer will eventually pay the full bill, so the seller owes the buyer a credit for the seller's share. Property taxes are the most common example because Texas tax bills cover the full calendar year but are paid at year-end. The portion of the annual tax bill from January 1 through the closing date is the seller's expense, so the seller receives a debit and the buyer receives a credit on the settlement statement.

The 12-Month/360-Day Method

The 12-month/360-day method, also called the banker's method, treats each month as having exactly 30 days and each year as having 360 days. The steps are:

- Identify the annual amount to be prorated
- Divide by 12 to get the monthly rate
- Divide the monthly rate by 30 to get the daily rate (the day of closing belongs to the seller)
- Multiply the monthly rate by the number of full months the seller owned the property before closing
- Multiply the daily rate by the number of days the seller owned the property in the closing month
- Add the two amounts to get the seller's total prorated share
- Subtract the seller's share from the annual total to get the buyer's share

Example: Jim and Beth are selling to Tim and Sue, closing on May 17. Annual real estate taxes are $1,950.

- Monthly rate: $1,950 divided by 12 = $162.50
- Daily rate: $162.50 divided by 30 = $5.42
- January through April (4 months): $162.50 x 4 = $650.00
- May 1 through May 17 (17 days): $5.42 x 17 = $92.14
- Jim and Beth's share: $650.00 + $92.14 = $742.14
- Tim and Sue's share: $1,950.00 - $742.14 = $1,207.86

The 365-Day Method

The 365-day method uses the actual number of days in the year (366 in a leap year). The steps are:

- Identify the annual amount to be prorated
- Divide by 365 (or 366) to get the daily rate
- Multiply the daily rate by the number of days the seller owned the property before closing to get the seller's share
- Subtract the seller's share from the annual total to get the buyer's share

Example: Greg and Jane are assuming Al and Kathy's insurance policy. The annual premium is $550, paid in advance on March 1. Closing is June 11.

- Daily rate: $550.00 divided by 365 = $1.51
- Al and Kathy's share (March 1 through June 11 = 103 days): $1.51 x 103 = $155.53
- Greg and Jane's share: $550.00 - $155.53 = $394.47
- Since Al and Kathy prepaid, $394.47 is credited to the sellers and debited to the buyers on the settlement statement

Prorating Rent

When a closing involves an income property, the month's rent is typically prorated because rent is collected in advance. The seller collected the full month's rent at the beginning of the month but will not own the property for the full period; therefore the seller owes the buyer a credit for the buyer's portion.

Example: Closing is set for March 23 and the tenant's rent is $950 per month. The seller owns the day of closing.

- Seller's days: 23
- Daily rent: $950 divided by 31 days in March = $30.65
- Seller's portion: $30.65 x 23 = $704.95
- Buyer's credit: $950.00 - $704.95 = $245.05; credit the buyer and debit the seller $245.05

Prorating Loan Interest

Interest on mortgage loans is paid in arrears. When a buyer's new loan closes mid-month, the buyer typically prepays interest for the remainder of the closing month. This ensures that the first full monthly payment, due the following month, covers only that full calendar month of interest.

Example: A buyer's new loan is $200,000 at 5 percent annual interest and the closing is August 20. The buyer owns the day of closing and the 360-day method is used.

- Buyer's days: 11 (August 20 through 31)
- Annual interest: $200,000 x 0.05 = $10,000
- Daily interest: $10,000 divided by 360 = $27.78
- Prepaid interest charge: $27.78 x 11 days = $305.58 debit to the buyer

For the seller's existing loan being paid off at closing, the lender typically provides a payoff figure that already includes accrued interest through the closing date. To illustrate: closing is on the 13th of September, seller's loan balance is $50,000 at 6 percent, the seller owns the day of closing, and the 360-day method is used.

- Seller's days: 13
- Annual interest: $50,000 x 0.06 = $3,000
- Daily interest: $3,000 divided by 360 = $8.33
- Interest charge for closing month: $8.33 x 13 days = $108.33 added to the seller's payoff amount

Conducting the Closing

The title closing, also called settlement, is the culmination of the real estate transaction. At closing, the buyer completes the financing arrangements and delivers the down payment and closing costs to escrow, the seller transfers title and pays off all outstanding liens and mortgages on the property, and both parties pay all required taxes, fees, and other charges.

Who Attends

The primary attendees at a closing are the buyer, who pays for the property and receives clear title; the seller, who conveys the property and receives the sale proceeds; and the closing or escrow agent, who prepares all documents and the settlement statements showing every debit and credit assigned to each party. Others who may attend but are not required include attorneys for the parties, a lender representative, the real estate agents, and a title company representative.

Where Closings Are Held

The sales contract typically specifies the closing location. A closing may be held at the title company, the lender's office, an attorney's office, the escrow agent's office, or in some circumstances the county recorder's office. Remote online notarization closings and hybrid closings, in which some documents are signed electronically and others are signed in person, have become increasingly common and are permitted in Texas.

The Broker's and Agent's Role at Closing

Most of the broker's work to facilitate a smooth closing happens during the period between the contract signing and the closing date. Just before closing, the agent should conduct a final walkthrough inspection with the buyer to confirm that the property's condition has not changed since the contract was signed and that no fixtures have been removed. This walkthrough protects the buyer and can trigger a contract amendment or escrow holdback if problems are found.

On the closing date, the broker may act as the closing agent, may be present to receive the commission check, or may not be present at all depending on local practice. The commission for the transaction is usually paid in a single check at closing. The broker deposits it into an escrow account and disburses the appropriate share to each cooperating agent after confirming that all required documentation is in order.

During the pre-closing period, the agent's responsibilities include:

- Communicating proactively with the client at every step so the client knows what is happening
- Communicating with the other party's agent to promote a cooperative path to closing
- Confirming that escrow instructions accurately reflect all terms of the purchase agreement
- Ordering or confirming the timely completion of all required inspections and delivery of reports
- Monitoring loan approval progress with the lender and helping the client understand the appraisal results
- Tracking all special provisions such as personal property inclusions
- Reviewing the title report for any issues that need to be addressed
- Confirming that the buyer has obtained homeowner's insurance and that a copy has been delivered to the escrow agent and lender

- Confirming that the seller has arrangements in place for moving out, including trash hauling and any agreed cleaning or repairs
- Ensuring that any pre-closing rental agreement for buyer occupancy before closing is signed and in place

Note: Licensees must not recommend specific service providers to clients in a way that creates an undisclosed conflict of interest. Accepting referral fees from inspectors, lenders, insurance agents, or other service providers could violate state licensing laws and RESPA.

Disbursement of Funds and IRS Reporting

After all closing documents are signed, the settlement agent arranges for the recording of the deed and the deed of trust or other security instrument. Following recording, the settlement agent disburses funds as directed by the contract, pays off any existing mortgage loans and other liens, and arranges for the title insurance policy to be issued to the purchaser. Several weeks after the closing, the buyer should receive the original deed and the title insurance policy.

The title to the property transfers when the deed is delivered to and accepted by the buyer. Delivery and acceptance must occur during the seller's lifetime. The deed must be signed by the seller, must identify both seller and buyer, must contain words of conveyance, and must include the correct legal description. Recording in the county clerk's office is not a legal requirement for the deed to be valid between the parties, but recording protects the buyer against subsequent third-party claims.

If a final walkthrough reveals unresolved repair or replacement issues, a portion of the seller's proceeds may be placed in escrow and held until the buyer confirms that the work has been completed. After the buyer signs off, the escrowed funds are released to the seller.

IRS Reporting Requirements

All real estate sales must be reported to the Internal Revenue Service after closing using Form 1099-S. The responsibility for completing and submitting this form falls to the person who conducted the closing, which may be the closing officer, the lender, the listing broker, or the buyer's broker. The form may also be filed by a US Treasury designee. There is no charge to the buyer for this IRS filing. The information reported includes the closing date, the gross proceeds, and the seller's identifying information.

Chapter 10 Snapshot Review

The following review summarizes the key rules and concepts from Chapter 10.

Transaction Process and Broker Roles

- The transaction process spans from accepted offer to post-closing and includes offer management, due diligence, title work, loan processing, closing preparation, and post-closing reporting
- The listing broker represents the seller, oversees the accuracy of all settlement statements, and ensures that all parties receive signed copies
- Under 2024 NAR settlement rules, cooperating brokers must have a signed written buyer representation agreement before showing any property; compensation is established in that agreement rather than through MLS
- The listing broker must obtain the seller's consent before offering a commission split to a cooperating broker; if tiered commission levels are offered to different broker types, that fact must be disclosed to the seller along with the potential impact on market exposure
- Cooperating brokers attend inspections, handle negotiations on the buyer's behalf, maintain communication with the listing broker, and coordinate document delivery throughout the transaction

Checklists and Closing Coordination

- Real estate transactions are checklist-driven; the TREC residential contract is itself structured as a checklist that prompts answers to key questions about the transaction
- A transaction should generate at least three checklists reviewed at preset dates between contract execution and closing
- A checklist is not a step-by-step instruction set but a simple tool to prevent oversight of routine but critical items
- A standard residential closing checklist covers executed documents, closing and possession dates, party names, broker commissions, attorney contacts, escrow details, property type, lease copies, abstract or title commitment, existing mortgage and assumption or payoff status, new mortgage terms and commitment deadline, seller carryback details, inspection status, insurance, personal property inventory, HOA status, lien searches, utility and tax verification, title defects, deed and title policy preparation, and file review

Loan Application and Processing

- The standard loan application is Fannie Mae Form 1003 and Freddie Mac Form 65; additional forms include permission to request a credit report, the Loan Estimate, and verifications of employment and deposit
- Under TRID, the Loan Estimate must be provided within three business days of application and must include all credit costs and the APR; it replaces the prior Good Faith Estimate and Truth in Lending Statement
- Standard information required at application: government-issued photo ID, two years of residential addresses, two years of employment history, gross monthly income from all sources, all debt account information, two to three months of bank statements, 30 days of pay stubs, and two years of W-2 forms

- Self-employed borrowers must provide two years of federal tax returns and a current year profit and loss statement
- The underwriter validates three things: the borrower (income, employment, funds, credit), the property (appraisal), and the title
- Lenders use a tri-merge credit report from Equifax, TransUnion, and Experian; the middle of the three scores is used; most conventional loan programs require a minimum score of 620
- FICO scores above 750 indicate very low risk; scores below 580 indicate high default risk and limit available loan programs
- Consumers are entitled to one free credit report per year from each bureau; errors must be disputed in writing and each bureau must respond within 30 days

RESPA and TRID

- RESPA applies to one-to-four family residential purchases financed by federally-related loans; it does not apply to seller-financed loans or to most loan assumptions
- TRID requires the Loan Estimate within three business days of application and the Closing Disclosure at least three business days before closing
- RESPA prohibits kickbacks and unearned referral fees for settlement services including title search, inspection, survey, appraisal, loan origination, credit reporting, and attorney services
- Affiliated business arrangements are permitted under RESPA if disclosed in writing, the consumer is free to use other providers, and no fees are exchanged solely for referrals
- CLO systems are permitted; only the borrower may pay the CLO fee; the broker must disclose that competing products exist outside the system
- Loan servicers must provide borrowers with an annual escrow statement summarizing account activity and disclosing any shortfall or overage

Inspections

- Inspections must be ordered as early as possible to allow time for reports, repair negotiations, and re-inspections before the closing date
- For every inspection: reports must be approved or rejected, required repairs must be completed and re-inspected, and all parties must receive final notification
- Common inspection types: standard home inspection (roof to foundation), pest inspection, soil inspection, structural inspection, and environmental inspection
- The buyer's agent should provide at least three inspector names rather than directing the buyer to a single provider, to avoid RESPA referral fee issues
- Inspection reports must be re-inspected after repairs and the results provided to lender and buyer before closing can proceed

Title Work and Escrow

- The seller must deliver marketable title at closing; title search, title commitment, and title insurance are the tools for accomplishing this
- Chain of title is the chronological record of ownership from the original government grant to the present; a break in the chain produces a clouded title requiring a quiet title suit
- Examples of title clouds: mechanic's lien, income or property tax lien, encroachment, zoning violation, defective deed signature, or incorrectly stated name

- Under Form 20-19 Paragraph 6, the title company has 20 days after contract receipt to deliver the title commitment, restrictive covenant copies, and all exception documents to the buyer; if not possible, a 15-day automatic extension applies
- The title commitment is not a title insurance policy; it shows the conditions under which the company will issue a policy
- Escrow is the process in which a neutral third party holds money and documents until all escrow conditions are satisfied; in Texas the escrow agent may be an attorney, title company, trust company, escrow company, or lender escrow department
- The preliminary title report identifies issues before closing so they can be resolved; it is not an insurance policy and reflects items the title company would exclude from coverage

Prorations

- Prorations divide closing-period expenses proportionately between buyer and seller based on their ownership periods
- Every prorated item appears as a debit to one party and a credit to the other for the same amount on the settlement statement
- Prepaid expenses (paid in advance): buyer is debited, seller is credited for the unused portion
- Accrued expenses (paid in arrears, such as property taxes): seller is debited, buyer is credited for the seller's share
- 12-month/360-day method: divide annual amount by 12 for monthly rate, divide by 30 for daily rate; seller owns closing day
- 365-day method: divide annual amount by 365 (or 366 in a leap year) for daily rate; multiply by seller's days of ownership
- Rent prorations: rent is collected in advance, so the seller owes the buyer a credit for the buyer's portion of the month
- Buyer's prepaid interest: calculated from closing day through end of closing month; equals daily interest rate times number of remaining days in the month
- Seller's payoff interest: lender typically provides a total payoff figure that already includes accrued daily interest through the closing date

Conducting the Closing and Post-Closing

- At closing: the buyer completes financing and delivers funds to escrow; the seller conveys title and pays off all liens; both parties pay required taxes, fees, and charges
- Closing may be held at the title company, lender's office, attorney's office, escrow agent's office, or through remote online notarization (permitted in Texas)
- The agent should conduct a final walkthrough with the buyer immediately before closing to confirm property condition; problems found can trigger a contract amendment or escrow holdback
- Commission is paid at closing in a single check; the broker deposits it to escrow and disburses cooperating agents' shares after confirming documentation is complete
- Title transfers when the deed is delivered to and accepted by the buyer; delivery and acceptance must occur during the seller's lifetime
- After closing, the settlement agent records the deed and security instrument, disburses all funds, pays off liens, and arranges for the title insurance policy to be issued
- All real estate sales must be reported to the IRS on Form 1099-S; responsibility falls to the closing officer, lender, listing broker, or buyer's broker, depending on who conducted the closing

CHAPTER 10 QUIZ:

TRANSACTION PROCESS AND CLOSING

1. Under the 2024 NAR settlement rules adopted in Texas, a cooperating broker must have which of the following in place before showing a buyer any property?
   a. Written seller consent authorizing the cooperating broker to show the property to a buyer-client
   b. A signed written buyer representation agreement with the buyer
   c. A pre-qualification letter from the buyer's lender confirming the buyer's financing ability
   d. Written authorization from TREC to act as a cooperating broker in the transaction

2. Under the TRID Rule, a lender must provide a borrower with a Loan Estimate by which deadline?
   a. On the day of closing, so all parties can review final credit costs together
   b. At least seven business days before the closing date
   c. Within ten calendar days of receiving the borrower's completed application
   d. Within three business days of receiving the borrower's application

3. When a licensee is asked by a buyer to recommend a home inspector, what practice should the licensee follow to comply with RESPA and avoid a conflict of interest?
   a. Provide the buyer with at least three inspector names to choose from rather than directing the buyer to a single provider
   b. Refer the buyer exclusively to an inspector who has completed TREC-certified continuing education
   c. Allow the listing broker to select the inspector to ensure consistency across all transaction parties
   d. Direct the buyer to the inspector who offers the lowest fee, because that reduces the buyer's overall closing costs

4. Under Paragraph 6 of the One to Four Family Residential Contract (Form 20-19), the title company has how many days after receiving the executed contract to furnish a title commitment to the buyer?
   a. 10 days, with an automatic 5-day extension if the commitment cannot be delivered in time
   b. 30 days, after which the buyer may terminate the contract and recover the earnest money
   c. 20 days, with an automatic extension of 15 additional days or until the closing date, whichever comes first
   d. 45 days, because the title search for a standard residential property typically takes at least that long

5. Which of the following is the most common example of an accrued expense that is prorated at a Texas residential closing?
   a. A homeowner's insurance premium that the seller paid in advance for the full calendar year
   b. A pest inspection fee that the seller paid at the beginning of the transaction
   c. A home warranty premium that the seller purchased as a closing concession for the buyer
   d. Property taxes, because Texas tax bills are typically paid at year-end

6. A seller is closing on May 17 and the annual property taxes are $1,950. Using the 12-month/360-day method, what is the daily tax rate?
   a. $5.42
   b. $5.34
   c. $162.50
   d. $5.21

7. A tenant pays $950 per month in rent and the closing is set for March 23. The seller owns the closing day. Using the 31 days in March, approximately how much rent credit does the buyer receive on the settlement statement?
   a. $213.45
   b. $319.57
   c. $245.05
   d. $176.50

8. When prorated items appear on a settlement statement, how does each prorated item show up for the two parties to the transaction?
   a. As a credit to both parties to reflect the shared nature of the ownership expense
   b. As a debit to one party and a credit to the other party for the same dollar amount
   c. As a debit to the party who will pay the expense after closing and no entry for the other party
   d. As a single line item allocated by percentage between the buyer and seller columns

9. What is the legal significance of the moment when a deed is delivered to and accepted by the buyer?
   a. The title becomes effective on the date the deed is recorded in the county clerk's office
   b. The title becomes effective on the date the seller signs the deed in front of a notary
   c. The title becomes effective on the date the settlement agent disburses the closing proceeds to all parties
   d. Title to the property transfers at that moment; delivery and acceptance must occur during the seller's lifetime

10. When a lender uses a tri-merge credit report to evaluate a borrower's creditworthiness, which score does the lender typically use when the three bureaus report different scores?
   a. The average of all three scores, rounded to the nearest whole number
   b. The middle of the three scores, not an average
   c. The highest of the three scores, to give the borrower the benefit of the best record
   d. The lowest of the three scores, to give the lender the most conservative view of the borrower's risk

11. A cloud on title discovered during the title search process may result from which of the following conditions?
   a. A title commitment that has not yet been reviewed and approved by the buyer's attorney
   b. An earnest money deposit that was not delivered to the escrow agent within the required number of days
   c. A mechanic's lien, a missing deed signature, or an incorrectly stated name in a prior recorded instrument
   d. A financing contingency that was not waived in writing by the buyer before the deadline

12. A buyer obtains a new loan of $200,000 at 5 percent annual interest and the closing occurs on August 20. Using the 360-day method, the buyer owns the closing day. Approximately how much prepaid interest does the buyer owe at closing for the remainder of August?

   a. $194.46
   b. $388.89
   c. $250.00
   d. $305.58

13. RESPA prohibits certain payments among settlement service providers. Which of the following is permitted under RESPA?

   a. Commission sharing among cooperating brokers and payments among MLS services
   b. A referral fee paid by a title company to a listing agent for sending closing business to that company
   c. A payment from a home inspector to a buyer's agent for recommending the inspector to buyer-clients
   d. A kickback from a lender to a real estate firm for directing buyers to apply for loans at that lender

14. Immediately before a closing, the buyer's agent should conduct a final walkthrough of the property with the buyer. What is the primary purpose of this walkthrough?

   a. To give the buyer an opportunity to renegotiate the sales price based on any new information
   b. To allow the title company to confirm that no new fixtures have been added since the survey was completed
   c. To confirm that the property's condition has not changed since the contract was signed and that no fixtures have been removed
   d. To allow the lender to verify that all lender-required repairs have been completed and documented

15. Which of the following best describes the purpose of a preliminary title report in a Texas residential transaction?

   a. It is a title insurance policy that takes effect immediately and protects the buyer from the date the report is issued
   b. It identifies problems with the title before closing so they can be resolved; it reflects items the title company would exclude from coverage if a policy were issued at that time
   c. It is a formal legal opinion from the county attorney confirming that no liens exist against the property
   d. It confirms that all inspections have been completed and all lender-required repairs have been documented and approved

Chapter 10 Case Study:
Transaction Process and Closing

The Situation

Lisa and Tom Mettling are closing on a home in Houston through Performance Programs Realty. Their agent, Dana Voss, has been managing the transaction for six weeks. The contract calls for a closing date of March 15, with possession upon funding and recording. The annual property taxes on the home are $6,600, and the seller has not yet paid them for the current year. The monthly rent on a tenant currently occupying a small guest cottage on the property is $900, due on the first of each month.

Three days before closing, Dana conducts a final walkthrough with the Mettlings and discovers that the seller has removed a built-in wine refrigerator from the kitchen that was listed as a fixture in the sales contract. The seller's agent says the seller considered it personal property and took it. Dana's clients are upset but Dana tells them the walkthrough finding is just a formality and they should proceed to closing to avoid losing their rate lock.

At the closing table, the Mettlings review the Closing Disclosure and notice that the property tax proration appears to reflect only two months of seller ownership rather than the correct amount for a March 15 closing. They also notice that the rent proration shows a credit to the buyer for the full month of March rather than just the buyer's portion. Dana tells them both figures look right to her and encourages them to sign.

Discussion Questions

Question 1

The final walkthrough revealed that the seller removed a built-in wine refrigerator that was identified as a fixture in the sales contract. Dana told the Mettlings it was just a formality and encouraged them to close anyway. Identify what options were available to the Mettlings at this point and explain what Dana should have advised instead.

____

____

____

____

____

Question 2

Using the 12-month/360-day method, calculate the correct property tax proration for a March 15 closing, assuming the seller owns the day of closing. Show your work and state which party is debited and which is credited. Then explain why an error in the proration matters even if the dollar difference is relatively small.

____

____

____

____

____

Question 3

The Closing Disclosure showed a rent credit to the buyer for the full month of March. The tenant pays $900 per month and the closing is March 15. Using the 30-day banker's method and assuming the seller owns the closing day, calculate the correct rent proration, state the correct debit and credit entries, and explain what Dana should have done when she noticed a discrepancy in the proration figures.

CHAPTER 11:

COMMON CONTRACT MISTAKES

Chapter Overview

Learning Objectives

Upon completing Chapter 11, the student will be able to:

1. Identify the most common mistakes licensees make when completing the One to Four Family Residential Contract (Form 20-19) and explain the consequences of each.
2. Correctly identify parties, property descriptions, checkbox elections, special provisions, default terms, signatures, effective dates, and addenda as required by TREC rules.
3. Distinguish between real property and personal property, explain how the classification can change through severance and affixing, and describe how to prevent disputes at closing.
4. Identify common title problems and explain their potential impact on a transaction, including how clouds on title arise and how they are resolved.
5. Apply practical best-practice guidelines to minimize contract errors and protect clients, the transaction, and the licensee's professional standing.

Contents

Contract Mistakes Overview

TREC has promulgated a comprehensive set of contract forms to protect the rights of buyers and sellers and to protect licensees from engaging in the unauthorized practice of law. Because most forms consist of relatively short fields to complete, it is easy to assume that errors are unlikely. In practice, however, licensees at every experience level routinely make mistakes when completing contracts, contingencies, amendments, and addenda.

This chapter examines the most common errors made when completing the One to Four Family Residential Contract (Form 20-19, effective July 1st, 2026), which is the standard TREC form for resale of one-to-four family residential properties. The categories of most frequent error are:

- The names of the parties to the contract
- The property description
- Checkboxes within individual paragraphs
- The Special Provisions paragraph
- The Default paragraph
- Signatures and initials
- The contract effective date
- Addenda identification and attachment

The Parties

Paragraph 1 of Form 20-19 requires the full legal names of both the seller and the buyer. One of the most frequent errors is the use of a name that is not the party's legal name. A social title, such as Mrs. Gray, is not a legal name and is insufficient.

For the seller, the name entered must match the name appearing on the property's current title exactly, assuming that name was correctly recorded when the seller acquired the property. If the name on the title is incorrect, that discrepancy must be corrected through a curative deed or other instrument before or at closing.

Because Texas is a community property state, each party's marital status must also be stated. Omitting marital status is one of the most commonly overlooked errors in this paragraph. A correct entry might read: Julia Ann Gray, a single person, as seller. For buyers who are married to each other, the correct form is: Barbara Jean Walsh and husband John Joseph Walsh, or Jane Doe and wife Mary Doe, reflecting both names and their relationship.

Errors in the parties paragraph can cloud the title, delay the closing, or require corrective instruments to be recorded. For a divorce situation, both spouses must sign the sales contract and, ideally, both should have signed the listing agreement at the outset. Obtaining a divorcing or estranged spouse's signature on the listing agreement early avoids a confrontation when an offer arrives.

The Property Description

Paragraph 2(A) of Form 20-19 requires the legal description of the property. A street address is never an adequate substitute for a legal description. The legal description must be sufficient for a competent surveyor to locate and identify the parcel.

A common error is omitting the section number from a subdivision legal description. An entry such as Lot 138, Block 16, Greenwood Hills Addition, City of Austin, Travis County, Texas is incomplete if the subdivision has multiple sections. The correct entry must specify the section: Lot 138, Block 16, Section 4 of Greenwood Hills Addition. The omission of the section number can make the description ambiguous and may affect the ability to insure the title or record the deed.

Best practice is to copy the legal description directly from the current deed, the title commitment, or the tax records and verify it against all three sources before using it in a contract. Any discrepancy among those sources is a potential title problem that should be resolved before the contract is executed.

Paragraph Checkboxes

Form 20-19 contains numerous checkboxes throughout its paragraphs. Failing to complete these elections is a frequent and consequential oversight.

Survey Checkbox

Paragraph 6(C) of the contract addresses the survey and requires the parties to elect one of two options. If the seller provides an existing survey that the title company or the lender finds unacceptable, the contract must specify whether the cost of a new survey falls on the seller or the buyer. Two checkboxes appear in the same sentence covering this situation. If neither box is checked, there is no agreement on who bears that cost, which can create a dispute that threatens the closing.

Possession Checkbox

Paragraph 10(A) of the contract addresses buyer's possession. The parties must elect whether possession will occur upon closing and funding, or pursuant to a TREC-promulgated temporary residential lease. If the parties do not check either box, or if they anticipate any possession arrangement other than immediate transfer at funding, a written temporary lease form must be used and the corresponding addendum identified in Paragraph 22 of the contract.

Any possession by the buyer before closing or by the seller after closing that is not governed by a written lease creates a tenancy at sufferance relationship. This can have serious insurance and liability implications for both parties. The contract reminds the parties to consult their insurance agents before any change in ownership or possession because coverage may be limited or terminated at that juncture.

Smart Devices Checkbox

Paragraph 10.B of the contract addresses Smart Devices. A Smart Device is defined as any device that connects to the internet to enable remote use, monitoring, and management of the property, items identified in any Non-Realty Items Addendum, or items in a fixture lease assigned to the buyer. At the time the seller delivers possession, the seller must deliver to the buyer written information containing all access codes, usernames, passwords, and applications the buyer will need to operate and control the Smart Devices, and must terminate and remove all of the seller's own access and connections from personal devices including phones and computers.

This paragraph is a common source of post-closing disputes. A seller who moves out and disconnects the smart home hub, removes the security camera app, or transfers the thermostat account without providing the buyer full access information leaves the buyer without the ability to control systems that may be essential to the property. Licensees should review Paragraph 10.B with sellers at the time of listing, compile a list of all Smart Devices on the property, and confirm that all credentials and connection transfers are completed before the keys are handed over.

Overlooked checkboxes throughout the contract can cause closing delays, create disputes between the parties, and expose the licensee to criticism for careless or incompetent practice. Licensees must review every page of every contract they handle for incomplete elections before the document leaves their hands.

Special Provisions

Paragraph 11 of Form 20-19 carries the following instruction directly on the form: "This paragraph is intended to be used only for additional informational items. An informational item is a statement that completes a blank in a contract form, discloses factual information, or provides instructions. Real estate brokers and sales agents are prohibited from practicing law and shall not add to, delete, or modify any provision of this contract unless drafted by a party to this contract or a party's attorney." Licensees must read that instruction carefully and follow it precisely.

The critical limitation is the word factual. A factual statement tells what a person will or will not do, such as the seller will leave the hot tub on the patio. What does not belong in Paragraph 11 is any statement that addresses what will happen if a condition is not met, because that type of language creates a legal right or remedy rather than describing a fact. Licensees are prohibited from writing legal rights and remedies into contracts. If parties ask a licensee to include such language, the licensee should advise them to consult a licensed attorney.

Specific examples of statements that do not belong in Paragraph 11:

- This contract is contingent upon an appraisal -- the words subject to and contingent upon are not factual statements and do not belong here; a financing contingency is addressed through the Third Party Financing Addendum (Form 40-11)
- The buyer will move into the home 48 hours prior to closing and funding -- this situation is governed by the Buyer's Temporary Residential Lease (Form 16-7), a TREC-promulgated form that must be used instead
- If the buyer does not receive the Seller's Disclosure of Property Condition within seven days, the buyer may terminate and receive the earnest money -- this right is already addressed in Paragraph 7(B)(2) of the contract and restating it in Paragraph 11 is redundant and potentially contradictory

Paragraph 11 is the appropriate location for straightforward factual business details that are specific to the transaction and not otherwise covered by the contract or a required addendum. Examples include items of personal property the seller agrees to leave, scheduled repairs the seller will complete before closing, or access arrangements during the inspection period.

The Default Paragraph

Paragraph 15 of Form 20-19 addresses what happens when a party defaults. If the buyer fails to comply, the seller may enforce specific performance or seek other legal remedies, or terminate the contract and retain the earnest money as liquidated damages. If the seller fails to comply, the buyer has the same options: enforce specific performance or seek other remedies, or terminate and recover the earnest money.

In practice, most licensees and parties move through this paragraph without stopping to discuss it. This is a missed opportunity. Reviewing the default paragraph thoroughly at the time of signing gives both parties a clear understanding of the consequences of non-performance. If the transaction later becomes contentious and one party threatens to walk away, a calm and accurate reminder of what default means under the contract often brings the situation back into perspective without further escalation.

A licensee who has reviewed the default paragraph with clients at the outset is also in a stronger position to help resolve disputes later, because the parties already understand what the contract provides rather than learning it for the first time in a moment of stress.

Signatures and Effective Date

Signatures and Initials

The final page of Form 20-19 provides signature lines for the buyer and seller. Every page of the contract also has a line for both parties' initials at the bottom. Missing signatures and missing initials are among the most frequent errors found in completed contracts.

Every addendum attached to the contract is part of the contract and requires all appropriate signatures and initials from both parties. A fully executed contract with an unsigned addendum is incomplete. The licensee must treat each addendum as a document requiring the same care and attention as the main contract form.

Under the Electronic Signatures in Global and National Commerce Act (ESIGN) and the Uniform Electronic Transactions Act (UETA), electronic signatures are legally equivalent to handwritten signatures. In Texas, electronic signatures are permitted on real estate contracts provided both parties agree in writing to the use of electronic execution. Many transactions today are executed entirely through electronic signature platforms such as DocuSign. When using electronic execution, the licensee must confirm that the consent to electronic signature has been completed by all parties before the contract is circulated for signing.

The Effective Date

Near the signature block on the final page of Form 20-19 is a blank for the effective date of the contract. This is the date of final acceptance, the date on which all parties have signed and the last party's acceptance has been communicated to the other side. The effective date must be entered by the listing broker. Every contractual deadline in the transaction is calculated from this date, so an omitted or incorrectly entered effective date can create confusion about when deadlines expire.

Because the effective date is recorded at the conclusion of what may have been a prolonged negotiation, it is easy to overlook in the relief of reaching final agreement. The wise licensee makes a habit of checking the effective date blank as the last step before delivering the executed contract to all parties.

Addenda

Paragraph 22 of Form 20-19 is the Agreement of Parties section, which lists all possible addenda and requires the parties to check each addendum that is being attached to and made part of the contract. Two errors involving addenda are extremely common:

- Checking an addendum in Paragraph 22 and then failing to physically attach it to the contract
- Attaching an addendum to the contract without checking it in Paragraph 22

Both errors create ambiguity about what is and is not part of the agreement. If a box in Paragraph 22 is checked but the addendum is not attached, the contract references an obligation or condition that neither party can read. If an addendum is attached but not listed in Paragraph 22, a court might find it was not incorporated into the contract. Every addendum check in Paragraph 22 must correspond to a physically attached and fully executed addendum, and every attached addendum must be identified in Paragraph 22.

As a practical matter, the licensee should assemble all addenda before beginning the signature process and confirm that the Paragraph 22 elections match the physical packet being signed. After all signatures are obtained, a final page count of the executed contract package confirms that nothing is missing.

Real Property vs. Personal Property

One of the most frequently contentious areas in a real estate transaction is determining which items convey with the property and which the seller is entitled to take. Understanding the distinction between real property and personal property is essential to preventing disputes.

Real property Ownership of real estate and the bundle of rights associated with owning it, including the right to use, possess, exclude, encumber, and transfer the land and everything permanently attached to it.

Personal property Ownership of anything that is not real estate, and the rights associated with owning it; may be tangible (physically existing items such as furniture, appliances, and vehicles) or intangible (abstract rights such as stocks, patents, and copyrights).

All real estate is tangible by nature. Personal property may be tangible or intangible. Boats, jewelry, appliances, and artwork are tangible personal property. Stocks, bonds, copyrights, trademarks, patents, and listing agreements are intangible personal property.

The primary test for distinguishing real from personal property is whether the item is permanently attached to the land or to a structure on the land. However, this classification is not immutable. The process of conversion can change an item's status:

Severance The conversion of real property to personal property by physically detaching it from the real estate, such as cutting down a tree, removing a built-in appliance, or detaching a ceiling fan.

Affixing (attachment) The conversion of personal property to real property by permanently attaching it to the real estate, such as installing a ceiling fan in a new home, assembling a masonry barbecue pit, or building a dock.

Preventing Disputes Over Property Classification

A wise listing agent compiles a complete written list at the time of listing identifying every item that will stay with the property and every item the seller intends to remove. This list should be reviewed with the seller and incorporated into the listing agreement or a separate written addendum. Items that are technically real property but that the seller intends to take, such as a ceiling fan from an estate, a custom chandelier, or a fruit tree planted in memory of a loved one, must be explicitly excluded in the listing and in the sales contract.

The buyer's agent should similarly confirm with the buyer every item the buyer expects to receive as part of the purchase, regardless of whether it is technically real or personal property, and ensure those items are specifically identified in the sales contract. Items that are commonly assumed to convey but often do not include window treatments, smart home devices, outdoor structures, storage systems, and specialty lighting fixtures.

Many of these disputes do not surface until the final walkthrough immediately before closing, when the buyer encounters a different or missing item for the first time. When a dispute arises at that stage, resolving it can be expensive and time-consuming. Licensees who have failed to clarify these items in writing sometimes find themselves personally replacing items to prevent a transaction from collapsing at the last moment.

Real-Life Examples of Property Classification Disputes

The following examples illustrate how these disputes arise:

- A flowering tree in the front yard had been planted by the seller's family in memory of a deceased relative. The seller dug it up and removed it before closing. The buyer had assumed it was part of the real estate and expected it to remain.
- A listing stated that the washer and dryer conveyed. The buyer first viewed a high-end modern set. At the final walkthrough, it had been swapped for an older set from the garage. Technically, a washer and dryer are personal property and a set was present, but the buyer's reasonable expectation was that the original set would be there.
- A glass-front curio cabinet in the dining room was built into a wall niche and appeared to be a permanent fixture. After closing, the buyer found it had been removed. Neither the listing nor the sales contract had addressed the cabinet. The buyer considered it real property; the seller considered it personal property.

In each case, explicit written identification of the item in the contract would have prevented the dispute entirely.

Title Problems

A seller is required to deliver marketable title at closing. Marketable title is one so free of defects that the buyer can be certain of not having to defend it. Any irregularity in the chain of title that would give a reasonable person pause before accepting a conveyance is called a cloud on title. A cloud reduces the marketability and value of the property because any prospective buyer aware of the cloud knows the seller may not be able to convey good title. The discovery of a cloud often gives the buyer a basis for terminating the contract.

Clouds on title range from minor clerical errors to serious unresolved legal claims. Common examples include:

- A misspelled property address or incorrect legal description in a prior deed
- A mortgage lien whose payoff and release has not been officially recorded
- A deed that was signed but never properly recorded
- An easement that was created but never recorded in the public record
- Unpaid property taxes or assessment liens
- A prior owner's failure to transfer mineral rights or other reserved interests
- A gap or missing link in the chronological chain of owners
- A pending lawsuit over ownership of all or part of the property

Many minor title defects can be resolved relatively quickly once identified. A misspelled name can be corrected by a curative or correction deed. An unrecorded release can be obtained from the former lienholder and recorded. However, any matter that requires court action, such as a quiet title suit or a pending ownership dispute, will take time and may delay or prevent the closing entirely.

Title problems are most likely to be identified during the title search and title commitment process. The licensee's role is to promptly communicate any discovered issues to the parties, help coordinate a resolution through the title company and the appropriate parties, and keep the transaction on track toward the closing date. Title insurance protects the buyer and lender against losses from covered title defects that were not discovered during the search.

Tips to Avoid Common Contract Mistakes

No licensee sets out to produce a contract full of errors. The following best practices reduce the risk of the mistakes described in this chapter and protect the licensee's clients, the transaction, and the licensee's own professional standing.

- Keep the contract neat and legible; sloppy or barely readable entries invite misreading and disputes
- Confirm that every blank on every page has been completed correctly before the contract is signed
- Always use the full legal name of each party; for sellers, match the name on the current title; always include marital status
- Double-check all numbers, figures, and calculations, including the sales price components in Paragraph 3 (3.A + 3.B = 3.C)
- Double-check all dates, especially the closing date, the option period expiration, financing deadlines, and the effective date
- Confirm that every party has initialed each page and any handwritten changes, and that all required signatures appear on the final page
- Ensure that clients receive a signed copy of the complete contract, including all addenda, as promptly as possible after execution
- Verify that every addendum checked in Paragraph 22 is physically attached and fully executed, and that every attached addendum is listed in Paragraph 22
- Copy the legal description from the current deed or title commitment and verify it against all available sources before entering it into the contract
- Explain the contract to clients in plain language, but do not interpret the legal ramifications of specific provisions; when legal interpretation is needed, direct clients to a licensed attorney
- Do not represent that a real estate contract does anything other than put the parties' agreement regarding the specific real property transaction in writing
- Do not accept poorly prepared contracts from other agents; an incomplete or error-ridden contract puts all parties and all licensees involved in the transaction at risk
- Review the default paragraph with clients at signing so they understand the consequences of non-performance before a dispute arises
- Complete a final page count of the executed contract package before delivering it to any party to confirm that all pages and addenda are present and signed

Chapter 11 Snapshot Review

The following review summarizes the key rules and concepts from Chapter 11.

Contract Mistakes and the Parties Paragraph

- TREC promulgates contract forms to protect buyers, sellers, and licensees; errors are common even among experienced licensees
- The eight most common error categories: party names, property description, checkboxes, Special Provisions, Default paragraph, signatures and initials, effective date, and addenda
- Always use each party's full legal name; for the seller, use the exact name shown on the current title
- Texas is a community property state; each party's marital status must be stated in Paragraph 1 (e.g., Julia Ann Gray, a single person; or Barbara Jean Walsh and husband John Joseph Walsh)
- In a divorce situation, both spouses must sign the contract; obtaining both signatures on the listing agreement from the start prevents confrontation when an offer arrives

Property Description and Checkboxes

- A street address is never an adequate legal description; the full legal description including lot, block, section, and subdivision name is required
- Omitting the section number from a subdivision description is a common error that can make the description ambiguous and affect title insurability
- Copy the legal description from the current deed or title commitment and verify it against the tax records
- Every checkbox election in the contract must be completed; incomplete elections can create disputes and delay closing
- Paragraph 6(C) survey checkbox: if the existing survey is unacceptable, the contract must specify who pays for a new one
- Paragraph 10(A) possession checkbox: the parties must elect possession at funding or by written temporary lease; any other possession arrangement creates a tenancy at sufferance with potential insurance and liability consequences

Special Provisions and Default

- Paragraph 11 is for informational items only: statements that complete a blank, disclose factual information, or provide instructions; licensees may not add, delete, or modify any contract provision unless it is drafted by a party or a party's attorney; do not use Paragraph 11 for language for which a promulgated addendum already exists
- A factual statement tells what a party will or will not do; language that creates a legal right or remedy does not belong in Paragraph 11 and requires an attorney
- Do not use the words contingent upon or subject to in Paragraph 11; use the appropriate TREC addendum instead
- Do not restate rights already addressed in other contract paragraphs; duplicative language can create contradictions
- Paragraph 15 (Default) should be reviewed with clients at signing; understanding the consequences of default in advance helps prevent disputes from escalating later

Signatures, Effective Date, and Addenda

- Every page of Form 20-19 requires buyer and seller initials at the bottom; the final page requires full signatures from all parties
- Every addendum is part of the contract and requires all appropriate signatures and initials
- Electronic signatures are permitted in Texas if both parties consent in writing; ESIGN and UETA make electronic signatures legally equivalent to handwritten signatures
- The effective date in the signature block must be completed by the listing broker; it is the date of final acceptance and is the reference point for all contractual deadlines
- Two common addenda errors: checking Paragraph 22 without attaching the addendum, and attaching an addendum without checking it in Paragraph 22
- Perform a final page count of the executed contract package before delivery to confirm all pages and addenda are present and signed

Real Property vs. Personal Property

- Real property is the land and everything permanently attached to it, plus the associated bundle of rights
- Personal property is everything that is not real estate; it may be tangible (boats, appliances, jewelry) or intangible (stocks, patents, copyrights)
- Severance converts real property to personal property by detaching it from the real estate (cutting a tree, removing a ceiling fan)
- Affixing converts personal property to real property by permanently attaching it to the real estate (installing a fixture, building a masonry structure)
- The listing agent should compile a written list at the outset identifying every item that will and will not convey; this list should be incorporated into the listing agreement and sales contract
- The buyer's agent should confirm every item the buyer expects to receive and have it specifically identified in the contract
- Most real-vs-personal property disputes surface at the final walkthrough; preventing them requires early, detailed written documentation

Title Problems

- Marketable title is one so free of defects that the buyer will not have to defend it; sellers are required to deliver marketable title at closing
- A cloud on title is any irregularity in the chain of title that would cause a reasonable person to pause before accepting a conveyance; it reduces value and marketability
- Common clouds: misspelled names or addresses in prior deeds, unrecorded mortgage releases, unrecorded easements, unpaid tax liens, reserved mineral rights that were never transferred, gaps in the chain of ownership, and pending title lawsuits
- Minor clerical defects can often be corrected quickly with a curative deed or an obtained and recorded release; matters requiring court action can delay or prevent closing
- Title problems are identified during the title search and title commitment process; the licensee coordinates resolution through the title company and the affected parties
- Title insurance protects the buyer and lender against financial loss from covered title defects not discovered during the search

Best Practices to Prevent Contract Mistakes

- Legible, complete contracts: fill every blank, check every required box, double-check all numbers and dates
- Full legal names and marital status for all parties; legal description copied from title records and verified
- All parties initial every page and any corrections; all required signatures on the final page of the contract and on every addendum
- Paragraph 22 elections match physically attached addenda; page count verified before delivery
- Effective date entered by the listing broker immediately upon final acceptance
- Explain contract provisions in plain language; direct clients to an attorney for legal interpretation
- Refuse to accept poorly prepared contracts from other agents; incomplete contracts expose all parties to risk

CHAPTER 11 QUIZ:

COMMON CONTRACT MISTAKES

1. In Paragraph 1 of Form 20-19, which of the following entries for a seller's name is unacceptable because it fails to meet the legal name requirement?
   a. Julia Ann Gray, a single person
   b. Barbara Jean Walsh and husband John Joseph Walsh
   c. Robert Alan Torres, a married man
   d. Mrs. Gray, as seller

2. Texas is a community property state. Which additional piece of information must always be included for each party in Paragraph 1 of Form 20-19?
   a. The party's marital status
   b. The party's Social Security number
   c. The party's date of birth
   d. The party's driver's license number

3. A legal description for a property in a subdivision with multiple sections reads: Lot 138, Block 16, Greenwood Hills Addition, City of Austin, Travis County, Texas. What critical element is missing from this description?
   a. The street address of the property
   b. The name of the county appraisal district
   c. The section number of the subdivision
   d. The property's tax identification number

4. What is the best practice for obtaining the legal description to use in a Texas residential sales contract?
   a. Use the property address that appears on the seller's most recent utility bill
   b. Copy the legal description from the current deed or title commitment and verify it against all available sources
   c. Ask the seller to write the legal description from memory based on what appears in the tax records
   d. Use the abbreviated description shown on the current mortgage statement

5. Paragraph 6(C) of Form 20-19 contains a survey checkbox requiring the parties to elect who pays for a new survey if the existing survey is unacceptable. What is the consequence if neither box is checked?
   a. There is no agreement on who bears the cost of a new survey, which can create a dispute that threatens the closing
   b. The cost of a new survey defaults to the buyer because the buyer typically benefits from a current survey
   c. The cost of a new survey defaults to the seller because the seller is required to deliver marketable title
   d. The contract automatically terminates because TREC rules require that every checkbox be completed before the contract is valid

6. If a buyer takes possession of a property before closing or a seller retains possession after closing without a written TREC-promulgated lease in place, what type of legal relationship is created?
   a. An estate for years, which requires proper written notice to terminate
   b. A month-to-month tenancy that automatically renews until either party gives 30 days' notice
   c. An implied license that the property owner may revoke at any time without notice
   d. A tenancy at sufferance, which can have serious insurance and liability consequences for both parties

7. A licensee wants to include a financing contingency in Paragraph 11 of Form 20-19 using the language that this contract is subject to the buyer obtaining financing. Why is this approach incorrect?
   a. Paragraph 11 is reserved for seller disclosures only and may not be used for buyer conditions
   b. The words subject to are reserved exclusively for use in addenda prepared by licensed attorneys
   c. Financing contingencies must be addressed through the Third Party Financing Addendum (Form 40-11), a TREC-promulgated form that exists for that purpose
   d. TREC rules prohibit any mention of financing in the body of the sales contract

8. Which of the following best describes why a licensee should review Paragraph 15 (Default) with clients at the time of contract signing?
   a. TREC requires licensees to obtain a written acknowledgment from clients confirming they have read the default paragraph
   b. The default paragraph is the only paragraph that requires separate initials from each party
   c. Reviewing the default paragraph protects the licensee from being held liable if either party later defaults
   d. Clients who understand the consequences of default in advance are better positioned to resolve disputes calmly if a problem arises later

9. Who is responsible for entering the effective date in the signature block of Form 20-19, and why is that date critical?
   a. The listing broker enters the effective date because every contractual deadline in the transaction is calculated from that date
   b. The buyer enters the effective date because the buyer initiates the transaction by making the offer
   c. The title company enters the effective date when it receives the executed contract and opens the file
   d. Either party may enter the effective date because it is simply a notation of the calendar date on which both parties happened to sign

10. Under the Electronic Signatures in Global and National Commerce Act (ESIGN) and the Uniform Electronic Transactions Act (UETA), electronic signatures on Texas real estate contracts are legally valid under which condition?
    a. Both parties must be physically present in the same location when the electronic signature is applied
    b. The electronic signature platform must be approved and certified by the Texas Real Estate Commission
    c. Both parties must consent in writing to the use of electronic execution
    d. Electronic signatures are valid on all documents except the deed, which must always bear an original handwritten signature

11. Two common errors involving addenda and Paragraph 22 of Form 20-19 frequently appear in completed contracts. Which of the following correctly describes one of those errors?
    a. Signing an addendum before the main contract is signed, which invalidates the addendum
    b. Checking an addendum in Paragraph 22 but failing to physically attach it to the contract
    c. Using a TREC-promulgated addendum for a purpose for which it was not specifically designed
    d. Attaching more than four addenda to a single contract without TREC approval

12. A seller removes a built-in ceiling fan from the dining room before closing, arguing it is personal property. The buyer expected it to remain. Which legal concept explains how the ceiling fan's classification may have changed when it was installed?
    a. Affixing, which converts personal property to real property by permanently attaching it to the real estate
    b. Severance, which converts personal property to real property by detaching it from the real estate
    c. Dedication, which transfers personal property to a public entity through a written instrument
    d. Escheat, which transfers ownership of abandoned property to the state after a statutory period
    d. A curative or correction deed is prepared, executed by the appropriate parties, and recorded to fix the error

13. A listing agent discovers during the title commitment process that an old mortgage lien on the property was paid off years ago but the release was never recorded. Which of the following correctly describes what must happen before closing?
    a. The buyer must waive the objection in writing because unrecorded mortgage releases do not affect the buyer's legal title
    b. The seller must obtain the release from the former lienholder and record it to clear the cloud on title
    c. The title company is required to issue the policy without exception because the underlying debt has been paid
    d. The parties must file a quiet title suit because an unrecorded mortgage release can only be cleared by a court order

14. To prevent disputes over which items convey with the property, what should a listing agent do at the time the listing agreement is signed?
    a. Advise the seller to remove all personal property from the home before the first showing so buyers are not confused
    b. Attach photographs of every item in the home to the listing agreement so there is a visual record of what was present
    c. Compile a written list identifying every item that will stay with the property and every item the seller intends to remove, and incorporate it into the listing agreement
    d. Instruct the seller to exclude all tangible personal property from the sale and negotiate those items separately after the contract is signed

Chapter 11 Case Study:
Common Contract Mistakes

The Situation

Mark Webb is a newly licensed sales agent at Performance Programs Realty. His sponsoring broker, Janet Mettling, has been reviewing his first independently prepared contract and found several problems before it was submitted to the seller.

In Paragraph 1, Mark identified the buyer as Mr. Brian Holloway without stating marital status or full legal name. For the seller, Mark copied the name from the MLS listing sheet, which read Pat Torres. The current deed on file at the county clerk's office shows the seller's name as Patricia Ann Torres, a married woman, and her husband does not appear anywhere in the contract.

In Paragraph 2(A), Mark entered the property's street address rather than the legal description. He told Janet the address was easier for the client to understand and that the legal description could be added later.

In Paragraph 11, the Special Provisions paragraph, Mark included the following language: This contract is contingent upon the buyer obtaining financing at an interest rate not to exceed 6.5 percent. If financing is not obtained on these terms within 21 days, this contract is void and the earnest money shall be returned to the buyer. Mark told Janet this was simpler than using the Third Party Financing Addendum.

Discussion Questions

Question 1

Janet found two problems in Paragraph 1. Identify both errors, explain why each one creates a risk for the transaction, and describe exactly how each entry should have been written.

____

____

____

____

____

Question 2

Mark entered the property's street address in the legal description blank and told Janet the legal description could be added later. Explain why a street address is legally insufficient, identify the risk created by leaving the legal description blank, and describe where Mark should obtain the correct legal description.

____

____

____

____

____

Question 3

Mark wrote a financing contingency directly into Paragraph 11 rather than using Form 40-11. Identify the two problems with his approach, explain what Paragraph 11 is actually for, and describe what Mark should have done instead.

Quiz Answer Key

Answer Key -- Chapter 1 Quiz: Texas Contract Law

1. c. 1939
2. a. The Texas Real Estate Commission
3. d. Nine
4. b. Three
5. a. Giving a client a legal opinion about the effect of a contract provision
6. d. The Texas Real Estate Commission
7. b. Thirteen
8. c. A deliberate act of deception committed to gain an unfair advantage over another person
9. d. That the licensee acted with intent to deceive
10. a. 60 days
11. c. Two years from the date of the event or from the date of discovery
12. b. Three times
13. a. One to Four Family Residential Contract (Form 20-19)
14. d. Terminate the contract for any reason during an agreed period in exchange for an option fee
15. b. The Buyer Representation Agreement
16. c. Two to three months
17. d. At the same time as the original contract
18. a. Nine
19. b. 90 days
20. c. Encourage the client to consult a licensed attorney for any legal questions

Answer Key -- Chapter 2 Quiz: Basics of Texas Real Estate Law

1. b. State government
2. d. The federal government establishes broad standards for property usage, fair housing, and environmental protection
3. a. The surface, everything beneath it to the earth's core, natural attachments, and air above to infinity
4. c. Land plus all man-made improvements permanently attached to that land
5. d. Possession, use, transfer, encumbrance, and exclusion
6. a. Separate estates that may be sold independently from surface ownership
7. c. The State of Texas

8. b. It belongs to the landowner above it

9. c. Whether the item is permanently attached to the land or to structures on the land

10. d. Real property is converted to personal property by detaching it from the land

11. a. Trade fixtures, which remain the tenant's personal property

12. b. Area preference

13. d. Immobility

14. a. Tenancy in common

15. c. It must be created by a written agreement that expressly states the intent to create a joint tenancy

16. b. The deceased tenant's interest passes automatically to the surviving joint tenants

17. a. All property earned or acquired by either spouse during the marriage, owned equally by both

18. d. Both spouses must sign the deed to eliminate any question about community property interest

19. b. A hybrid ownership combining fee simple title to a unit's airspace with a tenancy-in-common interest in common elements

20. c. In a cooperative, the owner holds stock in a corporation and a proprietary lease, not real property

21. b. Register the time-share plan with the Texas Real Estate Commission

22. c. A hybrid business entity combining limited liability protection with flexible management structure

23. d. The Federal Fair Housing Act of 1968

24. a. A personal property interest in emblements that the tenant retains the right to harvest

Answer Key -- Chapter 3 Quiz: Introduction to Contracts

1. b. Doing what a party agreed to do under the terms of the contract

2. d. Forbearance

3. a. Six

4. c. 18 years of age

5. d. The mutual exchange of promises between buyer and seller

6. a. It must be in writing and signed by the parties

7. c. A lease for a term of one year or less

8. b. A contract in which all terms are clearly stated by the parties, whether verbally or in writing

9. c. An implied agency relationship

10. d. From the moment the contract is formed, because both parties are bound by mutual promises

11. a. An option to purchase in which the seller is bound but the buyer is not obligated to buy

12. b. The contract has no legal effect and neither party can enforce it

13. d. Voidable

14. a. Four years from the date of the breach

15. c. Executory, because the most important obligations have not yet been performed

16. b. Before the purchaser signs the executory contract

Answer Key -- Chapter 4 Quiz: Ownership Rights and Limitations

1. c. Police power
2. b. Seven years
3. d. Just compensation at market value
4. a. Economic development that solely benefits a private party
5. b. Fee simple absolute
6. d. Determinable fee
7. a. Committing waste that impairs the value of future interest holders' rights
8. c. Reversionary interest
9. d. A private party's non-possessory interest in real property that limits the owner's full enjoyment of the bundle of rights
10. a. Easement appurtenant
11. c. Easement in gross
12. b. The encroachment may mature into an easement by prescription
13. a. A license that the farmer may revoke at any time
14. d. The borrower retains legal title and the lender holds only a security interest
15. b. The State of Texas
16. c. Even when the homestead is the separate property of one spouse
17. d. One-eighth
18. a. The Residential Lead-Based Paint Hazard Reduction Act
19. b. Lung cancer
20. c. Disclose the mold as a latent defect, even if it is no longer visible after repair work was performed

Answer Key -- Chapter 5 Quiz: Contracts Used in Texas Real Estate

1. b. A contract in which both parties exchange mutual promises and each is bound from the moment the contract is formed
2. d. Any lease for a term exceeding one year
3. a. Immediately, without delay, unless the seller has given specific written instructions to the contrary
4. c. Void, because it requires unlawful performance that violates fair housing law
5. d. It is a unilateral contract in which the seller is bound to sell but the buyer is not obligated to purchase
6. a. The listing broker still earns the commission because the broker holds the exclusive right regardless of who produces the buyer

7. c. Estate at sufferance

8. b. It signals the buyer's serious intent and may serve as liquidated damages if the buyer defaults

9. a. The vendor retains legal title while the vendee holds equitable title

10. d. They create a direct conflict between the broker's financial interest and the fiduciary duty to maximize the seller's proceeds

11. c. The landlord retains the consideration fee because it is non-refundable

12. b. It has a fixed beginning and ending date and terminates automatically without notice on the stated date

13. d. 90 days

14. a. Four years from the date of the breach

15. c. One broker has the marketing right but the seller may find a buyer independently without owing a commission

16. b. Showing property to a buyer

17. a. It arises from the conduct of the parties when no express agreement exists, such as when a licensee acts on a buyer's behalf without a signed representation agreement

18. c. A non-exclusive listing that allows the seller to engage multiple brokers simultaneously, with only the producing broker earning a commission

19. d. Pay the full amount due or deliver a promissory note equal to the balance under the same contract terms

20. b. Constructive eviction

21. a. The agent whose efforts were the proximate, efficient, and producing cause of the completed transaction

22. d. Specific performance

23. b. The land only, not improvements; the tenant typically develops the land at the tenant's expense over a long term

24. c. Percentage lease

25. a. A lease purchase agreement with a term exceeding 180 days

Answer Key -- Chapter 6 Quiz: The Texas Sales Contract

1. c. Reject the offer, which frees both parties and terminates the offer

2. a. Immediately, unless the seller has given specific written instructions directing otherwise

3. d. The original offer no longer exists because a counteroffer terminated it the moment the seller made it

4. a. To signal the buyer's serious intent and to serve as potential liquidated damages if the buyer defaults

5. c. Third Party Financing Addendum (Form 40-11)

6. d. On or before the effective date of the contract binding the buyer to purchase

7. b. The seller is exempt from the disclosure requirement because court-ordered foreclosures are among the eleven statutory exemptions

8. c. 1978

9. a. 15 percent

10. d. General warranty deed

11. b. Title insurance policy

12. a. A lease for a term of one year or less, which may be oral and is still enforceable

13. c. Four years from the date of the breach

14. d. Anticipatory breach

15. b. Specific performance

16. c. Costs are split equally between the parties, and the mediator cannot impose an outcome because mediation is non-binding

17. a. Only the property owner

18. d. The title company

19. b. The listing broker, upon receiving notification that the seller has accepted

20. c. Addendum for Seller's Disclosure of Information on Lead-Based Paint and Lead-Based Paint Hazards (Form 56-0)

21. d. The broker may not receive more than the commission that would have been earned at the full listing price

Answer Key -- Chapter 7 Quiz: Contingencies, Addenda, and Amendments

1. d. The right to exit the contract without default and to recover the earnest money

2. a. The contingency is deemed waived and the buyer becomes obligated to proceed with the purchase

3. c. Addendum Concerning Right to Terminate Due to Lender's Appraisal (Form 49-1)

4. b. It gives the buyer a specified number of days to obtain loan approval; if financing cannot be secured in time, the buyer may cancel and recover the earnest money

5. a. The financing contingency is waived and the buyer must close the transaction or be in default

6. d. 24 to 72 hours from the time the seller notifies the original buyer

7. b. The Termination Option in Paragraph 23 of Form 20-19, which gives the buyer an unrestricted right to terminate during the option period

8. c. In a settlement contingency, the seller is typically prohibited from accepting other offers; in a sale-and-settlement contingency, the seller retains the right to continue marketing

9. a. A written letter from the appropriate zoning authority confirming that the specified business may legally operate from the property address

10. d. Addendum for Property Subject to Mandatory Membership in a Property Owners Association (Form 36-11)

11. b. An addendum is executed at the same time as the original contract and is part of it from the start; an amendment modifies a contract that has already been fully ratified by all parties

12. c. Ten

13. d. A specific calendar date; entering vague language such as at lender's discretion violates TREC rules

14. **a.** VA and FHA transactions, where the lender's appraiser may generate a required repair list as a condition of loan approval

15. **c.** Third Party Financing Addendum (Form 40-11)

16. **a.** The VA Funding Fee

17. **d.** Seven days

18. **c.** Five hundred dollars

19. **b.** Terminate the contract and retain the earnest money

20. **d.** No prepayment penalty; the buyer may prepay all or any portion of the loan at any time without penalty

21. **a.** To formally release the seller from ongoing personal liability on a mortgage loan that the buyer has assumed

22. **b.** The seller, because those outcomes directly benefit the seller

23. **c.** The buyer must be a veteran with sufficient unused VA entitlement to substitute for the seller's entitlement

24. **a.** Retain an attorney to prepare the appropriate documents

25. **d.** A promissory note and a deed of trust

Answer Key -- Chapter 8 Quiz: Financing Real Estate

1. **b.** Lien theory, meaning the borrower retains legal title and the lender holds only a security interest

2. **d.** The Garn-St Germain Depository Institutions Act

3. **a.** In a single lump sum payment at the maturity date, after making periodic interest-only payments throughout the loan term

4. **c.** Trustor, beneficiary, and trustee

5. **d.** Pay off the entire remaining loan balance so the property can be conveyed free of the lender's lien

6. **a.** 20 days

7. **c.** 22 percent equity, corresponding to a 78 percent loan-to-value ratio

8. **b.** A promissory note and a deed of trust

9. **a.** Three business days

10. **d.** Ginnie Mae

11. **c.** The lender's fixed markup, added to the index rate to produce the note rate on the loan

12. **b.** When the seller's net proceeds at closing will be insufficient to pay off the existing mortgage balance and the seller requires the lienholder's consent to sell

13. **d.** The seller, while the buyer holds only equitable title and possesses the property

14. **a.** Race, color, religion, national origin, sex, marital status, age, or dependency on public assistance

15. **c.** Judicial foreclosure allows the lender to obtain a deficiency judgment against the borrower for any balance remaining after the sale

16. **b.** The refinancing of an existing mortgage or the taking out of a home equity loan on a primary residence

17. d. On the first Tuesday of each month at the courthouse, between 10 a.m. and 4 p.m.

18. a. Title search, inspection, survey, appraisal, loan origination, credit reporting, and attorney services, when no service has actually been rendered

19. c. The mechanic's lien priority dates from when work commenced or ended under state law, not from the date it was recorded

20. b. A writ of execution

21. a. Reduce the priority of an existing lien to a position behind a new lien that will be recorded in the future

22. d. When the amount of the forgiven debt exceeds the borrower's tax basis in the property

23. b. Jumbo loans

24. c. The FHA 203(k) loan combines home purchase financing with rehabilitation financing in a single loan, while the FHA 203(b) is a standard purchase loan

25. d. Redlining, in which lenders refused to make loans in certain neighborhoods based on the racial or economic composition of those areas

26. b. The borrower effectively makes 13 monthly payments per year, which shortens the loan term and reduces total interest paid

27. c. The release clause, also called the partial release clause

28. a. Payment history, which accounts for 35 percent of the score

29. d. Neither the first mortgage nor the second mortgage exceeds an 80 percent loan-to-value ratio, so PMI is not triggered on either loan

Answer Key -- Chapter 9 Quiz: Conveyance of Title

1. c. The grantor warrants the title against all claims whether they arose before or during the grantor's period of ownership

2. a. The covenant of seisin and the covenant against encumbrances

3. d. To clear a clouded title by conveying any and all interest a party may hold in the property

4. b. The owner may file a quiet title suit requiring the encumbering party to prove the validity of the interest in court

5. c. The possessor must consistently assert ownership of the property without the legal owner's permission

6. d. The possessor must bring a legal action to quiet title and obtain a court judgment establishing ownership

7. a. A property owner dies intestate with no recognized heirs, or property is abandoned for a statutory period

8. b. The seller holds legal title and the buyer holds equitable title during the contract period

9. d. It is written entirely in the testator's own handwriting, dated, and signed, and does not require any witnesses

10. c. Superior liens including real estate taxes, assessment taxes, federal estate taxes, and state inheritance taxes

11. a. The surviving spouse first, then children, then parents, then siblings, then more distant relatives

12. b. Constructive notice, because the law presumes that recorded information is available to and known by the public

13. c. In the Torrens system, the title certificate itself is the title; title passes only when the conveyance is registered directly on the certificate

14. d. The legal description of the property, the current owners of record, and any outstanding liens or encumbrances

15. a. An abstractor, who searches documents registered with the county recorder and other official sources and arranges them in chronological order

16. b. A forged deed appearing in the chain of title

17. d. It recapitulates the property description, the interest to be insured, the names of the insured parties, and any exceptions to coverage

18. a. Title insurance rates in Texas are set by the Texas Department of Insurance; the rate is the same regardless of which title company issues the policy

19. c. For as long as the owner or the owner's heirs hold the property or remain liable under any title warranties

20. b. The title company also issues an owner's title policy to the buyer

Answer Key -- Chapter 10 Quiz: Transaction Process and Closing

1. b. A signed written buyer representation agreement with the buyer

2. d. Within three business days of receiving the borrower's application

3. a. Provide the buyer with at least three inspector names to choose from rather than directing the buyer to a single provider

4. c. 20 days, with an automatic extension of 15 additional days or until the closing date, whichever comes first

5. d. Property taxes, because Texas tax bills are typically paid at year-end

6. a. $5.42

7. c. $245.05

8. b. As a debit to one party and a credit to the other party for the same dollar amount

9. d. Title to the property transfers at that moment; delivery and acceptance must occur during the seller's lifetime

10. b. The middle of the three scores, not an average

11. c. A mechanic's lien, a missing deed signature, or an incorrectly stated name in a prior recorded instrument

12. d. $305.58

13. a. Commission sharing among cooperating brokers and payments among MLS services

14. c. To confirm that the property's condition has not changed since the contract was signed and that no fixtures have been removed

15. b. It identifies problems with the title before closing so they can be resolved; it reflects items the title company would exclude from coverage if a policy were issued at that time

Answer Key -- Chapter 11 Quiz: Common Contract Mistakes

1. d. Mrs. Gray, as seller

2. a. The party's marital status

3. c. The section number of the subdivision

4. b. Copy the legal description from the current deed or title commitment and verify it against all available sources

5. a. There is no agreement on who bears the cost of a new survey, which can create a dispute that threatens the closing

6. d. A tenancy at sufferance, which can have serious insurance and liability consequences for both parties

7. c. Financing contingencies must be addressed through the Third Party Financing Addendum (Form 40-11), a TREC-promulgated form that exists for that purpose

8. d. Clients who understand the consequences of default in advance are better positioned to resolve disputes calmly if a problem arises later

9. a. The listing broker enters the effective date because every contractual deadline in the transaction is calculated from that date

10. c. Both parties must consent in writing to the use of electronic execution

11. b. Checking an addendum in Paragraph 22 but failing to physically attach it to the contract

12. a. Affixing, which converts personal property to real property by permanently attaching it to the real estate

13. b. The seller must obtain the release from the former lienholder and record it to clear the cloud on title

14. c. Compile a written list identifying every item that will stay with the property and every item the seller intends to remove, and incorporate it into the listing agreement

Case Study Debriefs

Chapter 1: Case Study Debrief Commentary

Question 1 -- The Missing Spouse Signature

Sandra's failure to obtain Donna Renfro's signature on the listing agreement is a foundational error rooted in Texas community property law and homestead rights. Texas requires both spouses to sign any document conveying or encumbering community property or homestead property. Even if the listing agreement was technically valid with only Carl's signature, the title company correctly identified that a deed from Carl alone could not convey clear title, because Donna's interest in the property had never been released.

Best practice requires the listing agent to identify all parties with an ownership interest in the property before accepting a listing. In a divorce situation, the agent should insist on both spouses signing the listing agreement at the outset, even if that conversation is uncomfortable. Obtaining Donna's signature on the listing agreement would not have resolved the divorce dispute, but it would have signaled her cooperation and positioned the closing to proceed without a last-minute title crisis. The agent should also have confirmed the ownership status of the property with the title company before listing it, which would have revealed the community property issue immediately.

The practical lesson is that title problems discovered at closing are far more damaging and expensive to resolve than title problems identified at the listing stage. A brief, upfront conversation with the title company or an attorney saves enormous difficulty later.

Question 2 -- Delayed Presentation of the Offer

TREC rules require immediate presentation of all offers. Sandra's 48-hour delay violated this requirement and placed her personal business interest, bringing in her own buyer, ahead of her fiduciary duty to the Renfros. The Canon of Ethics Rule 531.1 (Fidelity) requires that the agent's primary duty be to the client's interests at all times.

The consequences of this violation are significant. Sandra could face TREC disciplinary action, including possible suspension or revocation of her license, for failing to present an offer promptly. She could also face civil liability for tortious interference if her delay caused the seller financial harm. A tort is a negligent or wrongful act that constitutes a breach of a legal duty and causes damages to another person. If Marcus Webb had withdrawn his offer during the 48-hour window, or if the Renfros had accepted a worse offer because they were unaware of the better one, Sandra and PPC Realty could both be held liable.

Students should also recognize the ethical dimension. Sandra's competing obligation to her other buyer does not override her duty to present all offers immediately to her seller-client. The only permissible exception is when the seller has given specific written instructions directing the agent not to present certain types of offers. No such instruction existed here. The correct approach would have been to present Marcus Webb's offer immediately and allow the Renfros to decide how to proceed while awaiting the competing offer.

Question 3 -- Unauthorized Practice of Law

When Sandra explained the legal effect of terminating the contract on day eight versus day eleven of the option period, and offered her opinion on which approach would give Marcus the strongest legal position, she crossed from permissible brokerage activity into the unauthorized practice of law.

Texas law distinguishes between explaining what a contract says, which is permissible, and giving a legal opinion about the effect of a contract, which is prohibited. A licensee may help a party understand what a document says, but must not offer legal advice or opinions about the legal consequences of specific actions. Sandra's opinion about which termination date would give Marcus the strongest legal position was a legal conclusion, not a factual explanation.

Under TRELA, a license holder who gives legal advice in connection with an agency relationship or for consideration may have his or her license suspended or revoked. The National Association of REALTORS Code of Ethics, Article 13, reinforces this: licensees shall not engage in activities that constitute the unauthorized practice of law and shall recommend that legal counsel be obtained when the interests of any party require it.

The correct response to Marcus's question would have been to explain clearly what the Termination Option paragraph says about the option period and the mechanics of exercising it, and then to advise Marcus to consult a licensed attorney if he needed a legal opinion about the strategic consequences of each timing choice. This approach protects the client, protects the licensee, and honors the boundary between brokerage and legal practice.

Chapter 2: Case Study Debrief Commentary

Question 1 -- Mineral Rights and Separate Property

This question asks students to work through two distinct issues: the nature of Kevin's ownership interest in the home, and the character of mineral rights in Texas.

As to the home: property inherited by one spouse before or during the marriage is that spouse's separate property under Texas community property law. Kevin's home, inherited before the marriage and recorded in his name alone, qualifies as his separate property. Laura has no ownership interest in the home itself and no right to approve or block a mineral lease on that property's subsurface estate.

As to the mineral rights: Texas recognizes oil, gas, and other mineral rights as separate estates that may be owned, leased, and transferred independently of the surface. A surface owner who also holds the mineral estate may lease those rights to an operator without conveying the surface. Kevin, as the sole owner of separate property that includes the mineral estate, had the authority to sign the mineral lease with Performance Energy Programs without Laura's consent.

The adjacent lot purchased during the marriage with joint funds is community property. Both spouses own community property equally, and both must sign any conveyance or encumbrance of it. Had Performance Energy Programs approached Kevin about mineral rights beneath the adjacent lot, Laura's consent would have been required. This point is developed further in Question 2.

Dale Crosby's situation is a useful contrast. If the seller who conveyed Dale's property reserved the mineral rights at the time of sale, those rights stayed with the seller and did not pass to Dale. Dale's belief that he owns all rights to his land would be incorrect if the reservation was properly expressed in the deed and recorded. This illustrates the importance of reading the chain of title carefully and understanding what was and was not conveyed.

Question 2 -- Signature Requirements for Separate and Community Property

Tricia's advice was partially correct and partially incorrect, and the distinction matters significantly.

For the family home: because the home is Kevin's separate property, Kevin alone holds title and theoretically could sign a listing agreement and a deed without Laura's participation. However, Texas law and standard title company practice require both spouses to sign any conveyance of homestead property, even when the homestead is one spouse's separate property. If the Mettlings occupy the home as their principal residence, it qualifies as their homestead, and both spouses must sign. Tricia's advice that Laura did not need to sign was incorrect in this respect and could have created a title problem at closing identical to the one illustrated in the Chapter 1 case study.

For the adjacent lot: the lot was purchased during the marriage with funds from a joint account. It is community property, and both spouses own it equally. Community property cannot be transferred or encumbered without both spouses' signatures under any circumstances. Tricia's advice that Kevin could list and sell the lot alone because it would simplify the paperwork was flatly wrong. No convenience rationale overrides the community property signature requirement. A deed from Kevin alone on community property would not convey good title, and the title company would not insure the transaction.

This question reinforces a practical lesson: the most dangerous advice a licensee can give is incomplete advice that is partially correct. Tricia was right that separate property belongs to the titled spouse, but she failed to account for the homestead overlay and the community property nature of the second parcel. Both oversights had the potential to derail the closing.

Question 3 -- Encroachment and Adverse Possession

Dale Crosby's fence has stood four feet over the property line for at least twelve years without objection. This situation implicates the doctrine of adverse possession and potentially the related concept of an easement by prescription.

For adverse possession to succeed in Texas, the possessor must establish an open and notorious claim, hostile possession asserted without the owner's permission, and continuous occupation for the statutory period. The claimant must also hold a claim of right or color of title. Satisfying these criteria does not automatically transfer title. Dale would need to bring a quiet title action in court to obtain a judgment establishing his legal ownership of the encroaching strip of land. The court would then issue an order clearing the title record.

Twelve years of uncontested encroachment may be sufficient to meet the statutory period in Texas, depending on which statute applies to the specific circumstances. Whether Dale can succeed would depend on whether all elements are provable, including whether the Mettlings or Kevin's father had actual or constructive knowledge of the encroachment and whether any permissive use was ever granted. A permissive use, such as a verbal license, would defeat the hostility element.

As an alternative, if Dale does not seek to acquire title to the strip but simply wishes to preserve the right to maintain the fence in its current location, he might argue for an easement by prescription based on the same elements of open, continuous, and adverse use over the statutory period.

To prevent this outcome, the Mettlings or Kevin's father could have periodically inspected the boundary, objected to the fence placement, demanded its removal, or filed a quiet title action at any point within the statutory period. A current survey at the time of purchase or listing is the most reliable tool for detecting encroachments before they mature into legal claims. This underscores the practical value of ordering a survey early in every transaction rather than waiting until a lender requires one.

Chapter 3: Case Study Debrief Commentary

Question 1 -- Minor's Capacity and Voidable Contracts

Bryan lacks legal capacity to contract because he has not reached the age of majority, which is 18 in Texas. A contract signed by a minor is voidable, not void. The distinction is critical: a void contract has no legal effect from the beginning and neither party can enforce it. A voidable contract is valid on its face but may be cancelled by the party who holds the legal disability, which in this case is Bryan.

Bryan has the right to disaffirm the contract at any time before or within a reasonable time after turning 18. His parents cannot disaffirm on his behalf while he is still a minor, but they can advise him to do so, and Bryan has already communicated his intent to cancel. Upon disaffirmation, the contract is treated as though it never existed. Bryan is entitled to the return of his earnest money, and Carol Nguyen is released from her obligation to sell.

The right to disaffirm is lost if Bryan ratifies the contract after reaching 18. Ratification can occur expressly, by signing a new agreement confirming the contract, or implicitly, by continuing to perform under the contract after the age of majority without objecting. As long as Bryan disaffirms before turning 18 or promptly thereafter, he retains the right to cancel.

Question 2 -- Misrepresentation of Age and Carol's Recourse

Carol's argument that Bryan's misrepresentation should eliminate his right to disaffirm is understandable but generally does not succeed under Texas contract law. The purpose of the minority protection rule is to protect minors from the consequences of their own inexperience and poor judgment, including the judgment to misrepresent their age. Courts in most jurisdictions, including Texas, hold that a minor retains the right to disaffirm even if he or she lied about age to induce the other party's agreement.

This outcome can seem harsh to the adult party who acted in good faith. Carol accepted the offer believing Bryan was an adult, and she may have passed up other buyers during the contract period. However, the law places the risk of dealing with a minor on the adult party, not on the minor.

Carol may have a separate claim against Bryan for misrepresentation or fraud arising from the false statement about his age. This claim would exist outside the contract itself, in tort rather than in contract, because the contract has been disaffirmed. Whether that claim would succeed and what damages Carol could recover would depend on the specific facts and applicable law, but the availability of a potential tort claim does not prevent Bryan from exercising his contractual right to disaffirm.

Question 3 -- Statute of Frauds and the 18-Month Verbal Lease

The Texas Statute of Frauds requires that a lease for a term longer than one year be in writing and signed by both parties to be enforceable. The verbal agreement between the landlord and the prospective tenant is for 18 months, which exceeds the one-year threshold. As a result, the agreement is void and unenforceable regardless of how clearly both parties understood the terms or how firmly they believed they had a deal.

The one limited exception to the writing requirement is a lease of one year or less, which may be oral and is enforceable under Texas law. Had the parties agreed to a 12-month term, the verbal agreement would have been enforceable and the landlord could not simply walk away. The 18-month term placed this agreement squarely within the Statute of Frauds, and the absence of a written, signed lease is fatal to enforcement.

The tenant's options are limited. Because the lease is unenforceable, the tenant cannot compel the landlord to honor it or sue for specific performance of the lease itself. However, the tenant may have a claim for the out-of-pocket costs incurred in reasonable reliance on the agreement, such as renovation expenses, under a theory of promissory estoppel or detrimental reliance if the specific facts support it. The viability of such a claim would require legal advice. The practical lesson is clear: any lease for more than one year must be in writing and signed by both parties before either side spends money in reliance on it.

Chapter 4: Case Study Debrief Commentary

Question 1 -- Eminent Domain and Just Compensation

The city's authority to take the strip of land for road widening is grounded in the governmental power of eminent domain, which allows government entities to take private property for public use in exchange for just compensation. Road widening is a recognized public use, and the taking itself is legally permissible.

However, the constitutional protection the Mettlings hold is the right to just compensation at market value, not at tax-assessed value. Tax-assessed value and fair market value are often different figures, and the government's obligation under the Fifth Amendment and the Texas Constitution is to pay market value. The Mettlings are not required to accept the city's initial offer.

Under the Texas Landowner's Bill of Rights, the Mettlings have the right to hire an independent appraiser to assess the value of the strip and to retain an attorney to represent them in any condemnation proceeding. They are entitled to a hearing before a panel of three court-appointed special commissioners who will determine just compensation. If they are unsatisfied with the commissioners' award, they have the right to a full trial before a judge or jury and may appeal any adverse judgment. The Mettlings should not simply accept the tax-assessed value without first consulting an independent appraiser.

Question 2 -- Texas Surface Water Rights

The creek running along the edge of the Mettlings' property is surface water. Under Texas law, all surface water, including rivers, streams, creeks, and bays, is publicly owned by the State of Texas. The Mettlings do not own the water in the creek, and neither does Frank Pryor.

Because surface water is owned by the state, the right to use it is governed by the Doctrine of Prior Appropriation. Under this doctrine, a party who wants to use surface water must obtain a permit from the Texas Commission on Environmental Quality demonstrating a beneficial use for the water. Priority among competing permit holders is determined by the date the permit was issued.

Frank Pryor's use of the creek water without a permit is therefore unlawful regardless of how long he has been doing it. The fact that he has used the water openly for several years does not create any right to continue. The Mettlings cannot grant him permission to use it either, because the water is not theirs to grant. Frank would need to apply for and obtain a state water rights permit before his use is lawful. If he has a valid permit, his use may be lawful and the Mettlings would have no basis to object.

This question also illustrates an important distinction. Had Frank been drawing water from a well on his own property rather than from the creek, the analysis would be entirely different. Groundwater in Texas belongs to the landowner under the rule of capture, and Frank could pump it freely subject to applicable Groundwater Conservation District rules. The creek water, however, is surface water and belongs to the state.

Question 3 -- Mold Disclosure and the Licensee's Independent Duty

George Mettling's argument fails on both counts. Texas law requires sellers to disclose known material defects in the property, and a licensee has an independent duty to disclose material facts the licensee knows or should reasonably know, regardless of what the seller disclosed on the form.

The Mettlings noticed a musty smell in the master bathroom area for over a year before the inspection. A persistent musty smell is a recognized indicator of moisture intrusion or mold growth. The fact that the mold was physically inside the wall does not eliminate the obligation to disclose the conditions the Mettlings did observe. A seller cannot disclose only what is visible while remaining silent about sensory evidence of a problem that has been present for an extended period. The smell was a known condition, and mold is a latent defect that affects the value and habitability of the property. The Mettlings' failure to disclose it on the Seller's Disclosure Notice left the form materially incomplete.

Dana Voss bears her own independent liability. During the listing appointment, the Mettlings mentioned the musty smell to her directly. A licensee who learns of a condition that may constitute a material defect is required to disclose that information to prospective buyers regardless of what the seller discloses. Dana's failure to follow up on the smell and to independently ensure the disclosure was made exposed her to disciplinary action and potential civil liability. TRELA identifies failure to make required disclosures as grounds for revocation or suspension of a license.

The practical lesson is that mold often grows in areas that are not immediately visible, and any sensory evidence of moisture or organic growth should be treated as a known condition requiring disclosure. Both sellers and licensees benefit from erring on the side of full transparency rather than relying on the literal invisibility of a defect.

Chapter 5: Case Study Debrief Commentary

Question 1 -- Implied Agency and the Buyer Representation Agreement

Although Marcus and Tina never signed a buyer representation agreement, Marcus's conduct may have created an implied agency relationship. An implied contract arises from the conduct of the parties rather than from explicit words. When a licensee without a written agreement acts on a buyer's behalf by showing the property multiple times, answering detailed questions, and relaying negotiating positions to the seller, the licensee's actions suggest that an agency relationship exists. If Tina compensated Marcus or if Marcus expected compensation for those efforts, the existence of the implied agreement becomes very difficult to dispute.

The practical and legal problem with implied agency is that it creates duties and potential liabilities without the protections a written agreement provides. Marcus owed Tina fiduciary duties including loyalty, confidentiality, and full disclosure even without a signed contract, yet he had no written agreement defining the scope of his representation, his compensation, or the term of the relationship. Under the 2024 NAR settlement rules adopted in Texas, Marcus was required to have a signed buyer representation agreement in place before showing Tina the property. His failure to do so exposed him to both a disputed commission claim and potential disciplinary action.

Marcus should have presented Tina with a buyer representation agreement before the first showing and explained its purpose clearly. A signed agreement would have documented his role, protected his commission, and established the terms of representation in writing rather than leaving them to be inferred from conduct.

Question 2 -- Open Listing and Procuring Cause

Paula signed an open listing agreement with multiple brokers simultaneously. An open listing is a non-exclusive arrangement under which the seller may engage as many brokers as desired and owes a commission only to the broker who produces a ready, willing, and able buyer. If the seller finds a buyer independently, no commission is owed to anyone. Open listings are unilateral contracts: the seller's promise to pay is conditioned on the broker's act of producing the buyer, and no broker is obligated to participate.

Because only one broker can earn the commission under an open listing, disputes between competing brokers are resolved by determining who is the procuring cause of the sale. The procuring cause agent is the one whose efforts were the proximate, efficient, and producing cause of the completed transaction. This is not automatically the broker who first showed the property or who submitted the offer. It is the broker whose consistent efforts led the buyer to the decision to purchase.

On these facts, Marcus has the stronger procuring cause argument. He showed the property four times, cultivated the buyer's interest, answered detailed questions, and relayed negotiating positions. Greg Salinas showed the property once after Tina found it online on her own, and Tina submitted the offer through him after Marcus had already done the substantive work of bringing her to the point of purchase. However, procuring cause disputes are fact-specific and are sometimes resolved by arbitration. The outcome would depend on a careful examination of which broker's efforts were truly the efficient cause of Tina's decision to buy. A clearly written exclusive buyer representation agreement with Marcus at the outset would have eliminated this dispute entirely.

Question 3 -- Lease Purchase, Executory Contracts, and Texas Property Code

The arrangement between Paula and Tom is a lease purchase, also called a lease-to-own or rent-to-own agreement. Tom moved into the property, made monthly payments toward an eventual purchase, and agreed to receive a deed after two years. Because the arrangement involves a right or obligation to purchase combined with a period of possession exceeding 180 days, it is classified as an executory contract under Texas Property Code sections 5.061 and following.

Executory contracts of this type are subject to mandatory pre-execution disclosure requirements under Texas Property Code Chapter 5, Subchapter D. Before Tom signed any agreement, Paula was required to provide a survey or plat, copies of all liens and encumbrances affecting the property, a Seller's Disclosure Notice, and documentation of taxes and insurance. None of those disclosures appear to have been made, and critically, the agreement was never put in writing at all.

Tom's position is strengthened by the doctrine of part performance. Although the Texas Statute of Frauds generally requires real estate contracts to be in writing, a court may enforce an oral agreement to convey land when the party seeking enforcement has paid the purchase price, taken possession, and made improvements on the property with the seller's knowledge and permission. Tom has done all three: he made monthly payments, moved in with Paula's knowledge, and spent $6,000 on improvements. These facts present a strong part performance argument.

Tom's most practical remedies are a suit for specific performance asking the court to compel Paula to honor the agreement, or a suit for damages covering his payments, improvement costs, and any other reliance losses. Paula's failure to comply with Texas Property Code executory contract requirements also exposes her to statutory penalties. Both parties would have been far better protected by a written agreement, the involvement of an attorney, and proper title and escrow services from the beginning.

Chapter 6: Case Study Debrief Commentary

Question 1 -- Duty to Present Offers Immediately

TREC rules require immediate presentation of all offers. Sandra's two-day delay while attempting to negotiate a higher price was a clear violation of this rule and a breach of her fiduciary duty to the Mettlings under TREC Canon of Ethics Rule 531.1, which requires that the agent's primary obligation be to the client's interests at all times.

The consequences Sandra faces are both regulatory and civil. TREC may impose disciplinary action including suspension or revocation of her license for failing to present an offer promptly. She also faces potential civil liability for tortious interference. A tort is a negligent or wrongful act constituting a breach of a legal duty that causes damages to another person. When Hector withdrew his strong offer during Sandra's unauthorized delay, the Mettlings lost the opportunity to accept it. That lost opportunity is a quantifiable harm, and Sandra's conduct was its direct cause.

The only permissible basis for not presenting an offer immediately is a specific written instruction from the seller directing the agent not to present certain categories of offers, such as offers contingent on seller financing. No such instruction existed here. Sandra's belief that she was acting in her clients' best interests by seeking a higher price does not justify the delay. That judgment belonged to the Mettlings, not to Sandra.

Question 2 -- Lead-Based Paint Disclosure and Broker Responsibility

The federal Residential Lead-Based Paint Hazard Reduction Act requires disclosure of any known or potential lead-based paint hazards in residential properties built before 1978. The Mettlings' home, built in 1971, is a covered property. Before the contract was executed, Lisa was entitled to receive the EPA pamphlet titled Protect Your Family from Lead in Your Home, and Form 56-0 must be attached to the contract disclosing the sellers' knowledge of lead-based paint and acknowledging the buyer's rights.

Sandra's assumption that this was solely the seller's responsibility is incorrect. Real estate brokers are responsible for ensuring seller compliance with lead-based paint disclosure requirements. The broker's acknowledgment section of Form 56-0 exists precisely because the law places compliance responsibility on both the seller and the broker. Sandra had an independent obligation to confirm that the disclosure was completed and the pamphlet was delivered before the contract was finalized.

Failure to comply with the federal lead-based paint disclosure law can result in fines of up to $11,000 per violation. These penalties apply to brokers as well as sellers. Sandra's assumption that her responsibility ended at listing the property does not insulate her from federal enforcement. The disclosure requirement is non-negotiable for any pre-1978 property, and it was Sandra's professional duty to know and act on that requirement.

Question 3 -- Short Sale Disclosure and Misrepresentation to the Buyer

Sandra's representation that the transaction would close on schedule, made while she knew the lender had not confirmed a short payoff, is the source of significant legal exposure for both Sandra and the Mettlings.

For the Mettlings, the inability to deliver clear title at closing because the lender declined the short payoff constitutes a seller default. The Mettlings were unable to satisfy the seller's fundamental obligation under the contract, which is to convey the property free of liens that cannot be satisfied from the proceeds. Lisa is entitled to terminate the contract and recover her earnest money. Depending on the specific facts, Lisa may also have a claim for actual damages arising from the seller's failure, including moving costs, temporary housing expenses, and other foreseeable reliance losses.

For Sandra, knowingly representing to Lisa's agent that closing would proceed on schedule when she was aware that the lender had not approved the short payoff was a misrepresentation of a material fact. This creates personal exposure for Sandra in addition to the Mettlings' liability. A licensee who makes a false or misleading statement that a party relies on to her detriment may face both TREC disciplinary action and civil liability for misrepresentation.

The steps that should have been taken before the contract was executed are straightforward. Once the Mettlings disclosed that proceeds would fall short of the mortgage balance, Sandra should have advised them to contact the lender immediately and to use the TREC Short Sale Addendum (Form 45-2), which makes the contract contingent on the lienholder's written consent to the sale and agreement to accept the seller's net proceeds as full satisfaction. Proceeding without lender approval and without the appropriate addendum exposed all parties to foreseeable harm that proper use of the promulgated form would have prevented.

Chapter 7: Case Study Debrief Commentary

Question 1 -- The Option Period and the Amendment to Extend It

Rob's handling of the foundation crack was professionally negligent in two respects. First, his verbal reassurance that the finding was probably minor was an inappropriate response to a licensed inspector's written recommendation for further evaluation. Rob is not a structural engineer, and characterizing a professional's concern as minor without any expert basis was both inaccurate and potentially harmful to his clients. Second, and more critically, Rob failed to use the tool that exists precisely for this situation: Paragraph 7 of the TREC Amendment to Contract (Form 39-11), which allows the parties to extend the Termination Option period when additional inspections are needed.

An option period extension requires the seller's agreement, and the seller is not obligated to grant one. But the correct professional response when a significant finding arises late in the option period is to promptly notify the seller's agent, request an extension with a specific number of additional days, and document the agreement in a signed amendment. If the seller declines, the buyer must then decide whether to exercise the Termination Option with the information available or proceed without the follow-up report. That is the buyer's decision to make, not the agent's.

When the option period expired on day ten without a termination notice, the Mettlings lost their unrestricted right to terminate the contract for any reason. From that point forward, they could no longer exit the contract simply because they were uncomfortable with the foundation findings. Their only remaining exit options were the financing contingency and the sale contingency, both of which were subject to their own conditions and deadlines. The expiration of the Termination Option did not prevent the Mettlings from negotiating repairs through an amendment, but it did remove their safety net of unconditional exit.

Question 2 -- Financing Notification Deadline and the Waiver Consequence

The financing contingency under Form 40-11 requires the buyer to notify the seller in writing if financing cannot be obtained within the stated number of days. This is not a passive protection that simply allows the buyer to walk away if the loan falls through. It is an active obligation: the buyer must give written notice of the financing failure by the deadline, or the contingency is deemed waived.

Rob knew the loan had been declined on day 19. The correct course of action was to immediately prepare and deliver written notice to the seller's agent that the Mettlings were unable to obtain financing under the terms described in the addendum. That notice, delivered before day 21, would have triggered the contract's termination and entitled the Mettlings to a refund of their earnest money. Instead, day 21 passed without written notice.

The consequence of missing the written notice deadline is significant: the financing contingency was automatically waived and the Mettlings became obligated to close the transaction. They had no remaining basis to exit the contract without being in default and risking the loss of their earnest money. Rob's failure to notify was not merely a missed procedural step. It was a fundamental breach of his duty to act on his clients' behalf in a timely manner and directly exposed them to financial harm.

Rob's prior awareness of the co-signed car loan compounds the problem. A competent agent who knew about a potential debt-to-income issue at the application stage should have flagged it with the lender and discussed it with the clients before the contract was executed. The failure to investigate a known risk factor before recommending that the clients proceed is a separate professional failing from the missed notice deadline, but the two together illustrate how an agent's inattention at multiple stages of a transaction can cascade into serious client harm.

Question 3 -- Vague Date Language in an Amendment

TREC rules require that all date entries in the Amendment to Contract (Form 39-11) be specific calendar dates. The language financing deadline extended at lender's discretion that Rob entered in the date blank violates this requirement and constitutes a TREC rule violation.

The prohibition on vague date language exists for a straightforward reason: a date blank that does not contain a specific calendar date creates no enforceable deadline. If the financing notification deadline is extended to an unspecified date determined by a third party, neither the buyer nor the seller knows when the obligation expires, which party may act on it, or what triggers the next step. An ambiguous deadline is functionally no deadline at all, and a contract with unresolved ambiguities about material terms can give rise to disputes and, in some circumstances, destroy mutual agreement.

TREC has made clear that entering language such as at lender's discretion, to be determined, or upon loan approval in a date blank is the same as practicing law by adding terms that create legal uncertainty, which licensees are prohibited from doing. A licensee who enters vague language of this kind may face disciplinary action.

What Rob should have written was a specific calendar date: for example, the date that would give the Mettlings enough time to switch lenders and complete a new application, expressed as a concrete date such as June 15, 2025. If the new lender needed additional time beyond that date, another amendment could be prepared. Each extension should be a clean, documented agreement between the parties with a specific date, not an open-ended arrangement dependent on circumstances outside the contract.

Chapter 8: Case Study Debrief Commentary

Question 1 -- ARM Components and the Risk of Focusing on the Teaser Rate

An adjustable-rate mortgage is not a single fixed product. It is a loan whose interest rate changes over time based on a formula that combines a market index with a lender-set margin. Rita's reassurance that the initial rate was low enough to qualify easily is accurate as far as it goes, but it is also the least useful piece of information for a borrower making a long-term commitment.

The Mettlings should have been informed about every key ARM component before accepting the loan. The index is the market-based measure to which their rate will be tied after the fixed period, such as the Secured Overnight Financing Rate (SOFR) or a Treasury rate. The margin is the lender's fixed markup, typically two to three percentage points, added to the index to produce their actual note rate. The adjustment period is the interval at which the rate may change after the initial fixed period, which Rita described as annual. The periodic rate cap limits how much the rate can increase or decrease in any single adjustment period. The lifetime cap sets the maximum total rate increase over the life of the loan. The payment cap limits changes to the monthly payment amount but can cause negative amortization if the cap prevents full coverage of accrued interest.

The specific risk the Mettlings were not warned about is negative amortization. If future index increases push the note rate above what the payment cap allows the monthly payment to cover, the uncovered interest is added to the principal balance rather than paid down. The loan balance grows rather than shrinks, and the Mettlings could eventually owe more than the original $558,000 they borrowed. Rita's failure to explain these mechanics left the Mettlings with an incomplete picture of the financial commitment they were making.

Question 2 -- FIRPTA and the Buyer's Withholding Obligation

Cheryl Webb's response was inadequate. The situation she described, a foreign seller who has not filed U.S. tax returns, is precisely the circumstance that triggers the buyer's withholding obligation under the Foreign Investment in Real Property Tax Act (FIRPTA), which is addressed in Paragraph 20 of the standard residential contract (Form 20-19) under the heading Federal Requirements.

Under FIRPTA, when the seller of U.S. real property is a foreign person or entity as defined by the Internal Revenue Code, the buyer is required to withhold 15 percent of the purchase price at closing and remit it to the IRS along with the appropriate tax forms. This is not a discretionary step that the title company performs automatically. It is a legal obligation that falls on the buyer. If the buyer fails to withhold and the seller is in fact a foreign person, the buyer becomes personally liable for the tax that should have been withheld, plus potential penalties and interest.

In this transaction, the purchase price is $620,000. Fifteen percent of that is $93,000 that the Mettlings were obligated to withhold from Warren Oakes's proceeds at closing unless Warren could provide an affidavit of non-foreign status confirming he is not a foreign person, or unless a specific exemption applied. Cheryl's assurance that the title company would handle it was not only wrong about the process but left the Mettlings exposed to liability they did not know they were carrying. The correct advice would have been to alert the title company and lender immediately upon learning of Warren's foreign status so that appropriate withholding could be arranged before closing.

Question 3 -- Credit Report Errors and the Fair Credit Reporting Act

Rita's advice was professionally irresponsible. The fact that the lender uses the middle of three scores does not mean an error on one bureau's report can be safely ignored. The Fair Credit Reporting Act (FCRA) gives every consumer the right to dispute inaccurate information in a credit report, and each of the three major credit reporting agencies, Equifax, TransUnion, and Experian, is required to investigate a dispute and respond within 30 days.

Dan was entitled to write to all three agencies disputing the erroneous collection account. If the account could not be verified as accurate, the reporting agency was required to remove it. During an active loan application, a borrower who is waiting for an error correction should provide the lender with a written explanation of the discrepancy so the underwriter can evaluate the full credit picture. That step, which Rita failed to suggest, could have allowed the loan to proceed without prejudicing Dan's long-term credit standing.

The consequences of Rita's advice are illustrated directly by what happened two years later. The erroneous account remained on record as unresolved rather than disputed. When Dan applied for a home equity loan, the account had aged without resolution and contributed to a denial. Had the dispute been filed at the time of discovery, the error would likely have been removed and would not have appeared on any subsequent credit pull.

Rita's advice also reflects a misunderstanding of the FCRA's purpose. The law exists not just to protect lenders from bad credit risks but to protect consumers from the financial harm caused by inaccurate reporting. An agent or loan officer who tells a borrower not to exercise a federal consumer right because it is inconvenient for the current transaction is giving advice that serves neither the client's immediate nor long-term interests.

Chapter 9: Case Study Debrief Commentary

Question 1 -- Gap in the Chain of Title and the Judgment Lien

Both problems are clouds on title. A cloud on title is any irregularity in the chain of title that would cause a reasonable person to pause before accepting a conveyance. Each cloud reduces the marketability and value of the property and may give the buyer grounds to terminate the contract.

The first problem is a gap in the chain of title. Chain of title is the chronological succession of recorded owners from the original government grant to the present day. When Maria Elena Ochoa-Garza died without her estate being probated, there was no court proceeding to validate the transfer of ownership from the deceased to her heirs, no executor to execute a deed, and no recorded instrument conveying title to Rosa. As far as the public record reflects, the property still belongs to a deceased person. Rosa may have a valid equitable claim to the property, but she cannot demonstrate a clear, unbroken chain of title sufficient to deliver marketable title to the Mettlings.

Resolving this gap typically requires a formal probate proceeding for the mother's estate, even decades after the fact, to establish Rosa as the legal heir and authorize the issuance of a deed from the estate to Rosa. Alternatively, in some circumstances an affidavit of heirship supported by sworn statements from multiple disinterested parties who knew the family may be acceptable to the title company as a substitute for formal probate, depending on the age of the estate and the title company's underwriting standards. Either path requires time and likely attorney involvement.

The second problem is the recorded judgment lien from thirty years ago. A judgment lien attaches to real property as a result of a court-ordered money judgment and remains in the public record until it is satisfied and a release is recorded, or until a court orders its removal. The fact that Gil Trevino is deceased and his estate has been closed does not automatically extinguish the lien. Liens attach to property and transfer with it; a new owner acquires the property subject to any existing liens. Until the lien is formally released, the Mettlings would take title encumbered by an obligation that could theoretically be enforced by Trevino's successors-in-interest.

Resolving the judgment lien requires either locating Trevino's heirs or the administrator of his estate to obtain a release, or filing a quiet title suit asking a court to extinguish the lien on the grounds that it has been abandoned or is otherwise unenforceable. Neither path is instantaneous. Both require legal action, and the outcome of the quiet title route is not certain. The seller should be given a reasonable period to cure both defects before the Mettlings are required to close.

Question 2 -- Fiduciary Duty and the Agents' Conduct

Both agents failed their respective clients, though in different ways and with different consequences.

Frank Voss represented the seller. His characterization of both title defects as minor was inaccurate. A gap in the chain of title requiring probate of a deceased person's estate and an unresolved judgment lien of unknown enforceability are not minor clerical errors. They are material defects in the title that require legal action to resolve, and their resolution is not guaranteed on any particular timeline. By telling the Mettlings the issues were minor and suggesting they waive their title objection rights, Frank was acting entirely outside his role as the seller's agent. His duty ran to Rosa Ochoa, not to the buyers, and his interference with the buyers' decision about whether to exercise a contractual right they held exposed him to potential liability for misrepresentation. A seller's agent owes the buyer fair dealing but does not owe the buyer advice or counsel; what Frank did here crossed the line into providing guidance that was both outside his role and factually wrong.

Carol Webb represented the Mettlings. Her failure to intervene when Frank suggested the Mettlings waive their title objection rights was a direct breach of her fiduciary duty. A buyer's agent owes the buyer loyalty, full disclosure, and the duty to investigate and disclose all facts relevant to the buyer's decision. The title objection right exists specifically to protect buyers from being compelled to accept property with title defects they have not had a reasonable opportunity to evaluate. Carol should have immediately advised the Mettlings not to waive anything without first understanding what each defect meant legally and what remediation would require. She should have directed them to consult a licensed attorney before making any decision about the title objections.

The practical outcome of both agents' failures is that the Mettlings were in danger of closing on a property with a broken chain of title and an unresolved lien, without ever having exercised the rights the contract gave them to demand that those defects be cured. A competent buyer's agent treats the title commitment review as a critical step in the transaction, not a formality to be disposed of quickly to avoid awkwardness with the seller's agent. Title problems that surface at the commitment stage are far easier and less expensive to address than title problems discovered after closing, when the buyer has already taken possession and the seller's leverage to act has largely disappeared.

Chapter 10: Case Study Debrief Commentary

Question 1 -- Walkthrough Findings and the Agent's Duty

The final walkthrough is not a formality. Its purpose is to confirm that the property's condition has not changed since the contract was signed and that no fixtures have been removed. A built-in wine refrigerator listed as a fixture in the contract is real property that conveys with the sale. The seller had no right to remove it.

At the point of the walkthrough discovery, the Mettlings had several options. They could have refused to close until the refrigerator was returned or replaced. They could have negotiated a price reduction or escrow holdback equal to the refrigerator's value and documented the agreement in a contract amendment before closing. They could have sought damages from the seller for breach of contract. Proceeding to closing without addressing the issue would typically constitute a waiver of the claim.

Dana's advice to close anyway to protect the rate lock placed the lender's deadline above the clients' contractual rights. A rate lock is a real concern, but it does not eliminate the buyer's right to receive what the contract promised. Dana should have immediately contacted the seller's agent, documented the discrepancy in writing, and presented the Mettlings with their options rather than dismissing the issue. An escrow holdback or a same-day amendment would have preserved both the closing timeline and the clients' rights.

Question 2 -- Property Tax Proration (12-Month/360-Day Method)

Annual taxes: $6,600. Monthly rate: $6,600 divided by 12 = $550.00. Daily rate: $550.00 divided by 30 = $18.33.

The seller owns January, February, and 15 days of March. January through February is two full months: $550.00 x 2 = $1,100.00. March 1 through March 15 is 15 days: $18.33 x 15 = $274.95. Seller's total share: $1,100.00 + $274.95 = $1,374.95.

The correct entry on the settlement statement is a debit to the seller of $1,374.95 and a credit to the buyer of $1,374.95. If the Closing Disclosure showed only two months of seller ownership, the seller's proration would have been only $1,100.00, meaning the seller was underpaying by $274.95 and the buyer was receiving $274.95 less credit than entitled. Even modest proration errors matter because the settlement statement is a legal document, and a buyer who signs it without objection may have limited recourse afterward. Dana's responsibility was to review all figures for accuracy before closing, not to reassure clients that whatever the escrow agent prepared must be correct.

Question 3 -- Rent Proration and Dana's Responsibility

Monthly rent: $900. The seller owns the closing day, March 15, so the seller owns days 1 through 15 (15 days) and the buyer owns days 16 through 31 (16 days). Using the 30-day banker's method: daily rate = $900 divided by 30 = $30.00.

Seller's portion: $30.00 x 15 days = $450.00. Buyer's portion: $900.00 minus $450.00 = $450.00. The buyer is entitled to a credit of $450.00, not the full $900.00. The correct settlement statement entry is a debit to the seller of $450.00 and a credit to the buyer of $450.00.

If the Closing Disclosure showed a full-month credit to the buyer, the seller was being overcharged by $450.00. Dana's job was to catch exactly this kind of error before the closing table, not to tell clients the figures look right without checking the math. The listing broker is responsible for the accuracy of all settlement statements, and the buyer's agent has an independent duty to confirm that the closing documents reflect the agreed contract terms. When a client identifies a potential discrepancy in a closing document, the correct response is to pause, verify the calculation, and if an error exists, request a corrected Closing Disclosure before signatures are obtained.

Chapter 11: Case Study Debrief Commentary

Question 1 -- Errors in Paragraph 1

The first error is identifying the buyer only as Mr. Brian Holloway without including his marital status. Texas is a community property state, and Paragraph 1 requires the marital status of every party. The correct entry would read Brian Holloway, a single man, or Brian Holloway and wife [full name], depending on the buyer's actual status. Without this information, the contract is incomplete and the title company cannot determine whose signatures will be needed to convey a clear title in any future transaction.

The second error is using the name Pat Torres, copied from the MLS listing sheet, rather than the name on the current deed. The seller's name in Paragraph 1 must match the name on the title exactly. The deed shows Patricia Ann Torres, a married woman. Using a nickname or informal version of the name creates a discrepancy between the contract and the title records, which can produce a cloud on title and may require a curative instrument to correct. Equally significant, the husband's name does not appear anywhere in the contract. Because the property is the seller's homestead and because Texas requires both spouses to sign any deed conveying homestead property, the husband must be identified in Paragraph 1 and must sign the contract and the deed. Proceeding without him would prevent clear title from being conveyed at closing.

Question 2 -- Legal Description

A street address is never a legally sufficient property description. Real estate is non-homogeneous; no two parcels are identical, and a street address can be changed, duplicated, or mistakenly applied to the wrong parcel. A legal description must be precise enough for a competent surveyor to locate and identify the specific parcel without reference to any other document. All instruments that transfer or encumber real property, including sales contracts, require a proper legal description.

Leaving the blank empty and planning to add the description later is not acceptable practice. A contract with an incomplete legal description may not be enforceable, and there is no guarantee that the description added later will match what all parties intended. The risk of a dispute over which property was actually under contract is real. The correct source for the legal description is the current deed, the title commitment, or the county tax records, and Mark should verify the description against all three before entering it into the contract.

Question 3 -- Financing Contingency in Paragraph 11

Mark's entry has two problems. First, Paragraph 11 is designated only for factual statements and business details. TREC rules expressly prohibit licensees from adding language to Paragraph 11 for which a promulgated addendum or form already exists. A financing contingency is precisely the kind of provision for which TREC has promulgated a mandatory form: the Third Party Financing Addendum (Form 40-11). Writing that contingency into Paragraph 11 instead is a TREC rule violation and potentially constitutes unauthorized practice of law.

Second, the language Mark used creates legal rights and remedies by declaring the contract void and directing the return of earnest money upon a specific condition. That type of language goes well beyond a factual statement. Licensees may not draft provisions that create contractual rights or remedies; only an attorney may do so. Paragraph 11 is the right place to note things like the seller will leave the riding lawn mower, not to construct contingency mechanisms.

Mark should have checked the Third Party Financing Addendum box in Paragraph 3.B of the contract, attached Form 40-11, and filled in the loan terms, the number of days for the buyer to obtain approval, and the other required fields. That addendum was designed specifically to address financing contingencies in a legally complete and TREC-compliant way, and using it would have protected both the buyer and the licensee.

INDEX

If you liked Essentials of Contract Law in Texas, check out the other titles of Performance Programs Company!

Looking for a Texas-specific real estate principles textbook? Get what all the students love -- Principles of Real Estate Practice in Texas!

Principles of Real Estate Practice in Texas is invaluable reference material for real estate professionals. Its 625-pages contain the essentials of real estate law, principles, and practices taught in real estate schools and colleges across Texas.

Where can you buy Principles of Real Estate Practice in Texas?
Principles Real Estate Practice in Texas is available as a printed book or e-book through nearly all online retailers.

Cramming for the Texas real estate exam? You need Texas Real Estate License Exam Prep!

Texas Real Estate License Exam Prep (TX-RELEP) is a 300-page modern learning tool designed to prepare real estate candidates to pass Texas' Pearson Vue licensing exam. TX-RELEP contains six different sections to provide the knowledge and practice necessary to succeed with both Texas and national questions.

Where can you buy Texas Real Estate License Exam Prep?

Texas Real Estate License Exam Prep is available as a printed book or e-book through nearly all online retailers.

Struggling with real estate math? The solution to that equation is Real Estate Math Express!

Real Estate Math Express is a concise, easy-to-study test preparation guide to help real estate students improve their real estate math scores to pass the state licensing test. The primary feature of Real Estate Math Express is that it contains all necessary formulas and practice questions in 100+ pages.

Where can you buy Real Estate Math Express?
Real Estate Math Express is available as a printed book or e-book through nearly all online retailers.

Publisher Contact
Ryan Mettling
Performance Programs Company
6810 190th Street East, Bradenton, FL 34211
941-677-6043
ryan@performanceprogramscompany.com
www.performanceprogramscompany.com

www.ingramcontent.com/pod-product-compliance
Ingram Content Group UK Ltd.
Pitfield, Milton Keynes, MK11 3LW, UK
UKHW051241300926
15471UKWH00015B/1525